PROPERTY
Cases, Concepts, Critiques

PROPERTY
Cases, Concepts, Critiques

Edited by

Lawrence C. Becker *and* **Kenneth Kipnis**

PRENTICE-HALL, INC., *Englewood Cliffs, New Jersey 07632*

Library of Congress Cataloging in Publication Data
Main entry under title:

Property : cases, concepts, critiques.

Bibliography: p.
  1. Property—United States. 2. Property. I. Becker,
Lawrence C. II. Kipnis, Kenneth.
KF561.P68 1984   346.7304   83–21123
ISBN 0–13–730912–0   347.3064

For Adam Benjamin Smith-Kipnis

Cover design: Ben Santora
Manufacturing buyer: Harry Baisley

Excerpt from "Postscript" of W. H. Auden's "Prologue: The Birth of Architecture," from *W. H. Auden: Collected Poems,* edited by Edward Mendelson. Copyright © 1965 by W. H. Auden. Reprinted by permission of Random House, Inc., and Faber and Faber Ltd.

William Empson's "Legal Fiction" from *Collected Poems of William Empson,* copyright 1949, 1977 by William Empson. Reprinted by permission of Harcourt Brace Jovanovich, Inc., and Chatto and Windus Ltd.

Excerpt from *The People, Yes* by Carl Sandburg, copyright 1936 by Harcourt Brace Jovanovich, Inc.; copyright 1964 by Carl Sandburg. Reprinted by permission of the publisher.

Printed in the United States of America

10   9   8   7   6   5   4   3   2   1

ISBN 0-13-730912-0

PRENTICE-HALL INTERNATIONAL, INC., *London*
PRENTICE-HALL OF AUSTRALIA PTY. LIMITED, *Sydney*
EDITORA PRENTICE-HALL DO BRASIL, LTDA., *Rio de Janeiro*
PRENTICE-HALL CANADA INC., *Toronto*
PRENTICE-HALL OF INDIA PRIVATE LIMITED, *New Delhi*
PRENTICE-HALL OF JAPAN, INC., *Tokyo*
PRENTICE-HALL OF SOUTHEAST ASIA PTE. LTD., *Singapore*
WHITEHALL BOOKS LIMITED, *Wellington, New Zealand*

CONTENTS

A NOTE TO THE READER

When arranging the contents of this book, we assumed that reading a group of concrete but puzzling cases would be a good way to begin the study of the philosophic issues in property theory. Such a beginning creates a profitable level of frustration—a sense of bafflement which leads naturally to interest in the otherwise fairly dry discussion of the concept of property. Once some headway is made with definitions, readers are ready to pursue questions of justification—in the Critiques part of the book.

There are, of course, other plausible ways of studying these materials. We expect that most users will do at least some reorganizing. One reader has suggested, for example, that the organization be reversed: Critiques, then Concepts, then Cases. Another has said that spotting the cases throughout the text—next to the articles each is most closely related to—would be an improvement. But since a topical approach is likely to be the most popular alternative to the one we prefer—and since seeing such an ordering of the contents can be useful for an understanding of the interconnectedness of these materials—we provide on the following pages a topical reorganization of the contents. The topics need not be taken up in the order listed, of course. Nor is it always necessary to follow the suggested order within each topic.

TOPICAL TABLE
OF CONTENTS

INTRODUCTION

Property rights are fundamental to our society. In fact, as long as one is careful to include state or social ownership along with private ownership, it is fair to say that property rights are fundamental to *all* societies. Furthermore, many of the most important conflicts among today's political systems are disagreements about property rights. Should individuals be able to hold land as private property? Should they be able to own the means of production? Should they be able to accumulate wealth without limit? Should they be able to pass their wealth on to their children? How much property can the state tax or take away? For what purposes may the state tax? What *counts* as property? (Can one "own" a job, for example? Or future pension benefits?) Who owns the air, and the sea, and the moon? These and other questions require serious thinking about property; they provoke important philosophic, legal, and political debate. This book presents some of the most basic elements of that debate.

The literature on property is vast. No anthology like this one can pretend to be comprehensive, but a careful choice of material can do at least three things: (1) It can display some of the most perplexing disputes about property rights. That is the purpose of the Cases part of this book. (2) It can clarify the concepts of ownership and property as a preliminary to a deepened understanding of property problems. That is the purpose of the Concepts part. And (3) it can present the major lines of moral and political attack on property, as well as the defense of it. That is the purpose of the Critiques part.

In making our choices about what material to include, we tried to stay with what is fundamental rather than merely fashionable, substantive rather than merely current. The reading is sometimes difficult because the problems are difficult. In the section introductions we have provided a brief summary for each piece to clarify its argument. Cross-references and notes about related reading are included where appropriate. It is our hope that this book will provide the philosophical materials necessary to the fruitful study of the institution of property—and thus to the fruitful study of the societies of which it is a central feature.

The editors wish to express their gratitude to the publisher's anonymous reviewers whose thoughtful suggestions significantly improved this book and to Judith Farb, Carolyn Stevens, Madeline Spickard, Bea Verin, Sachiko Sugimoto, Floris Sakamoto, Renée McHarris, and Renee Kojima who provided assistance in the long and tedious process of preparing the manuscript. Special thanks are due for the contributions and help of Sara Lyn Smith, Haskell Fain, Annette Appell, and Fred Bender. Hollins College, the University of Hawaii, and Lake Forest College also supported this project with funds for research and duplicating services.

PART ONE
CASES

Everyone has the right to own property alone as well as in association with others. No one shall be arbitrarily deprived of his property.

> Universal Declaration of Human Rights (United Nations General Assembly, 1948), Article 17

No person . . . shall . . . be deprived of life, liberty or property without due process of law; nor shall private property be taken for public use, without just compensation.

> Constitution of the United States of America, Amendment V

Some thirty inches from my nose
The frontier of my Person goes,
And all the untilled air between
Is private *pagus* or demesne.
Stranger, unless with bedroom eyes
I beckon you to fraternize,
Beware of rudely crossing it:
I have no gun, but I can spit.

> W. H. Auden, "Prologue: The Birth of Architecture"

Law makes long spokes of the short stakes of men.
Your well fenced out real estate of mind
No high flat of the nomad citizen
Looks over, or train leaves behind.

Your rights extend under and above your claim
Without bound; you own land in Heaven and Hell;
Your part of earth's surface and mass the same,
Of all cosmos' volume, and all stars as well.

Your rights reach down where all owners meet, in Hell's
Pointed exclusive conclave, at earth's centre
(Your spun farm's root still on that axis dwells);
And up, through galaxies, a growing sector.

You are nomad yet; the lighthouse beam you own
Flashes, like Lucifer, through the firmament.
Earth's axis varies; your dark central cone
Wavers, a candle's shadow, at the end.

> William Empson,
> "Legal Fiction"

OVERVIEW

The legal materials on property are voluminous. We present here a small
selection of cases bearing directly on important philosophical issues in
property law. The judicial opinions included consider questions such as
the following: What kinds of things can be owned? How does something
that is unowned by *any*one become the property of *some*one? When can a
community, acting through its government, take private property? What
counts as a "taking"? When must compensation be paid? Readers who
pursue the bibliographical references given at the end of each section and
at the end of the book will have the materials for a fairly comprehensive
understanding of these major philosophical questions.

One caution: We have not attempted to illustrate the numerous and
varied technical problems involved in defining the *extent* of particular
property rights. (Can you drill straight down and pump up water that is
under someone else's land? Can you will your property to persons born
years after your death?) Nor have we tried to cover the issues involved in
transferring title. (Suppose someone buys a car with a phony check and
then sells it to you?) Nor have we included cases on taxation. These
matters and others have important philosophical aspects and readers possessing ingenuity should be able to find their way into even these topics
through the bibliographical references provided.

The cases that follow illustrate in a general way the manner in which
property questions are presented to judges and the manner in which
judges understand them. They fit comfortably into both traditional and
contemporary philosophical discussions of property. They provide a set
of concrete points of reference that may profitably be kept in mind when
reading the more abstract selections of Parts Two and Three. In returning to these reference points, the reader will, we believe, develop a sense
of what is at stake in the effort to secure a responsible understanding of
the proper place of property rights. These cases can help us to appreciate
how difficult and important it is to develop that understanding.

SECTION ONE
WHAT CAN BE PROPERTY?

When we think of property, we usually think first of material things: personal possessions, houses, land. But a moment's reflection reveals that much of the wealth held as property is neither valuable nor tangible in quite the same way that those things are. Money, for example, takes most of its value from social practices, agreements, expectations—not from the material it is made of. Copyrights and patents protect what is called intellectual property. It is a short but startling step to the thought that all sorts of other things can be property. The four cases in this section each consider whether certain things should count as property: a new life form, the news, a job, a place on the welfare rolls.

In the first case, *Diamond* v. *Chakrabarty*, the issue is whether a new, genetically engineered bacterium can be patented. Ananda M. Chakrabarty, working for the General Electric Company, had developed an organism capable of digesting crude oil. In seeking a patent, his company is endeavoring to have its ownership of the new type of organism legally recognized. This would mean that anyone who wanted to use the bacteria (or their offspring)—say, to clean up an oil spill—would first have to get permission from the General Electric Company, at least as long as the patent is in effect. General Electric would have an exclusive legal right to the type of organism that Chakrabarty developed. To fail to obtain permission would be to infringe upon the patent. Ruling that the micro-organism is a nonnaturally occurring composition of matter (Chakrabarty's "handiwork") with "the potential for significant utility," the Supreme Court holds that the bacterium is patentable. (Though the Court does not do so here, one might ask what the limits of such patentability might be: Could businesses compete for new, improved models of human beings?)

In the next case, *International News Service* v. *Associated Press,* the Supreme Court is concerned about the ownership of news. When a newspaper publishes an item in its pages, does the news in the story become common property or is it somehow still the property of the organization that gathered it, even after it is released to the public? The defendant, International News Service, had obtained news from the bulletins issued by its competitor, Associated Press, and had then sold the stories to other newspapers. The Associated Press contended that the appropriation and sale of news that it had gathered violated its property right in the news and was unfair business competition. In arriving at its decision, the Court considers the "practical needs and requirements" of the news-gathering business and the question of when property is abandoned. While the Court does not consider that news once published is property, it holds that it is nonetheless "quasi property" and lets stand a lower court ruling that International News Service may not use news gathered by Associated Press until after its commercial value has passed. "He who has fairly paid the price should have the beneficial use of the property."

In a dissenting opinion, Justice Brandeis points out that the law often permits people to reap where they have not sown. The specification of the dimensions of property rights in news can affect the public interest in ways that should be taken into account by comprehensive legislation, not by judicial decision. Courts are "ill equipped" to make the necessary investigations.

Perry et al. v. *Sindermann* raises the question of whether a job can be held as property. Robert Sindermann had been a teacher in the Texas state college system for ten years and had been terminated by Odessa College without official explanation and without opportunity to challenge the reasons for the dismissal. If Odessa College had had a tenure system (and if Sindermann had had tenure), then the College would have had to have shown that it had "adequate cause" to fire him. But while Odessa College had "no tenure system" (as the Faculty Guide put it), there had been an "understanding fostered by the college administration" that faculty could normally and reasonably expect to have their contracts renewed. Sindermann claimed that his expectation of continued employment constituted a property interest. Since property may not be taken, constitutionally, without "due process of law," if his job was his property in some sense, he was entitled, at a minimum, to a fair hearing before being dismissed by the Board of Regents acting on behalf of the State of Texas. The United States Supreme Court rules here that a "person's interest in a benefit is a 'property' interest for due process purposes if there are . . . rules or mutually explicit understandings that support his claim of entitlement to the benefit and that he may invoke at a hearing." Accordingly, Sindermann is entitled to the hearing he did not receive.

The fourth and last case in this section, *Goldberg* v. *Kelly,* raises a similar issue: "whether a State that terminates public assistance payments to a particular recipient without affording him the opportunity for an evidentiary hearing prior to termination denies the recipient procedural due process in violation of the Due Process Clause of the Fourteenth Amendment." Are welfare benefits a gratuity, a continuing gift that the government can terminate at will? Or are people entitled to them, so that the government cannot, in fairness, cut them off without good cause? In arriving at its decision, the Supreme Court balances the government's interest in "conserving fiscal and administrative resources" against the welfare recipient's "brutal need" and the "Nation's basic commitment . . . to foster the dignity and well-being of all persons within its borders." The Court rules that welfare benefits are not "mere charity" and that due process requires an adequate hearing *before* the government can terminate them.

In his dissenting opinion, Justice Black laments that it "strains credulity to say that the government's promise of charity . . . is property . . . when the government denies that the individual is honestly entitled to receive such a payment." He is concerned as well that the difficulty the Court creates in getting ineligible people off the rolls may lead to investigative delay in placing eligible people on the rolls.

Diamond v. Chakrabarty

UNITED STATES SUPREME COURT

CHIEF JUSTICE BURGER delivered the opinion of the Court.

We granted certiorari to determine whether a live, human-made micro-organism is patentable subject matter under 35 U. S. C. § 101.

I

In 1972, respondent Chakrabarty, a microbiologist, filed a patent application, assigned to the General Electric Company. The application asserted 36 claims related to Chakrabarty's invention of "a bacterium from the genus *Pseudomonas* containing therein at least two stable energy-generating plasmids, each of said plasmids providing a separate hydrocarbon degradative pathway."[1] This human-made, genetically engineered bacterium is

---

447 U.S. 303 (1979). Footnotes renumbered and locations of deleted citations marked with double asterisk (**). [Eds.]

[1]Plasmids are hereditary units physically separate from the chromosomes of the cell. In prior research, Chakrabarty and an associate discovered that plasmids control the oil

capable of breaking down multiple components of crude oil. Because of this property, which is possessed by no naturally occurring bacteria, Chakrabarty's invention is believed to have significant value for the treatment of oil spills.[2]

Chakrabarty's patent claims were of three types: first, process claims for the method of producing the bacteria; second, claims for an inoculum comprised of a carrier material floating on water, such as straw, and the new bacteria; and third, claims to the bacteria themselves. The patent examiner allowed the claims falling into the first two categories but rejected claims for the bacteria. His decision rested on two grounds: (1) that micro-organisms are "products of nature," and (2) that as living things they are not patentable subject matter under 35 U. S. C. § 101. . . .

The Constitution grants Congress broad power to legislate to "promote the Progress of Science and the useful Arts, by securing for limited times to authors and inventors the exclusive right to their respective writings and discoveries." Art. I, § 8. The patent laws promote this progress by offering inventors exclusive rights for a limited period as an incentive for their inventiveness and research efforts. *Kewanee Oil Co.* v. *Bicron Corp.*, 416 U. S. 470, 480–481 (1974); *Universal Oil Co.* v. *Globe Co.*, 322 U. S. 471, 484 (1944). The authority of Congress is exercised in the hope that "[t]he productive effort thereby fostered will have a positive effect on society through the introduction of new products and processes of manufacture into the economy, and the emanations by way of increased employment and better lives for our citizens." *Kewanee, supra,* at 480.

The question before us in this case is a narrow one of statutory interpretation requiring us to construe 35 U. S. C. § 101, which provides:

> "Whoever invents or discovers any new and useful process, machine, manufacture, or composition of matter, or any new and useful improvement thereof, may obtain a patent therefor, subject to the conditions and requirements of this title."

Specifically, we must determine whether respondent's micro-organism constitutes a "manufacture" or "composition of matter" within the meaning of the statute.[3]

---

degradation abilities of certain bacteria. In particular, the two researchers discovered plasmids capable of degrading camphor and octane, two components of crude oil. In the work represented by the patent application at issue here, Chakrabarty discovered a process by which four different plasmids, capable of degrading four different oil components, could be transferred to and maintained stably in a single *Pseudomonas* bacteria, which itself has no capacity for degrading oil.

[2]At present, biological control of oil spills requires the use of a mixture of naturally occurring bacteria, each capable of degrading one component of the oil complex. In this way, oil is decomposed into simpler substances which can serve as food for aquatic life. However, for various reasons, only a portion of any such mixed culture survives to attack the oil spill. By breaking down multiple components of oil, Chakrabarty's micro-organism promises more efficient and rapid oil-spill control.

[3]This case does not involve the other "conditions and requirements" of the patent laws, such as novelty and nonobviousness. 35 U. S. C. §§ 102, 103.

III

In cases of statutory construction we begin, of course, with the language of the statute.** And "unless otherwise defined, words will be interpreted as taking their ordinary, contemporary, common meaning."** We have also cautioned that courts "should not read into the patent laws limitations and conditions which the legislature has not expressed."**

Guided by these canons of construction, this Court has read the term "manufacture" in § 101 in accordance with its dictionary definition to mean "the production of articles for use from raw materials prepared by giving to these materials new forms, qualities, properties, or combinations whether by hand labor or by machinery."** Similarly, "composition of matter" has been construed consistent with its common usage to include "all compositions of two or more substances and . . . all composite articles, whether they be the results of chemical union, or of mechanical mixture, or whether they be gases, fluids, powders, or solids."** In choosing such expansive terms as "manufacture" and "composition of matter," modified by the comprehensive "any," Congress plainly contemplated that the patent laws would be given wide scope.

The relevant legislative history also supports a broad construction. The Patent Act of 1793, authored by Thomas Jefferson, defined statutory subject matter as "any new and useful art, machine, manufacture, or composition of matter, or any new or useful improvement [thereof]." Act of Feb. 21, 1793, ch. 11, § 1, 1 Stat. 318. The Act embodied Jefferson's philosophy that "ingenuity should receive a liberal encouragement." V Writings of Thomas Jefferson, at 75–76.** Subsequent patent statutes in 1836, 1870, and 1874 employed this same broad language. In 1952, when the patent laws were recodified, Congress replaced the word "art" with "process," but otherwise left Jefferson's language intact. The Committee Reports accompanying the 1952 act inform us that Congress intended statutory subject matter to "include anything under the sun that is made by man." S. Rep. No. 1979, 82d Cong., 2d Sess., 5 (1952); H. R. Rep. No. 1923, 82d Cong., 2d Sess., 6 (1952).*

This is not to suggest that § 101 has no limits or that it embraces every discovery. The laws of nature, physical phenomena, and abstract ideas have been held not patentable.** Thus, a new mineral discovered in the earth or a new plant found in the wild is not patentable subject matter. Likewise, Einstein could not patent his celebrated law that $E = mc^2$; nor could Newton have patented the law of gravity. Such discoveries are "manifestations of . . . nature, free to all men and reserved exclusively to none."**

Judged in this light, respondent's micro-organism plainly qualifies as patentable subject matter. His claim is not to a hitherto unknown natural phenomenon, but to a nonnaturally occurring manufacture or composition of matter—a product of human ingenuity "having a distinctive name, character [and] use."** The point is underscored dramatically by com-

---

*Footnote omitted [Eds.].

parison of the invention here with that in *Funk* [*Funk Seed Co.* v. *Kalo Co.*, 333 U. S. 127 (1948)]. There, the patentee had discovered that there existed in nature certain species of root-nodule bacteria which did not exert a mutually inhibitive effect on each other. He used that discovery to produce a mixed culture capable of inoculating the seeds of leguminous plants. Concluding that the patentee had discovered "only some of the handiwork of nature," the Court ruled the product nonpatentable:

> "Each of the species of root-nodule bacteria contained in the package infects the same group of leguminous plants which it always infected. No species acquires a different use. The combination of the six species produces no new bacteria, no change in the six bacteria, and no enlargement of the range of their utility. Each species has the same effect it always had. The bacteria perform in their natural way. Their use in combination does not improve in any way their natural functioning. They serve the same ends nature originally provided and act quite independently of any effort by the patentee." 333 U. S., at 127.

Here, by contrast, the patentee has produced a new bacterium with markedly different characteristics from any found in nature and one having the potential for significant utility. His discovery is not nature's handiwork, but his own; accordingly it is patentable subject matter under § 101.

International News Service v. Associated Press

UNITED STATES SUPREME COURT

MR. JUSTICE PITNEY delivered the opinion of the court:

The parties are competitors in the gathering and distribution of news and its publication for profit in newspapers throughout the United States. The Associated Press, which was complainant in the district court, is a co-operative organization, incorporated under the Membership Corporations Law of the state of New York, its members being individuals who are either proprietors or representatives of about 950 daily newspapers published in all parts of the United States. . . . Complainant gathers in all parts of the world, by means of various instrumentalities of

---

248 U.S. 215 (1918). Locations of deleted citations marked with double asterisk (**). [Eds.]

its own, by exchange with its members, and by other appropriate means, news and intelligence of current and recent events of interest to newspaper readers, and distributes it daily to its members for publication in their newspapers. . . .

Defendant is a corporation organized under the laws of the state of New Jersey, whose business is the gathering and selling of news to its customers and clients, consisting of newspapers published throughout the United States, under contracts by which they pay certain amounts at stated times for defendant's service. . . .

The only matter that has been argued before us is whether defendant may lawfully be restrained from appropriating news taken from bulletins issued by complainant or any of its members, or from newspapers published by them, for the purpose of selling it to defendant's clients. Complainant asserts that defendant's admitted course of conduct in this regard both violates complainant's property right in the news and constitutes unfair competition in business. And notwithstanding the case has proceeded only to the stage of a preliminary injunction, we have deemed it proper to consider the underlying questions, since they go to the very merits of the action and are presented upon facts that are not in dispute. As presented in argument, these questions are: (1) Whether there is any property in news; (2) whether, if there be property in news collected for the purpose of being published, it survives the instant of its publication in the first newspaper to which it is communicated by the newsgatherer; and (3) whether defendant's admitted course of conduct in appropriating for commercial use matter taken from bulletins or early editions of Associated Press publications constitutes unfair competition in trade. . . .

Complainant's news matter is not copyrighted. It is said that it could not, in practice, be copyrighted, because of the large number of despatches that are sent daily; and, according to complainant's contention, news is not within the operation of the Copyright Act. Defendant, while apparently conceding this, nevertheless invokes the analogies of the law of literary property and copyright, insisting as its principal contention that, assuming complainant has a right of property in its news, it can be maintained (unless the Copyright Act be complied with) only by being kept secret and confidential; and that upon the publication with complainant's consent of uncopyrighted news by any of complainant's members in a newspaper or upon a bulletin board, the right of property is lost, and the subsequent use of the news by the public or by defendant for any purpose whatever becomes lawful. . . .

In considering the general question of property in news matter, it is necessary to recognize its dual character, distinguishing between the substance of the information and the particular form or collocation of words in which the writer has communicated it.

No doubt news articles often possess a literary quality, and are the subject of literary property at the common law. . . .

But the news element—the information respecting current events contained in the literary production—is not the creation of the writer, but is a report of matters that ordinarily are publici juris; it is the history of the day. It is not to be supposed that the framers of the Constitution, when they empowered Congress "to promote the progress of science and useful arts, by securing for limited times to authors and inventors the exclusive right to their respective writings and discoveries" (Const. art. 1, § 8, ¶ 8), intended to confer upon one who might happen to be the first to report a historic event the exclusive right for any period to spread the knowledge of it.

We need spend no time, however, upon the general question of property in news matter at common law, or the application of the Copyright Act, since it seems to us the case must turn upon the question of unfair competition in business. And, in our opinion, this does not depend upon any general right of property analogous to the common-law right of the proprietor of an unpublished work to prevent its publication without his consent; nor is it foreclosed by showing that the benefits of the Copyright Act have been waived. We are dealing here not with restrictions upon publication, but with the very facilities and processes of publication. The peculiar value of news is in the spreading of it while it is fresh; and it is evident that a valuable property interest in the news as news cannot be maintained by keeping it secret. Besides, except for matters improperly disclosed, or published in breach of trust or confidence, or in violation of law, none of which is involved in this branch of the case, the news of current events may be regarded as common property. What we are concerned with is the business of making it known to the world, in which both parties to the present suit are engaged. That business consists in maintaining a prompt, sure, steady, and reliable service designed to place the daily events of the world at the breakfast table of the millions at a price that, while of trifling moment to each reader, is sufficient in the aggregate to afford compensation for the cost of gathering and distributing it, with the added profit so necessary as an incentive to effective action in the commercial world. The service thus performed for newspaper readers is not only innocent, but extremely useful in itself, and indubitably constitutes a legitimate business. . . .

Obviously, the question of what is unfair competition in business must be determined with particular reference to the character and circumstances of the business. The question here is not so much the rights of either party as against the public, but their rights as between themselves.**
And although we may and do assume that neither party has any remaining property interest as against the public in uncopyrighted news matter after the moment of its first publication, it by no means follows that there is no remaining property interest in it as between themselves. For, to both of them alike, news matter, however little susceptible of ownership or dominion in the absolute sense, is stock in trade, to be gathered at the cost of enterprise, organization, skill, labor, and money, and to be distributed and sold to those who will pay money for it, as for any other merchandise. Regarding the news, therefore, as but the material out of which both parties are seeking to make profits at the same time and in the same field, we hardly can fail to recognize that for this purpose, and as between them,

it must be regarded as quasi property, irrespective of the rights of either as against the public. . . .

The right of the purchaser of a single newspaper to spread knowledge of its contents gratuitously, for any legitimate purpose not unreasonably interfering with complainant's right to make merchandise of it, may be admitted; but to transmit that news for commercial use, in competition with complainant,—which is what defendant has done and seeks to justify,—is a very different matter. In doing this defendant, by its very act, admits that it is taking material that has been acquired by complainant as the result of organization and the expenditure of labor, skill, and money and which is salable by complainant for money, and that defendant, in appropriating it and selling it as its own, is endeavoring to reap where it has not sown, and by disposing of it to newspapers that are competitors of complainant's members is appropriating to itself the harvest of those who have sown. . . . The transaction speaks for itself, and a court of equity ought not to hesitate long in characterizing it as unfair competition in business.

The underlying principle is much the same as that which lies at the base of the equitable theory of consideration in the law of trusts,—that he who has fairly paid the price should have the beneficial use of the property.** It is no answer to say that complainant spends its money for that which is too fugitive or evanescent to be the subject of property. That might, and for the purposes of the discussion we are assuming that it would, furnish an answer in a common-law controversy. But in a court of equity, where the question is one of unfair competition, if that which complainant has acquired fairly at substantial cost may be sold fairly at substantial profit, a competitor who is misappropriating it for the purpose of disposing of it to his own profit and to the disadvantage of complainant cannot be heard to say that it is too fugitive or evanescent to be regarded as property. It has all the attributes of property necessary for determining that a misappropriation of it by a competitor is unfair competition because contrary to good conscience.

The contention that the news is abandoned to the public for all purposes when published in the first newspaper is untenable. Abandonment is a question of intent, and the entire organization of the Associated Press negatives such a purpose. The cost of the service would be prohibitive if the reward were to be so limited. No single newspaper, no small group of newspapers, could sustain the expenditure. Indeed, it is one of the most obvious results of defendant's theory that, by permitting indiscriminate publication by anybody and everybody for purposes of profit in competition with the news gatherer, it would render publication profitless, or so little profitable as in effect to cut off the service by rendering the cost prohibitive in comparison with the return. The practical needs and requirements of the business are reflected in complainant's by-laws, which have been referred to. Their effect is that publication by each member must be deemed not by any means an abandonment of the news to the world for any and all purposes, but a publication for limited purposes; for the benefit of the readers of the bulletin or the newspaper as such; not for the purpose of making merchandise of it as news, with the result of depriving complainant's other members of their reasonable opportunity to obtain just returns for their expenditures. . . .

There is some criticism of the injunction that was directed by the district court upon the going down of the mandate from the circuit court of appeals. In brief, it restrains any taking or gainfully using of the complainant's news, either bodily or in substance, from bulletins issued by the complainant or any of its members, or from editions of their newspapers, *"until its commercial value as news to the complainant and all of its members has passed away."* The part complained of is the clause we have italicized; but if this be indefinite, it is no more so than the criticism. Perhaps it would be better that the terms of the injunction be made specific, and so framed as to confine the restraint to an extent consistent with the reasonable protection of complainant's newspapers, each in its own area and for a specified time after its publication, against the competitive use of pirated news by defendant's customers. But the case presents practical difficulties; and we have not the materials, either in the way of a definite suggestion of amendment, or in the way of proofs, upon which to frame a specific injunction; hence, while not expressing approval of the form adopted by the district court, we decline to modify it at this preliminary stage of the case, and will leave that court to deal with the matter upon appropriate application made to it for the purpose.

The decree of the Circuit Court of Appeals will be affirmed.

• • •

MR. JUSTICE BRANDEIS, dissenting.

• • •

News is a report of recent occurrences. The business of the news agency is to gather systematically knowledge of such occurrences of interest and to distribute reports thereof. The Associated Press contended that knowledge so acquired is property, because it costs money and labor to produce and because it has value for which those who have it not are ready to pay; that it remains property and is entitled to protection as long as it has commercial value as news; and that to protect it effectively, the defendant must be enjoined from making, or causing to be made, any gainful use of it while it retains such value. An essential element of individual property is the legal right to exclude others from enjoying it. If the property is private, the right of exclusion may be absolute; if the property is affected with a public interest, the right of exclusion is qualified. But the fact that a product of the mind has cost its producer money and labor, and has a value for which others are willing to pay, is not sufficient to insure to it this legal attribute of property. The general rule of law is, that the noblest of human productions—knowledge, truths ascertained, conceptions, and ideas—become, after voluntary communication to others, free as the air to common use. Upon these incorporeal productions the attribute of property is continued after such communication only in certain classes of cases where public policy has seemed to demand it. These exceptions are confined to productions which, in some degree, involve creation, invention, or discovery. But by no means all such are endowed with this attribute of property. The creations which are recognized as property by the common law are literary, dramatic, musical, and other artistic creations; and these have also protection under the copyright statutes. The inventions and discoveries upon which this attribute of property is conferred only by statute are the few comprised within the patent law. There are also many other cases in which courts interfere to prevent curtailment of plaintiff's enjoyment of incorporeal productions; and in which the right to relief is often called a property right, but is such only in a special sense. In those cases, the plaintiff has no absolute right to the protection of his production; he has merely the qualified right to be protected as against the defendant's acts, because of the special relation in which the latter stands or the wrongful method or means employed in acquiring the knowledge or the manner in which it is used. Protection of this character is afforded where the suit is based upon breach of contract or of trust, or upon unfair competition. . . .

Plaintiff . . . contended that defendant's practice constitutes unfair competition because there is "appropriation without cost to itself of values created by" the plaintiff; and it is upon this ground that the decision of this court appears to be based. To appropriate and use for profit, knowledge and ideas produced by other men, without making compensation or even acknowledgment, may be inconsistent with a finer sense of propriety; but, with the exceptions indicated above, the law has heretofore sanctioned the practice. Thus it was held that one may ordinarily make and sell anything in any form, may copy with exactness that which another has produced, or may otherwise use his ideas without his consent and without the payment of compensation, and yet not inflict a legal injury. . . .

That competition is not unfair in a legal sense, merely because the profits gained are unearned, even if made at the expense of a rival, is shown by many cases. . . . He who follows the pioneer into a new market, or who engages in the manufacture of an article newly introduced by another, seeks profits due largely to the labor and expense of the first adventurer; but the law sanctions, indeed encourages, the pursuit.* He who makes a city known through his product must submit to sharing the resultant trade with others who, perhaps for that reason, locate there later. . . .

The means by which the International News Service obtains news gathered by the Associated Press is also clearly unobjectionable. It is taken from papers bought in the open market or from bulletins publicly posted. No breach of contract,** or of trust** and neither fraud nor force, are involved. The manner of use is likewise unobjectionable. No reference is made by word or by act to the Associated Press, either in transmitting the

*Footnote omitted [Eds.].

news to subscribers, or by them in publishing it in their papers. Neither the International News Service nor its subscribers is gaining or seeking to gain in its business a benefit from the reputation of the Associated Press. They are merely using its product without making compensation.** That, they have a legal right to do; because the product is not property, and they do not stand in any relation to the Associated Press, either of contract or of trust, which otherwise precludes such use. The argument is not advanced by characterizing such taking and use a misappropriation. . . .

Nor is the use made by the International News Service of the information taken from papers or bulletins of Associated Press members legally objectionable by reason of the purpose for which it was employed. The acts here complained of were not done for the purpose of injuring the business of the Associated Press. Their purpose was not even to divert its trade, or to put it at a disadvantage by lessening defendant's necessary expenses. The purpose was merely to supply subscribers of the International News Service promptly with all available news. . . .

The rule for which the plaintiff contends would effect an important extension of property rights and a corresponding curtailment of the free use of knowledge and of ideas; and the facts of this case admonish us of the danger involved in recognizing such a property right in news, without imposing upon newsgatherers corresponding obligations. A large majority of the newspapers and perhaps half the newspaper readers of the United States are dependent for their news of general interest upon agencies other than the Associated Press. The channel through which about 400 of these papers received, as the plaintiff alleges, "a large amount of news relating to the European war of the greatest importance and of intense interest to the newspaper reading public," was suddenly closed. The closing to the International News Service of these channels for foreign news (if they were closed) was due not to unwillingness on its part to pay the cost of collecting the news, but to the prohibitions imposed by foreign governments upon its securing news from their respective countries and from using cable or telegraph lines running therefrom. For aught that appears, this prohibition may have been wholly undeserved; and at all events the 400 papers and their readers may be assumed to have been innocent. For aught that appears, the International News Service may have sought then to secure temporarily by arrangement with the Associated Press the latter's foreign news service. For aught that appears, all of the 400 subscribers of the International News Service would gladly have then become members of the Associated Press, if they could have secured election thereto.* It is possible, also, that a large part of the readers of these papers were so situated that they could not secure prompt access to papers served by the Associated Press. The prohibition of the foreign governments might as well have been extended to the channels through which news was supplied to the more than a thousand other daily papers in the United States not served by the Associated Press; and a large part of their readers may also be so located that they cannot procure prompt access to papers served by the Associated Press.

*Footnote omitted [Eds.].

A legislature, urged to enact a law by which one news agency or newspaper may prevent appropriation of the fruits of its labors by another, would consider such facts and possibilities and others which appropriate inquiry might disclose. Legislators might conclude that it was impossible to put an end to the obvious injustice involved in such appropriation of news without opening the door to other evils, greater than that sought to be remedied. . . .

Or legislators dealing with the subject might conclude that the right to news values should be protected to the extent of permitting recovery of damages for any unauthorized use, but that protection by injunction should be denied. . . .

Or again, a legislature might conclude that it was unwise to recognize even so limited a property right in published news as that above indicated; but that a news agency should, on some conditions, be given full protection of its business; and to that end a remedy by injunction as well as one for damages should be granted, where news collected by it is gainfully used without permission. If a legislature concluded** that, under certain circumstances, news-gathering is a business affected with a public interest, it might declare that, in such cases, news should be protected against appropriation only if the gatherer assumed the obligation of supplying it at reasonable rates and without discrimination, to all papers which applied therefor. . . .

Courts are ill-equipped to make the investigations which should precede a determination of the limitations which should be set upon any property right in news, or of the circumstances under which news gathered by a private agency should be deemed affected with a public interest. Courts would be powerless to prescribe the detailed regulations essential to full enjoyment of the rights conferred, or to introduce the machinery required for enforcement of such regulations. Considerations such as these should lead us to decline to establish a new rule of law in the effort to redress a newly disclosed wrong, although the propriety of some remedy appears to be clear.

Perry et al. v. Sindermann

UNITED STATES SUPREME COURT

MR. JUSTICE STEWART delivered the opinion of the Court.

From 1959 to 1969 the respondent, Robert Sindermann, was a teacher in the state college system of the State of Texas. After teaching

408 U.S. 593 (1971). Footnotes renumbered. [Eds.]

for two years at the University of Texas and for four years at San Antonio Junior College, he became a professor of Government and Social Science at Odessa Junior College in 1965. He was employed at the college for four successive years, under a series of one-year contracts. He was successful enough to be appointed, for a time, the cochairman of his department.

During the 1968–1969 academic year, however, controversy arose between the respondent and the college administration. The respondent was elected president of the Texas Junior College Teachers Association. In this capacity, he left his teaching duties on several occasions to testify before committees of the Texas Legislature, and he became involved in public disagreements with the policies of the college's Board of Regents. In particular, he aligned himself with a group advocating the elevation of the college to four-year status—a change opposed by the Regents. And, on one occasion, a newspaper advertisement appeared over his name that was highly critical of the Regents.

Finally, in May 1969, the respondent's one-year employment contract terminated and the Board of Regents voted not to offer him a new contract for the next academic year. The Regents issued a press release setting forth allegations of the respondent's insubordination.* But they provided him no official statement of the reasons for the nonrenewal of his contract. And they allowed him no opportunity for a hearing to challenge the basis of the nonrenewal.

The respondent then brought this action in Federal District Court. He alleged primarily that the Regents' decision not to rehire him was based on his public criticism of the policies of the college administration and thus infringed his right to freedom of speech. He also alleged that their failure to provide him an opportunity for a hearing violated the Fourteenth Amendment's guarantee of procedural due process. The petitioners—members of the Board of Regents and the president of the college—denied that their decision was made in retaliation for the respondent's public criticism and argued that they had no obligation to provide a hearing.* On the basis of these bare pleadings and three brief affidavits filed by the respondent,* the District Court granted summary judgment for the petitioners. It concluded that the respondent had "no cause of action against the [petitioners] since his contract of employment terminated May 31, 1969, and Odessa Junior College has not adopted the tenure system."*

The Court of Appeals reversed the judgment of the District Court. 430 F. 2d 939. First, it held that, despite the respondent's lack of tenure, the nonrenewal of his contract would violate the Fourteenth Amendment if it in fact was based on his protected free speech. Since the actual reason for the Regents' decision was "in total dispute" in the pleadings, the court remanded the case for a full hearing on this contested issue of fact. *Id.,* at 942–943. Second, the Court of Appeals held that, despite the respondent's lack of tenure, the failure to allow him an opportunity for a hear-

---

*Footnote omitted [Eds.].

ing would violate the constitutional guarantee of procedural due process if the respondent could show that he had an "expectancy" of re-employment. It, therefore, ordered that this issue of fact also be aired upon remand. *Id.,* at 943–944. We granted a writ of certiorari, 403 U. S. 917, and we have considered this case along with *Board of Regents* v. *Roth, ante,* p. 564.

I

The first question presented is whether the respondent's lack of a contractual or tenure right to re-employment, taken alone, defeats his claim that the nonrenewal of his contract violated the First and Fourteenth Amendments. We hold that it does not.

. . .

II

The respondent's lack of formal contractual or tenure security in continued employment at Odessa Junior College, though irrelevant to his free speech claim, is highly relevant to his procedural due process claim. But it may not be entirely dispositive.

We have held today in *Board of Regents* v. *Roth, ante,* p. 564, that the Constitution does not require opportunity for a hearing before the nonrenewal of a nontenured teacher's contract, unless he can show that the decision not to rehire him somehow deprived him of an interest in "liberty" or that he had a "property" interest in continued employment, despite the lack of tenure or a formal contract. In *Roth* the teacher had not made a showing on either point to justify summary judgment in his favor.

Similarly, the respondent here has yet to show that he has been deprived of an interest that could invoke procedural due process protection. As in *Roth,* the mere showing that he was not rehired in one particular job, without more, did not amount to a showing of a loss of liberty.[1] Nor did it amount to a showing of a loss of property.

But the respondent's allegations—which we must construe most favorably to the respondent at this stage of the litigation—do raise a genuine issue as to his interest in continued employment at Odessa Junior College. He alleged that this interest, though not secured by a formal contractual tenure provision, was secured by a no less binding understanding fostered by the college administration. In particular, the respondent alleged that the college had a *de facto* tenure program, and that he had tenure under that program. He claimed that he and others legiti-

---

[1]The Court of Appeals suggested that the respondent might have a due process right to some kind of hearing simply if he *asserts* to college officials that their decision was based on his constitutionally protected conduct. 430 F. 2d, at 944. We have rejected this approach in *Board of Regents* v. *Roth, ante,* at 575 n. 14.

mately relied upon an unusual provision that had been in the college's official Faculty Guide for many years:

> *"Teacher Tenure:* Odessa College has no tenure system. The Administration of the College wishes the faculty member to feel that he has permanent tenure as long as his teaching services are satisfactory and as long as he displays a cooperative attitude toward his co-workers and his superiors, and as long as he is happy in his work."

Moreover, the respondent claimed legitimate reliance upon guidelines promulgated by the Coordinating Board of the Texas College and University System that provided that a person, like himself, who had been employed as a teacher in the state college and university system for seven years or more has some form of job tenure.[2] Thus, the respondent offered to prove that a teacher with his long period of service at this particular State College had no less a "property" interest in continued employment than a formally tenured teacher at other colleges, and had no less a procedural due process right to a statement of reasons and a hearing before college officials upon their decision not to retain him.

We have made clear in *Roth, supra,* at 571–572, that "property" interests subject to procedural due process protection are not limited by a few rigid, technical forms. Rather, "property" denotes a broad range of interests that are secured by "existing rules or understandings." *Id.,* at 577. A person's interest in a benefit is a "property" interest for due process purposes if there are such rules or mutually explicit understandings that support his claim of entitlement to the benefit and that he may invoke at a hearing. *Ibid.*

[2]The relevant portion of the guidelines, adopted as "Policy Paper 1" by the Coordinating Board on October 16, 1967, reads:
"A. Tenure
    "Tenure means assurance to an experienced faculty member that he may expect to continue in his academic position unless adequate cause for dismissal is demonstrated in a fair hearing, following established procedures of due process.
    "A specific system of faculty tenure undergirds the integrity of each academic institution. In the Texas public colleges and universities, this tenure system should have these components:
    "(1) Beginning with appointment to the rank of full-time instructor or a higher rank, the probationary period for a faculty member shall not exceed seven years, including within this period appropriate full-time service in all institutions of higher education. This is subject to the provision that when, after a term of probationary service of more than three years in one or more institutions, a faculty member is employed by another institution, it may be agreed in writing that his new appointment is for a probationary period of not more than four years (even though thereby the person's total probationary period in the academic profession is extended beyond the normal maximum of seven years).

• • •

    "(3) Adequate cause for dismissal for a faculty member with tenure may be established by demonstrating professional incompetence, moral turpitude, or gross neglect of professional responsibilities."
The respondent alleges that, because he has been employed as a "full-time instructor" or professor within the Texas College and University System for 10 years, he should have "tenure" under these provisions.

A written contract with an explicit tenure provision clearly is evidence of a formal understanding that supports a teacher's claim of entitlement to continued employment unless sufficient "cause" is shown. Yet absence of such an explicit contractual provision may not always foreclose the possibility that a teacher has a "property" interest in re-employment. For example, the law of contracts in most, if not all, jurisdictions long has employed a process by which agreements, though not formalized in writing, may be "implied." 3 A. Corbin on Contracts §§ 561–572A (1960). Explicit contractual provisions may be supplemented by other agreements implied from "the promisor's words and conduct in the light of the surrounding circumstances." *Id.*, at § 562. And, "[t]he meaning of [the promisor's] words and acts is found by relating them to the usage of the past." *Ibid.*

A teacher, like the respondent, who has held his position for a number of years, might be able to show from the circumstances of this service—and from other relevant facts—that he has a legitimate claim of entitlement to job tenure. Just as this Court has found there to be a "common law of a particular industry or of a particular plant" that may supplement a collective-bargaining agreement, *Steelworkers* v. *Warrior & Gulf Co.*, 363 U. S. 574, 579, so there may be an unwritten "common law" in a particular university that certain employees shall have the equivalent of tenure. This is particularly likely in a college or university, like Odessa Junior College, that has no explicit tenure system even for senior members of its faculty, but that nonetheless may have created such a system in practice. See C. Byse & L. Joughin, Tenure in American Higher Education 17–28 (1959).[3]

In this case, the respondent has alleged the existence of rules and understandings, promulgated and fostered by state officials, that may justify his legitimate claim of entitlement to continued employment absent "sufficient cause." We disagree with the Court of Appeals insofar as it held that a mere subjective "expectancy" is protected by procedural due process, but we agree that the respondent must be given an opportunity to prove the legitimacy of his claim of such entitlement in light of "the policies and practices of the institution." 430 F. 2d, at 943. Proof of such a property interest would not, of course, entitle him to reinstatement. But such proof would obligate college officials to grant a hearing at his request, where he could be informed of the grounds for his nonretention and challenge their sufficiency.

Therefore, while we do not wholly agree with the opinion of the Court of Appeals, its judgment remanding this case to the District Court is

Affirmed.

---

[3]We do not now hold that the respondent has any such legitimate claim of entitlement to job tenure. For "[p]roperty interests . . . are not created by the Constitution. Rather, they are created and their dimensions are defined by existing rules or understandings that stem from an independent source such as state law. . . ." *Board of Regents* v. *Roth, supra,* at 577. If it is the law of Texas that a teacher in the respondent's position has no contractual or other claim to job tenure, the respondent's claim would be defeated.

Goldberg, Commissioner of Social Services of the City of New York v. Kelly et al.

UNITED STATES SUPREME COURT

MR. JUSTICE BRENNAN delivered the opinion of the Court.

The question for decision is whether a State that terminates public assistance payments to a particular recipient without affording him the opportunity for an evidentiary hearing prior to termination denies the recipient procedural due process in violation of the Due Process Clause of the Fourteenth Amendment.

This action was brought in the District Court for the Southern District of New York by residents of New York City receiving financial aid under the federally assisted program of Aid to Families with Dependent Children (AFDC) or under New York State's general Home Relief program.* Their complaint alleged that the New York State and New York City officials administering these programs terminated, or were about to terminate, such aid without prior notice and hearing, thereby denying them due process of law. . . .*

Pursuant to subdivision (b), the New York City Department of Social Services promulgated Procedure No. 68-18. A caseworker who has doubts about the recipient's continued eligibility must first discuss them with the recipient. If the caseworker concludes that the recipient is no longer eligible, he recommends termination of aid to a unit supervisor. If the latter concurs, he sends the recipient a letter stating the reasons for proposing to terminate aid and notifying him that within seven days he may request that a higher official review the record, and may support the request with a written statement prepared personally or with the aid of an attorney or other person. If the reviewing official affirms the determination of ineligibility, aid is stopped immediately and the recipient is informed by letter of the reasons for the action. Appellees' challenge to this procedure emphasizes the absence of any provisions for the personal appearance of the recipient before the reviewing official, for oral presentation of evidence, and for confrontation and cross-examination of adverse witnesses.* However, the letter does inform the recipient that he may request a post-termination "fair hearing."* This is a proceeding before an independent state hearing officer at which the recipient may appear personally, offer oral evidence, confront and cross-examine the

---

397 U.S. 254 (1970). Footnotes renumbered and locations of deleted citations marked with double asterisk (**). [Eds.]

*Footnote omitted [Eds.].

witnesses against him, and have a record made of the hearing. If the recipient prevails at the "fair hearing" he is paid all funds erroneously withheld.* HEW Handbook, pt. IV. §§ 6200–6500; 18 NYCRR §§ 84.2– 84.23. A recipient whose aid is not restored by a "fair hearing" decision may have judicial review. N. Y. Civil Practice Law and Rules, Art. 78 (1963). The recipient is so notified, 18 NYCRR § 84.16.

I

The constitutional issue to be decided, therefore, is the narrow one whether the Due Process Clause requires that the recipient be afforded an evidentiary hearing *before* the termination of benefits.* The District Court held that only a pre-termination evidentiary hearing would satisfy the constitutional command, and rejected the argument of the state and city officials that the combination of the post-termination "fair hearing" with the informal pre-termination review disposed of all due process claims. The court said: "While post-termination review is relevant, there is one overpowering fact which controls here. By hypothesis, a welfare recipient is destitute, without funds or assets. . . . Suffice it to say that to cut off a welfare recipient in the face of . . . 'brutal need' without a prior hearing of some sort is unconscionable, unless overwhelming considerations justify it."** The court rejected the argument that the need to protect the public's tax revenues supplied the requisite "overwhelming consideration." "Against the justified desire to protect public funds must be weighed the individual's overpowering need in this unique situation not to be wrongfully deprived of assistance. . . . While the problem of additional expense must be kept in mind, it does not justify denying a hearing meeting the ordinary standards of due process. Under all the circumstances, we hold that due process requires an adequate hearing before termination of welfare benefits, and the fact that there is a later constitutionally fair proceeding does not alter the result."** Although state officials were party defendants in the action, only the Commissioner of Social Services of the City of New York appealed. We noted probable jurisdiction, 394 U. S. 971 (1969), to decide important issues that have been the subject of disagreement in principle between the three-judge court in the present case and that convened in *Wheeler* v. *Montgomery*, No. 14, *post*, p. 280, also decided today. We affirm.

Appellant does not contend that procedural due process is not applicable to the termination of welfare benefits. Such benefits are a matter of statutory entitlement for persons qualified to receive them.[1] Their termi-

---

*Footnote omitted [Eds.].

[1]It may be realistic today to regard welfare entitlements as more like "property" than a "gratuity." Much of the existing wealth in this country takes the form of rights that do not fall within traditional common-law concepts of property. It has been aptly noted that

"[s]ociety today is built around entitlement. The automobile dealer has his franchise, the doctor and lawyer their professional licenses, the worker his union membership,

nation involves state action that adjudicates important rights. The constitutional challenge cannot be answered by an argument that public assistance benefits are "a 'privilege' and not a 'right.' "** Relevant constitutional restraints apply as much to the withdrawal of public assistance benefits as to disqualification for unemployment compensation,** or to denial of a tax exemption,** or to discharge from public employment.** * The extent to which procedural due process must be afforded the recipient is influenced by the extent to which he may be "condemned to suffer grievous loss,"** and depends upon whether the recipient's interest in avoiding that loss outweighs the governmental interest in summary adjudication. Accordingly, as we said in *Cafeteria & Restaurant Workers Union* v. *McElroy*, 367 U. S. 886, 895 (1961), "consideration of what procedures due process may require under any given set of circumstances must begin with a determination of the precise nature of the government function involved as well as of the private interest that has been affected by governmental action."**

It is true, of course, that some governmental benefits may be administratively terminated without affording the recipient a pre-termination evidentiary hearing.* But we agree with the District Court that when welfare is discontinued, only a pre-termination evidentiary hearing provides the recipient with procedural due process.** For qualified recipients, welfare provides the means to obtain essential food, clothing, housing, and medical care.** Thus the crucial factor in this context—a factor not present in the case of the blacklisted government contractor, the discharged government employee, the taxpayer denied a tax exemption, or virtually anyone else whose governmental entitlements are ended—is that termination of aid pending resolution of a controversy over eligibility may deprive an *eligible* recipient of the very means by which to live while he waits. Since he lacks independent resources, his situation becomes immediately desperate. His need to concentrate upon finding the means for daily subsistence, in turn, adversely affects his ability to seek redress from the welfare bureaucracy.*

Moreover, important governmental interests are promoted by affording recipients a pre-termination evidentiary hearing. From its founding the Nation's basic commitment has been to foster the dignity and

---

contract, and pension rights, the executive his contract and stock options; all are devices to aid security and independence. Many of the most important of these entitlements now flow from government: subsidies to farmers and businessmen, routes for airlines and channels for television stations; long term contracts for defense, space, and education; social security pensions for individuals. Such sources of security, whether private or public, are no longer regarded as luxuries or gratuities; to the recipients they are essentials, fully deserved, and in no sense a form of charity. It is only the poor whose entitlements, although recognized by public policy, have not been effectively enforced."

Reich, Individual Rights and Social Welfare: The Emerging Legal Issues, 74 Yale L. J. 1245, 1255 (1965). See also Reich, The New Property, 73 Yale L. J. 733 (1964).

*Footnote omitted [Eds.].

well-being of all persons within its borders. We have come to recognize that forces not within the control of the poor contribute to their poverty.* This perception, against the background of our traditions, has significantly influenced the development of the contemporary public assistance system. Welfare, by meeting the basic demands of subsistence, can help bring within the reach of the poor the same opportunities that are available to others to participate meaningfully in the life of the community. At the same time, welfare guards against the societal malaise that may flow from a widespread sense of unjustified frustration and insecurity. Public assistance, then, is not mere charity, but a means to "promote the general Welfare, and secure the Blessings of Liberty to ourselves and our Posterity." The same governmental interests that counsel the provision of welfare, counsel as well its uninterrupted provision to those eligible to receive it; pre-termination evidentiary hearings are indispensable to that end.

Appellant does not challenge the force of these considerations but argues that they are outweighed by countervailing governmental interests in conserving fiscal and administrative resources. These interests, the argument goes, justify the delay of any evidentiary hearing until after discontinuance of the grants. Summary adjudication protects the public fisc by stopping payments promptly upon discovery of reason to believe that a recipient is no longer eligible. Since most terminations are accepted without challenge, summary adjudication also conserves both the fisc and administrative time and energy by reducing the number of evidentiary hearings actually held.

We agree with the District Court, however, that these governmental interests are not overriding in the welfare context. The requirement of a prior hearing doubtless involves some greater expense, and the benefits paid to ineligible recipients pending decision at the hearing probably cannot be recouped, since these recipients are likely to be judgment-proof. But the State is not without weapons to minimize these increased costs. Much of the drain on fiscal and administrative resources can be reduced by developing procedures for prompt pre-termination hearings and by skillful use of personnel and facilities. Indeed, the very provision for a post-termination evidentiary hearing in New York's Home Relief program is itself cogent evidence that the State recognizes the primacy of the public interest in correct eligibility determinations and therefore in the provision of procedural safeguards. Thus, the interest of the eligible recipient in uninterrupted receipt of public assistance, coupled with the State's interest that his payments not be erroneously terminated, clearly outweighs the State's competing concern to prevent any increase in its fiscal and administrative burdens. As the District Court correctly concluded, "[t]he stakes are simply too high for the welfare recipient, and the possibility for honest error or irritable misjudgment too great, to allow termination of aid without giving the recipient a chance, if he so desires,

*Footnote omitted [Eds.].

to be fully informed of the case against him so that he may contest its basis and produce evidence in rebuttal."** . . .

Affirmed

• • •

Mr. Justice Black, dissenting.

In the last half century the United States, along with many, perhaps most, other nations of the world, has moved far toward becoming a welfare state, that is, a nation that for one reason or another taxes its most affluent people to help support, feed, clothe, and shelter its less fortunate citizens. The result is that today more than nine million men, women, and children in the United States receive some kind of state or federally financed public assistance in the form of allowances or gratuities, generally paid them periodically, usually by the week, month, or quarter.[2] Since these gratuities are paid on the basis of need, the list of recipients is not static, and some people go off the lists and others are added from time to time. These ever-changing lists put a constant administrative burden on government and it certainly could not have reasonably anticipated that this burden would include the additional procedural expense imposed by the Court today. . . .

The more than a million names on the relief rolls in New York,[3] and the more than nine million names on the rolls of all the 50 States were not put there at random. The names are there because state welfare officials believed that those people were eligible for assistance. Probably in the officials' haste to make out the lists many names were put there erroneously in order to alleviate immediate suffering, and undoubtedly some people are drawing relief who are not entitled under the law to do so. Doubtless some draw relief checks from time to time who know they are not eligible, either because they are not actually in need or for some other reason. Many of those who thus draw undeserved gratuities are without sufficient property to enable the government to collect back from them any money they wrongfully receive. But the Court today holds that it would violate the Due Process Clause of the Fourteenth Amendment to stop paying those people weekly or monthly allowances unless the government first affords them a full "evidentiary hearing" even though welfare officials are persuaded that the recipients are not rightfully entitled to receive a penny under the law. In other words, although some recipients might be on the lists for payment wholly because of deliberate fraud on their part, the Court holds that the government is helpless and must continue, until after an evidentiary hearing, to pay money that it does not

---

[2]This figure includes all recipients of Old-age Assistance, Aid to Families with Dependent Children, Aid to the Blind, Aid to the Permanently and Totally Disabled, and general assistance. In this case appellants are AFDC and general assistance recipients. In New York State alone there are 951,000 AFDC recipients and 108,000 on general assistance. In the Nation as a whole the comparable figures are 6,080,000 and 391,000. U. S. Bureau of the Census, Statistical Abstract of the United States: 1969 (90th ed.), Table 435, p. 297.

[3]See n. 2, *supra*.

owe, never has owed, and never could owe. I do not believe there is any provision in our Constitution that should thus paralyze the government's efforts to protect itself against making payments to people who are not entitled to them.

Particularly do I not think that the Fourteenth Amendment should be given such an unnecessarily broad construction. That Amendment came into being primarily to protect Negroes from discrimination, and while some of its language can and does protect others, all know that the chief purpose behind it was to protect ex-slaves.** The Court, however, relies upon the Fourteenth Amendment and in effect says that failure of the government to pay a promised charitable instalment to an individual deprives that individual of *his own property,* in violation of the Due Process Clause of the Fourteenth Amendment. It somewhat strains credulity to say that the government's promise of charity to an individual is property belonging to that individual when the government denies that the individual is honestly entitled to receive such a payment. . . .

The procedure required today as a matter of constitutional law finds no precedent in our legal system. Reduced to its simplest terms, the problem in this case is similar to that frequently encountered when two parties have an ongoing legal relationship that requires one party to make periodic payments to the other. Often the situation arises where the party "owing" the money stops paying it and justifies his conduct by arguing that the recipient is not legally entitled to payment. The recipient can, of course, disagree and go to court to compel payment. But I know of no situation in our legal system in which the person alleged to owe money to another is required by law to continue making payments to a judgment-proof claimant without the benefit of any security or bond to insure that these payments can be recovered if he wins his legal argument. Yet today's decision in no way obligates the welfare recipient to pay back any benefits wrongfully received during the pre-termination evidentiary hearings or post any bond, and in all "fairness" it could not do so. These recipients are by definition too poor to post a bond or to repay the benefits that, as the majority assumes, must be spent as received to insure survival.

The Court apparently feels that this decision will benefit the poor and needy. In my judgment the eventual result will be just the opposite. While today's decision requires only an administrative, evidentiary hearing, the inevitable logic of the approach taken will lead to constitutionally imposed, time-consuming delays of a full adversary process of administrative and judicial review. In the next case the welfare recipients are bound to argue that cutting off benefits before judicial review of the agency's decision is also a denial of due process. Since, by hypothesis, termination of aid at that point may still "deprive an *eligible* recipient of the very means by which to live while he waits," *ante,* at 264, I would be surprised if the weighing process did not compel the conclusion that termination without full judicial review would be unconscionable. After all, at each step, as the majority seems to feel, the issue is only one of weighing the government's pocketbook against the actual survival of the recipient, and surely that balance must always tip in favor of the individual. Similarly today's decision requires only the opportunity to have the benefit of counsel at the administrative hearing, but it is difficult to believe that the same reasoning process would not require the appointment of counsel, for otherwise the right to counsel is a meaningless one since these people are too poor to hire their own advocates. Cf. *Gideon* v. *Wainwright,* 372 U. S. 335, 344 (1963). Thus the end result of today's decision may well be that the government, once it decides to give welfare benefits, cannot reverse that decision until the recipient has had the benefits of full administrative and judicial review, including, of course, the opportunity to present his case to this Court. Since this process will usually entail a delay of several years, the inevitable result of such a constitutionally imposed burden will be that the government will not put a claimant on the rolls initially until it has made an exhaustive investigation to determine his eligibility. While this Court will perhaps have insured that no needy person will be taken off the rolls without a full "due process" proceeding, it will also have insured that many will never get on the rolls, or at least that they will remain destitute during the lengthy proceedings followed to determine initial eligibility.

For the foregoing reasons I dissent from the Court's holding. The operation of a welfare state is a new experiment for our Nation. For this reason, among others, I feel that new experiments in carrying out a welfare program should not be frozen into our constitutional structure. They should be left, as are other legislative determinations, to the Congress and the legislatures that the people elect to make our laws.

Suggestions for Further Reading

Previous Supreme Court decisions with a bearing on the question of whether the "laws of nature, physical phenomena, and abstract ideas" are patentable include *Parker* v. *Flook,* 437 U.S. 584 (1978); *Gottschalk* v. *Benson,* 409 U.S. 63 (1973); and *Funk Seed Co.* v. *Kalo Co.,* 333 U.S. 127 (1948).

As a way of opening a more general study of the legal materials on intellectual property, consult the Note by Joseph E. Kovacs, "Beyond the Realm of Copyright: Is There Legal Sanctuary for the Merchant of Ideas?" 41 *Brooklyn Law Review* 284 (1974), and the text of the new copyright law, Public Law 94553, which revised Title 17 of the U.S. Code, and became effective on January 1, 1978. Relevant legal casebooks include E. Ernest Goldstein, ed., *Patent, Trademark and Copyright Law* (Mineola, N.Y.:

Foundation Press, 1959); and Benjamin Kaplan and Ralph S. Brown, Jr., eds., *Copyright,* 2d ed. (Mineola, N.Y.: Foundation Press, 1974).

With regard to the *Goldberg* case, readers may be interested to know that in *Mathews* v. *Ehlridge,* 424 U.S. 319 (1976), the Court refused to extend the *Goldberg* result to the payment of Social Security Disability Benefits. For a summary of the law on these issues, see Laurence H. Tribe, *American Constitutional Law* (Mineola, N.Y.: Foundation Press, 1978), chap. 10, sect. 12–16 (and especially sect. 12).

For material related to *Perry et al.* v. *Sindermann,* readers can consult the comment on "Unemployment as a Taking without Just Compensation," 43 *Southern California Law Review* 488 (1970). *Board of Regents* v. *Roth,* 408 U.S. 564 (1971), concerns tenured teachers, and *Bishop* v. *Wood,* 426 U.S. 341 (1975), raises a comparable issue about police officers.

SECTION TWO
ACQUISITION

The two cases in this section concern issues arising in the acquisition of property. If something is unowned (abandoned or a part of "nature") and if we agree that a person can come to own it simply by occupying it or taking possession of it, how then do we decide when a person has done *enough* to count as occupation or possession? The underlying question can be asked in many important contexts. Think of explorers, the gold rush, homesteading, fishing rights, and so on. Often, possession has been considered to be enough to create a presumption of ownership. It has been, as lawyers say, the "root of title." But the problematic nature of possession shows the need for sophisticated theory on even this most basic of property questions: Who has it?

Almost two centuries ago Lodowick Post chased a wild fox across some unowned land in Queens County, New York. Before he could seize it, a man named Pierson intercepted the fox, killed it, and carried it off. Post sued, claiming that the fox was his, and won in the trial court (the justice's court). But Pierson appealed and the Supreme Court of New York considers the case in *Pierson* v. *Post*. Relying upon "ancient writers upon general principles of law," the Court holds for Pierson. Since Post had neither deprived the fox of its natural liberty nor subjected it to his control, he has no basis for legal action against Pierson. To hold otherwise "would prove a fertile source of quarrels and litigation."

In his dissenting opinion, Judge Livingston expresses his view that the opinions of sportsmen ought to count for more than those of the ancient authorities. The law should provide "the greatest possible encouragement" for those who would pursue the "noxious beast." A more appropriate ruling would have allowed Post to acquire property in the fox provided "he be within reach" of it or have "a reasonable prospect" of taking it.

Haslem v. *Lockwood* focuses on the ownership of eighteen heaps of horse manure. Thomas Haslem had had them gathered up on the evening of April 6, 1869, intending to cart them off the next day. But on the following morning, William Lockwood came along and, seeing the heaps of manure, took them away himself. Haslem sued to recover his property (trover), but lost, He then appealed, claiming that the trial judge had erred. It is this claim that Judge Park considers after hearing the arguments of the attorneys, here summarized by the court reporter. Judge Park determines that the manure is personal property that has been abandoned by the owners of the horses. It is not part of the real estate (property held in land). The Borough of Stamford, which owned the land upon which the abandoned personal property rested, apparently did not object to people hauling the filthy nuisance away. Holding for Haslem, Judge Park rules that the plaintiff-appellant (Haslem), having increased the value of the manure by gathering it up into heaps, does not lose his property right in the manure if he leaves it for a reasonable time in order to procure the necessary means to take it away. Therefore the lower court did err and a new trial is required.

Pierson v. Post

SUPREME COURT OF NEW YORK

This was an action of trespass on the case, commenced in a justice's court by the present defendant against the now plaintiff.

The declaration stated that Post, being in possession of certain dogs and hounds under his command, did, "upon a certain wild and uninhabited, unpossessed and waste land, called the beach, find and start one of those noxious beasts called a fox," and whilst there hunting, chasing and pursuing the same with his dogs and hounds, and when in view thereof, Pierson, well knowing the fox was so hunted and pursued, did, in the sight of Post, to prevent his catching the same, kill and carry it off. A

3 Caines 175 (1805).

verdict having been rendered for the plaintiff below, the defendant there sued. . . .

TOMPKINS, J., delivered the opinion of the court. This cause comes before us on a return to a certiorari directed to one of the justices of Queens county.

The question submitted by the counsel in this cause for our determination is, whether Lodowick Post, by the pursuit with his hounds in the manner alleged in his declaration, acquired such a right to, or property in the fox, as will sustain an action against Pierson for killing and taking him away?

The cause was argued with much ability by the counsel on both sides, and presents for our decision a novel and nice question. It is admitted, that a fox is an animal ferae naturae, and that property in such animals is acquired by occupancy only. These admissions narrow the discussion to the simple question of what acts amount to occupancy, applied to acquiring right to wild animals?

If we have recourse to the ancient writers upon general principles of law, the judgment below is obviously erroneous. Justinian's Institutes, lib. 2, tit. I, sect. 13, and Fleta, lib. III, c. II, page 175, adopt the principle, that pursuit alone, vests no property or right in the huntsman; and that even pursuit accompanied with wounding, is equally ineffectual for that purpose, unless the animal be actually taken. The same principle is recognised by Bracton, lib. II, c. I, page 8.

Puffendorf, lib. IV, c. 6, sec. 2, §10, defines occupancy of beasts ferae naturae, to be the actual corporal possession of them, and Bynkershoek is cited as coinciding in this definition. It is indeed with hesitation that Puffendorf affirms that a wild beast mortally wounded, or greatly maimed, cannot be fairly intercepted by another, whilst the pursuit of the person inflicting the wound continues. The foregoing authorities are decisive to show that mere pursuit gave Post no legal right to the fox, but that he became the property of Pierson, who intercepted and killed him.

It therefore only remains to inquire whether there are any contrary principles, or authorities, to be found in other books, which ought to induce a different decision. Most of the cases which have occurred in England, relating to property in wild animals, have either been discussed and decided upon the principles of their positive statute regulations, or have arisen between the huntsman and the owner of the land upon which beasts ferae naturae have been apprehended; the former claiming them by title of occupancy, and the latter ratione soli. Little satisfactory aid can, therefore, be derived from the English reporters.

Barbeyrac, in his notes on Puffendorf, does not accede to the definition of occupancy by the latter, but, on the contrary, affirms that actual bodily seizure is not, in all cases, necessary to constitute possession of wild animals. He does not, however, *describe* the acts which, according to his ideas, will amount to an appropriation of such animals to private use, so as to exclude the claims of all other persons, by title of occupancy, to the same animals; and he is far from averring that pursuit alone is sufficient for that purpose. To a certain extent, and as far as Barbeyrac appears to me to go, his objections to Puffendorf's definition of occupancy are reasonable and correct. That is to say, that actual bodily seizure is not indispensable to acquire right to, or possession of, wild beasts; but that, on the contrary, the mortal wounding of such beasts, by one not abandoning his pursuit, may, with the utmost propriety, be deemed possession of him; since thereby, the pursuer manifests an unequivocal intention of appropriating the animal to his individual use, has deprived him of his natural liberty, and brought him within his certain control. So, also, encompassing and securing such animals with nets and toils, or otherwise intercepting them, in such a manner as to deprive them of their natural liberty, and render escape impossible, may justly be deemed to give possession of them to those persons who, by their industry and labor, have used such means of apprehending them. . . . The case now under consideration is one of mere pursuit, and presents no circumstances or acts which can bring it within the definition of occupancy by Puffendorf, . . . or the ideas of Barbeyrac upon that subject. . . .

We are the more readily inclined to confine possession or occupancy of beasts ferae naturae within the limits prescribed by the learned authors above cited, for the sake of certainty, and preserving peace and order in society. If the first seeing, starting or pursuing such animals, without having so wounded, circumvented or ensnared them, so as to deprive them of their natural liberty, and subject them to the control of their pursuer, should afford the basis of actions against others for intercepting and killing them, it would prove a fertile source of quarrels and litigation.

However uncourteous or unkind the conduct of Pierson towards Post, in this instance, may have been, yet his act was productive of no injury or damage for which a legal remedy can be applied. We are of the opinion the judgment below was erroneous, and ought to be reversed.

Livingston, J. [dissenting]. . . . This is a knotty point, and should have been submitted to the arbitration of sportsmen, without poring over Justinian, Fleta, Bracton, Puffendorf, Locke, Barbeyrac or Blackstone, all of whom have been cited; they would have had no difficulty in coming to a prompt and correct conclusion. . . . But the parties have referred the question to our judgment, and we must dispose of it as well as we can, from the partial lights we possess, leaving to a higher tribunal* the correction of any mistake which we may be so unfortunate as to make. By the pleadings it is admitted, that a fox is a "wild and noxious beast." Both parties have regarded him as the law of nations does a pirate, "hostem humani generis," and although "de mortuis nil nisi bonum" be a maxim of our profession, the memory of the deceased has not been spared. His depredations on farmers and on barn yards, have not been forgotten; and to put him to death wherever found, is allowed to be meritorious, and of public benefit. Hence it follows, that our decision should have in view the greatest possible encouragement to the destruction of an animal so cunning and ruthless in his career. But who would keep a pack of hounds; or what gentleman, at the sound of the horn and at peep of day would mount his steed, and for hours together, "sub jove frigido" or a vertical sun, pursue the windings of

---

*The Supreme Court of New York is not that state's highest court. In 1805 it was subordinate to the Court of Errors, now transformed into the Court of Appeals [Eds.].

this wily quadruped, if, just as night came on, and his stratagems and strength were nearly exhausted, a saucy intruder, who had not shared in the honors or labours of the chase, were permitted to come in at the death, and bear away in triumph the object of pursuit? Whatever Justinian may have thought of the matter, it must be recollected that his code was compiled many hundred years ago, and it would be very hard indeed, at the distance of so many centuries, not to have a right to establish a rule for ourselves. In his day, we read of no order of men who made it a business, in the language of the declaration in this cause, "with hounds and dogs to find, start, pursue, hunt, and chase," these animals, and that too, without any other motive than the preservation of Roman poultry; if this diversion had been then in fashion, the lawyers who composed his institutes, would have taken care not to pass it by without suitable encouragement. If any thing, therefore, in the digests or pandects shall appear to militate against the defendant in error, who, on this occasion, was the fox hunter, we have only to say tempora mutantur; and if men themselves change with the times, why should not laws also undergo an alteration? . . .

Now, as we are without any municipal regulations of our own, . . . we are at liberty . . . [to hold] that property in animals ferae naturae, may be acquired without bodily touch or manucaption, provided the pursuer be within reach, or have a *reasonable* prospect (which certainly existed here) of taking, what he has *thus* discovered [with] an intention of converting to his own use.

When we reflect also that the interest of our husbandmen, the most useful of men in any community, will be advanced by the destruction of a beast so pernicious and incorrigible, we cannot greatly err in saying that a pursuit like the present, through waste and unoccupied lands, which must inevitably and speedily have terminated in corporal possession, or bodily seisin, confers such a right to the object of it as to make anyone a wrong doer who shall interfere and shoulder the spoil. The *justice's* judgment ought therefore, in my opinion, to be affirmed.

Haslem v. Lockwood

SUPREME COURT OF ERRORS,
STATE OF CONNECTICUT

Trover, for a quantity of manure; brought before a justice of the peace and appealed by the defendant to the Court of Common Pleas for

37 Conn. 500 (1871). Locations of deleted citations marked with double asterisk (**).
[Eds.].

the county of Fairfield, and tried in that court, on the general issue closed to the court, before BREWSTER, J.

On the trial it was proved that the plaintiff employed two men to gather into heaps, on the evening of April 6th, 1869, some manure that lay scattered along the side of a public highway, for several rods, in the borough of Stamford, intending to remove the same to his own land the next evening. The men began to scrape the manure into heaps at six o'clock in the evening, and after gathering eighteen heaps, or about six cart-loads, left the same at eight o'clock in the evening in the street. The heaps consisted chiefly of manure made by horses hitched to the railing of the public park in, and belonging to, the borough of Stamford, and was all gathered between the center of the highway and the park; the rest of the heaps consisting of dirt, straw and the ordinary scrapings of highways. The defendant on the next morning, seeing the heaps, endeavored without success to ascertain who had made them, and inquired of the warden of the borough if he had given permission to any one to remove them, and ascertained from him that he had not. He thereupon, before noon on that day, removed the heaps and also the rest of the manure scattered along the side of the highway adjacent to the park, to his own land.

The plaintiff and defendant both claimed to have received authority from the warden to remove the manure before the 6th of April, but in fact neither had any legal authority from the warden, or from any officer of the borough or of the town. The borough of Stamford was the sole adjoining proprietor of the land on which the manure lay scattered before it was gathered by the plaintiff. No notice was left on the heaps or near by, by the plaintiff or his workmen, to indicate who had gathered them, nor had the plaintiff or his workmen any actual possession of the heaps after eight o'clock in the evening on the 6th of April.

Neither the plaintiff while gathering, nor the defendant while removing the heaps, was interfered with or opposed by any one. The removal of the manure and scrapings was calculated to improve the appearance and health of the borough. The six loads were worth one dollar per load. The plaintiff, on ascertaining that the defendant had removed the manure, demanded payment for the same, which the defendant refused. Neither the plaintiff nor defendant owned any land adjacent to the place where the manure lay. The highway was kept in repair by the town of Stamford.

On the above facts the plaintiff claimed, and prayed the court to rule, that the manure was personal property which had been abandoned by its owners and became by such abandonment the property of the first person who should take possession of the same, which the plaintiff had done by gathering it into heaps, and that it was not and never had been a part of the real estate of the borough or of any one else who might be regarded as owning the fee of the soil. He further claimed that if it was a part of the real estate, it was taken without committing a trespass, and with the tacit consent of the owners of such real estate, and that thereby it became his personal property of which he was lawfully possessed, and at least that he had acquired such an interest in it as would enable him to hold it against any person except the owner of the land or some person claiming under the owner.

The defendant claimed, upon the above facts, that the manure being dropped upon and spread out over the surface of the earth was a part of the real estate, and belonged to the owner of the fee, subject to the public easement; that the fee was either in the borough of Stamford or the town of Stamford, or in the parties who owned the lands adjacent; that therefore the scraping up of the manure, mixed with the soil, if real estate, did not change its nature to that of personal estate, unless it was removed, whether the plaintiff had the consent of the owner of the fee or not; and that, unless the heaps became personal property, the plaintiff could not maintain his action. The defendant further claimed, as matter of law, that if the manure was always personal estate, or became personal estate after being scraped up into heaps, the plaintiff, by leaving it from eight o'clock in the evening until noon the next day, abandoned all right of possession which he might have had, and could not, therefore, maintain his action.

The court ruled adversely to the claims of the plaintiff and held that on the facts proved the plaintiff had not made out a sufficient interest in, or right of possession to, the subject matter in dispute, to authorize a recovery in the suit, and rendered judgment for the defendant.

The plaintiff moved for a new trial for error in this ruling of the court.

Curtis and Hoyt [Counsel for the plaintiff-appellant], in support of the motion.

1. The manure in question was personal property abandoned by its owners.**

2. It never became a part of the real estate on which it was abandoned.**

3. It being personal property abandoned by its owners, and lying upon the highway, and neither the owners of the fee nor the proper authorities of the town and borough having by any act of theirs shown any intention to appropriate the same, it became lawful for the plaintiff to gather it up and remove it from the highway, providing he did not commit a trespass, and removed it without objection from the owners of the land.** And no trespass was in fact committed. No person interfered with the plaintiff or made any objection. This court cannot presume a trespass to have been committed.**

4. But if the manure had become a part of the real estate, yet when it was gathered into heaps by the plaintiff it was severed from the realty and became personal estate.** And being gathered without molestation from any person owning or claiming to own the land, it is to be considered as having been taken by the tacit consent of such owner.**

5. The plaintiff therefore acquired not only a valid legal possession, but a title by occupancy, and by having expended labor and money upon the property. Such a title is a good legal title against every person but the true owner.

6. If the plaintiff had a legal title then he had the constructive possession. If he had legal possession, and only left the property for a short time intending to return and take it away, then he might maintain an action against a wrong doer for taking it away.** The leaving of property for a short time, intending to return, does not constitute an abandonment. The property is still to be considered as in the possession of the plaintiff.

Olmstead [Counsel for the defendant-respondent], contra.

1. The manure mixed with the dirt and ordinary scrapings of the highway, being spread out over the surface of the highway, was a part of the *real estate*, and belonged to the owner of the fee, subject to the public easement.**

2. The scraping up of the manure and dirt into piles, if the same was a part of the real estate, did not change its nature to that of *personal property*, unless there was a severance of it from the realty by removal, (which there was not), whether the plaintiff had the consent of the owner of the fee or not, which consent it is conceded the plaintiff did not have.

3. Unless the scraping up of the heaps made their substance *personal property*, the plaintiff could not maintain his action either for trespass or trespass on the case.

4. In trespass *de bonis asportatis*, or trover, the plaintiff must have had the *actual possession*, or a right to the immediate possession, in order to recover.**

5. If the manure was always personal estate, it being spread upon the surface of the earth, it was in possession of the owner of the fee, who was not the plaintiff.** The scraping of it into heaps, unless it was removed, would not change the *possession* from the owner of the fee to the plaintiff. The plaintiff therefore never had the *possession*.

6. If the heaps were personal property the plaintiff never had any right in the property, but only *mere possession*, if anything, which he abandoned by leaving the same upon the public highway from 8 o'clock in the evening until 12 o'clock the next day, without leaving any notice on or about the property, or any one to exercise control over the same in his behalf.**

PARK, Judge. We think the manure scattered upon the ground, under the circumstances of this case, was personal property. The cases referred to by the defendant to show that it was real estate are not in point. The principle of those cases is, that manure made in the usual course of husbandry upon a farm is so attached to and connected with the realty that, in the absence of any express stipulation to the contrary, it becomes appurtenant to it. The principle was established for the benefit of agriculture. It found its origin in the fact that it is essential to the successful cultivation of a farm that the manure, produced from the droppings of cattle and swine fed upon the products of the farm, and composted with earth and vegetable matter taken from the land, should be used to supply the drain made upon the soil in the production of crops, which otherwise would become impoverished and barren; and in the fact that manure so produced is generally regarded by farmers in this country as a part of the realty and has been so treated by landlords and tenants from time immemorial.**

But this principle does not apply to the droppings of animals driven by travelers upon the highway. The highway is not used, and cannot be used, for the purpose of agriculture. The manure is of no benefit whatsoever to it, but on the contrary is a detriment; and in cities and large villages it becomes a nuisance, and is removed by public officers at public expense. The finding in this case is, "that the removal of the manure and scrapings was calculated to improve the appearance and health of the borough." It is therefore evident that the cases relied upon by the defendant have no application to the case.

But it is said that if the manure was personal property, it was in the possession of the owner of the fee, and the scraping it into heaps by the plaintiff did not change the possession, but it continued as before, and that therefore the plaintiff cannot recover, for he neither had the possession nor the right to the immediate possession.

The manure originally belonged to the travelers whose animals dropped it, but it being worthless to them was immediately abandoned; and whether it then became the property of the borough of Stamford which owned the fee of the land on which the manure lay, it is unnecessary to determine; for, if it did, the case finds that the removal of the filth would be an improvement to the borough, and no objection was made by any one to the use that the plaintiff attempted to make of it. Considering the character of such accumulations upon highways in cities and villages, and the light in which they are everywhere regarded in closely settled communities, we cannot believe that the borough in this instance would have had any objection to the act of the plaintiff in removing a nuisance that affected the public health and the appearance of the streets. At all events, we think the facts of the case show a sufficient right in the plaintiff to the immediate possession of the property as against a mere wrong doer.

The defendant appears before the court in no enviable light. He does not pretend that he had a right to the manure, even when scattered upon the highway, superior to that of the plaintiff; but after the plaintiff had changed its original condition and greatly enhanced its value by his labor, he seized and appropriated to his own use the fruits of the plaintiff's outlay, and now seeks immunity from responsibility on the ground that the plaintiff was a wrong doer as well as himself. The conduct of the defendant is in keeping with his claim, and neither commends itself to the favorable consideration of the court. The plaintiff had the peaceable and quiet possession of the property; and we deem this sufficient until the borough of Stamford shall make complaint.

It is further claimed that if the plaintiff had a right to the property by virtue of occupancy, he lost the right when he ceased to retain the actual possession of the manure after scraping it into heaps.

We do not question the general doctrine, that where the right by occupancy exists, it exists no longer than the party retains the actual possession of the property, or till he appropriates it to his own use by removing it to some other place. If he leaves the property at the place where it was discovered, and does nothing whatsoever to enhance its value or change its nature, his right by occupancy is unquestionably gone. But the question is, if a party finds property comparatively worthless, as the plaintiff found the property in question, owing to its scattered condition upon the highway, and greatly increases its value by his labor and expense, does he lose his right if he leaves it a reasonable time to procure the means to take it away, when such means are necessary for its removal?

Suppose a teamster with a load of grain, while traveling the highway, discovers a rent in one of his bags, and finds that his grain is scattered upon the road for the distance of a mile. He considers the labor of collecting his corn of more value than the property itself, and he therefore abandons it, and pursues his way. *A* afterwards finds the grain in this condition and gathers it kernel by kernel into heaps by the side of the road, and leaves it a reasonable time to procure the means necessary for its removal. While he is gone for his bag, *B* discovers the grain thus conveniently collected in heaps and appropriates it to his own use. Has *A* any remedy? If he has not, the law in this instance is open to just reproach. We think under such circumstances *A* would have a reasonable time to remove the property, and during such reasonable time his right to it would be protected. If this is so, then the principle applies to the case under consideration.

A reasonable time for the removal of this manure had not elapsed when the defendant seized and converted it to his own use. The statute regulating the rights of parties in the gathering of sea-weed, gives the party who heaps it upon a public beach twenty-four hours in which to remove it, and that length of time for the removal of the property we think would not be unreasonable in most cases like the present one.

We therefore advise the Court of Common Pleas to grant a new trial.

In this opinion the other judges concurred.

Suggestions for Further Reading

For an overview of the conceptual problems of possession, see A. James Casner and W. Barton Leach, *Cases and Text on Property*, 2d ed. (Boston: Little, Brown, 1969), 9–98, and the extensive bibliography therein. For analysis of the use of possession to justify ownership claims, see Lawrence

C. Becker, *Property Rights: Philosophic Foundations* (London and Boston: Routledge & Kegan Paul, 1977), chap. 3; and Richard A. Epstein, "Possession as the Root of Title," 13 *Georgia Law Review* 1221 (1980).

On the legal questions concerning abandonment, many helpful references and definitions can be found under "Abandonment" in *Black's Law Dictionary*, 4th ed. (St. Paul: West, 1968). See also the case of Chester the parrot, otherwise known as *Conti* v. *ASPCA*, 77 Misc. 2d 61, 333 N.Y.S. 2d 288 (1974), reprinted in A. James Casner's *1976 Supplement to Casner and Leach's Text and Cases on Property* (Boston: Little, Brown, 1976), 31–33.

SECTION THREE
TAKINGS AND RIGHTS
IN CONFLICT

The Constitution of the United States, in Amendments Five and Fourteen, forbids the taking of private property for public purposes unless due process of law is observed and just compensation is paid to the owner. When the government moves people out of their homes in order to build a dam or a highway, it is taking their property and must pay them for it. "Takings" law, as it is called, raises some very vexing problems, problems that are the focus of this section.

The first case here, *United States* v. *Sioux Nation of Indians,* arises out of events during a colorful if somewhat sordid period of American history. The Supreme Court, sitting in 1980, considers whether the Sioux are entitled to compensation for lands taken from them during the Black Hills gold rush. Many famous names from the Old West figure prominently in the history of the taking: Red Cloud and Sitting Bull, Sheridan and Custer, Fort Laramie and Little Big Horn. Though the legal issue is less widely known than the history, it is important nonetheless. Did the government's 1876 "agreement" with the Sioux, in the aftermath of Custer's defeat at Little Big Horn, amount to a taking for which just compensation must be paid? The government had argued that, in forcing the 1876 agreement, it was acting in its capacity as trustee of Indian lands. The Sioux had been given food rations in exchange for the land. The Sioux Nation had replied that the rations were not intended to amount to the full value of the land. Accordingly, the government had not been acting as a trustee, exchanging on behalf of the Sioux one form of property for another of equal value. Rather, it was exercising its power of eminent domain, taking the Black Hills for public purposes. The government must therefore pay just compensation. The Court agrees with the Sioux Nation and upholds a lower court opinion ordering payment of over $100 million to the Sioux. We reprint here only portions of the history of the taking and some of the main arguments in the case. We have omitted the discussion of the procedural matters that kept the case in litigation for so long.

The next case in this section, *Kaiser Aetna* v. *United States,* concerns the ownership of navigable waterways. Since waterways are so important to the commerce of the country, the general legal rule is that they must be treated as public property. They cannot be privately owned. But what happens when a company, at its own expense, turns a pond—a private pond under Hawaii state law—into a navigable waterway? Can the government require that the marina be open to the public? The Supreme Court here says yes. But, ordinarily, the government does not have to pay compensation when it moves to protect the public's right of access to navigable waterways. Must it do so here? The Supreme Court says yes again. The "right to exclude" cannot be taken without just compensation. The case raises an issue we will consider again: the control of essential resources.

The final cases in this section concern the relationship between property rights and the right to free expression enjoyed by Californians under their state constitution. PruneYard Shopping Center, privately owned, had enforced a rule prohibiting noncommercial "publicly expressive activity" on its premises. The United States Supreme Court had earlier decided (in *Lloyd* v. *Tanner*) that the First Amendment of the United States Constitution did not permit citizens to circulate handbills at an Oregon shopping mall in violation of the policy of the shopping center management. California decisions (*Diamond II*) had followed the federal precedent. But shopping centers, like PruneYard, had since become recognized as having significant importance in the life of suburban areas. And the freedom of expression at issue in these cases is not the freedom of expression of the Federal Constitution but, rather, that secured by the California State Constitution.

A security guard working for PruneYard had informed a group of high school students that they would have to leave the shopping center because they were soliciting the signatures of shoppers for a petition to be sent to Washington. The students left but brought suit against the shopping center in the Superior Court of Santa Clara County, asking the Court to order the shopping center to permit on its premises solicitation of signatures for petitions to the government. The Superior Court denied the students' request for an injunction. They then appealed to the California Supreme Court and its decision, in *Robins* v. *Pruneyard Shopping Center,* is reprinted here. The Court considers that the power to regulate property is "capable of expansion to meet new conditions of modern life."

It notes that shopping centers can provide "an essential and invaluable forum" for the exercise of those rights to speech and petition that are more broadly secured by the California Constitution than they seem to be by the Federal Constitution. Overruling *Diamond II*, the Court rules that reasonably exercised speech and petition in private shopping centers are protected by the California Constitution. In a dissenting opinion, Justice Richardson argues that in *Lloyd* the United States Supreme Court had given the owners of shopping centers a property right broad enough to permit them to exclude persons coming onto the premises for noncommercial purposes, a right that may not be abrogated by the California Constitution.

The owner of PruneYard Shopping Center challenged the California decision in the United States Supreme Court. The issue in *PruneYard Shopping Center* v. *Robins* is "whether state constitutional provisions, which permit individuals to exercise free speech and petition rights on the property of a privately owned shopping center to which the public is invited, violate the shopping center owner's property rights under the Fifth and Fourteenth Amendments. . . . " The Court distinguishes the facts in *PruneYard* from those in *Kaiser Aetna* v. *United States* and considers that the California rights of free expression and petition on private shopping center property do not "unreasonably impair the value or use" of the property. Accordingly, regulation here does not amount to a taking, and the owner's property rights have not been infringed. Though in general agreement with the ruling opinion, Justice Blackmun dissents from its view that the federal government lacks the authority "to define 'property' in the first instance."

United States v. Sioux Nation of Indians

UNITED STATES SUPREME COURT

MR. JUSTICE BLACKMUN delivered the opinion of the Court.

This case concerns the Black Hills of South Dakota, the Great Sioux Reservation, and a colorful, and in many respects tragic, chapter in the history of the Nation's West. . . .

For over a century now the Sioux Nation has claimed that the

448 U.S. 371 (1980). Footnotes renumbered and locations of deleted citations marked with double asterisk (**). [Eds.]

United States unlawfully abrogated the Fort Laramie Treaty of April 29, 1868, 15 Stat. 635, in Art. II of which the United States pledged that the Great Sioux Reservation, including the Black Hills, would be "set apart for the absolute and undisturbed use and occupation of the Indians herein named."**[1] The Fort Laramie Treaty was concluded at the culmination of the Powder River War of 1866–1867, a series of military engagements in which the Sioux tribes, led by their great chief, Red Cloud, fought to protect the integrity of earlier-recognized treaty lands from the incursion of white settlers.

• • •

The years following the treaty brought relative peace to the Dakotas, an era of tranquility that was disturbed, however, by renewed speculation that the Black Hills, which were included in the Great Sioux Reservation, contained vast quantities of gold and silver.*

• • •

Having promised the Sioux that the Black Hills were reserved to them, the United States Army was placed in the position of having to threaten military force, and occasionally to use it, to prevent prospectors and settlers from trespassing on lands reserved to the Indians. For example, in September 1874, General Sheridan sent instructions to Brigadier General Alfred H. Terry, Commander of the Department of Dakota, at Saint Paul, directing him to use force to prevent companies of prospectors from trespassing on the Sioux reservation. At the same time, Sheridan let it be known that he would "give a cordial support to the settlement of the Black Hills," should Congress decide to "open up the country for settlement, by extinguishing the treaty rights of the Indians."** [2] Sheridan's instructions were published in local newspapers.**[2]

Eventually, however, the Executive Branch of the Government de-

---

[1]The boundaries of the reservation included approximately half the area of what is now the State of South Dakota, including all of that State west of the Missouri River save for a narrow strip in the far western portion. The reservation also included a narrow strip of land west of the Missouri and north of the border between North and South Dakota.

*Footnote omitted [Eds.].

[2]General William Tecumseh Sherman, Commanding General of the Army, as quoted in the Saint Louis Globe in 1875, described the military's task in keeping prospectors out of the Black Hills as "the same old story, the story of Adam and Eve and the forbidden fruit. [D.] Jackson, [Custer's Gold], at 112 [(1966)]. In an interview with a correspondent from the Bismarck Tribune, published September 2, 1874, Custer recognized the military's obligation to keep all trespassers off the reservation lands, but stated that he would recommend to Congress "the extinguishment of the Indian title at the earliest moment practicable for military reasons." [H.] Krause & [G.] Olson [Prelude to Glory], at 233 [(1974)]. Given the ambivalence of feeling among the commanding officers of the Army about the practicality and desirability of its treaty obligations, it is perhaps not surprising that one chronicler of Sioux history would describe the Government's efforts to dislodge invading settlers from the Black Hills as "feeble." F. Hans, The Great Sioux Nation 522 (1964 reprint).

cided to abandon the Nation's treaty obligation to preserve the integrity of the Sioux territory. In a letter dated November 9, 1875, to Terry, Sheridan reported that he had met with President Grant, the Secretary of the Interior, and the Secretary of War, and that the President had decided that the military should make no further resistance to the occupation of the Black Hills by miners, "it being his belief that such resistance only increased their desire and complicated the troubles." *Id.*, at 59. These orders were to be enforced "quietly," *ibid.*, and the President's decision was to remain "confidential." *Id.*, at 59–60 (letter from Sheridan to Sherman).

With the Army's withdrawal from its role as enforcer of the Fort Laramie Treaty, the influx of settlers into the Black Hills increased. The Government concluded that the only practical course was to secure to the citizens of the United States the right to mine the Black Hills for gold. Toward that end, the Secretary of the Interior, in the spring of 1875, appointed a commission to negotiate with the Sioux. The commission was headed by William B. Allison. The tribal leaders of the Sioux were aware of the mineral value of the Black Hills and refused to sell the land for a price less than $70 million. The commission offered the Indians an annual rental of $400,000, or payment of $6 million for absolute relinquishment of the Black Hills. The negotiations broke down.*

In the winter of 1875–1876, many of the Sioux were hunting in the unceded territory north of the North Platte River, reserved to them for that purpose in the Fort Laramie Treaty. On December 6, 1875, for reasons that are not entirely clear, the Commissioner of Indian Affairs sent instructions to the Indian agents on the reservation to notify those hunters that if they did not return to the reservation agencies by January 31, 1876, they would be treated as "hostiles." Given the severity of the winter, compliance with these instructions was impossible. On February 1, the Secretary of the Interior nonetheless relinquished jurisdiction over all hostile Sioux, including those Indians exercising their treaty-protected hunting rights, to the War Department. The Army's campaign against the "hostiles" led to Sitting Bull's notable victory over Custer's forces at the battle of the Little Big Horn on June 25. That victory, of course, was short-lived, and those Indians who surrendered to the Army were returned to the reservation, and deprived of their weapons and horses, leaving them completely dependent for survival on rations provided them by the Government. . . .

In August 1876, . . . Congress requested the President to appoint another commission to negotiate with the Sioux for the cession of the Black Hills.

This commission, headed by George Manypenny, arrived in the Sioux country in early September and commenced meetings with the head men of the various tribes. . . .

The commissioners brought with them the text of a treaty that had been prepared in advance. The principal provisions of this treaty were

---

*Footnote omitted. [Eds.].

that the Sioux would relinquish their rights to the Black Hills and other lands west of the one hundred and third meridian, and their rights to hunt in the unceded territories to the north, in exchange for subsistence rations for as long as they would be needed to ensure the Sioux' survival. In setting out to obtain the tribes' agreement to this treaty, the commission ignored the stipulation of the Fort Laramie Treaty that any cession of the lands contained within the Great Sioux Reservation would have to be joined in by three-fourths of the adult males. Instead, the treaty was presented just to Sioux chiefs and their leading men. It was signed by only 10% of the adult male Sioux population.[3]

Congress resolved the impasse by enacting the 1876 "agreement" into law as the Act of Feb. 28, 1877 (1877 Act). 19 Stat. 254. The Act had the effect of abrogating the earlier Fort Laramie Treaty, and of implementing the terms of the Manypenny Commission's "agreement" with the Sioux leaders.[4]

---

[3]The commission's negotiations with the chiefs and head men is described by [D.] Robinson, [A History of the Dakota or Sioux Indians], at 439–442 [(1904)]. He states: "As will be readily understood, the making of a treaty was a forced put, so far as the Indians were concerned. Defeated, disarmed, dismounted, they were at the mercy of a superior power and there was no alternative but to accept the conditions imposed upon them. This they did with as good grace as possible under all of the conditions existing." *Id.*, at 442.

Another early chronicler of the Black Hills region wrote of the treaty's provisions in the following chauvinistic terms:

"It will be seen by studying the provisions of this treaty, that by its terms the Indians from a material standpoint lost much and gained but little. By the first article they lose all rights to the unceded territory in Wyoming from which white settlers had then before been altogether excluded; by the second they relinquish all right to the Black Hills, and the fertile valley of the Belle Fourche in Dakota, without additional material compensation; by the third conceding the right of way over the unceded portions of their reservation; by the fourth they receive such supplies only, as were provided by the treaty of 1868, restricted as to the points for receiving them. The only real gain to the Indians seems to be embodied in the fifth article of the treaty [Government's obligation to provide subsistence rations]. The Indians, doubtless, realized that the Black Hills was destined soon to slip out of their grasp, regardless of their claims, and therefore thought it best to yield to the inevitable, and accept whatever was offered to them.

"They were assured of a continuance of their regular daily rations, and certain annuities in clothing each year, guaranteed by the treaty of 1868, and what more could they ask or desire, than that a living be provided for themselves, their wives, their children, and all their relations, including squaw men, indirectly, thus leaving them free to live their wild, careless, unrestrained life, exempt from all the burdens and responsibilities of civilized existence? In view of the fact that there are thousands who are obliged to earn their bread and butter by the sweat of their brows, and that have hard work to keep the wolf from the door, they should be satisfied." [A.] Tallent, [The Black Hills], at 133–134 [(1977 reprint of 1899 ed.)].

[4]The 1877 Act "ratified and confirmed" the agreement reached by the Manypenny Commission with the Sioux tribes. 19 Stat. 254. It altered the boundaries of the Great Sioux Reservation by adding some 900,000 acres of land to the north, while carving out virtually all that portion of the reservation between the one hundred and third and one hundred and fourth meridians, including the Black Hills, an area of well over 7 million acres. The Indians also relinquished their rights to hunt in the unceded lands recognized by the Fort Laramie Treaty, and agreed that three wagon roads could be cut through their reservation. *Id.*, at 255.

In exchange, the Government reaffirmed its obligation to provide all annuities called

The passage of the 1877 Act legitimized the settlers' invasion of the Black Hills, but throughout the years it has been regarded by the Sioux as a breach of this Nation's solemn obligation to reserve the Hills in perpetuity for occupation by the Indians. One historian of the Sioux Nation commented on Indian reaction to the Act in the following words:

> "The Sioux thus affected have not gotten over talking about that treaty yet, and during the last few years they have maintained an organization called the Black Hills Treaty Association, which holds meetings each year at the various agencies for the purpose of studying the treaty with the intention of presenting a claim against the government for additional reimbursement for the territory ceded under it. Some think that Uncle Sam owes them about $9,000,000 on the deal, but it will probably be a hard matter to prove it." F. Fiske, The Taming of the Sioux 132 (1917).

Fiske's words were to prove prophetic.

● ● ●

The Sioux, after years of lobbying, succeeded in obtaining from Congress the passage of a special jurisdictional act which provided them a forum for adjudication of all claims against the United States "under any treaties, agreements, or laws of Congress or for the misappropriation of any of the funds or lands of said tribe or band or bands thereof." Act of June 3, 1920, 41 Stat. 738. Pursuant to this statute, the Sioux, in 1923, filed a petition with the Court of Claims alleging that the Government had taken the Black Hills without just compensation, in violation of the Fifth Amendment. . . . *

On March 13, 1978, Congress passed a statute providing for Court of Claims review of the merits [of the Sioux Nation case]. . . .

Acting pursuant to that statute, a majority of the Court of Claims, sitting en banc, in an opinion by Chief Judge Friedman [held] that the 1877 Act effected a taking of the Black Hills and of rights of way across the reservation. *Sioux Nation* v. *United States,* 220 Ct. Cl.—, 601 F. 2d 1157

---

for by the Fort Laramie Treaty, and "to provide all necessary aid to assist the said Indians in the work of civilization; to furnish to them schools and instruction in mechanical and agricultural arts, as provided for by the treaty of 1868." *Id.,* at 256. In addition, every individual was to receive fixed quantities of beef or bacon and flour, and other foodstuffs, in the discretion of the Commissioner of Indian Affairs, which "shall be continued until the Indians are able to support themselves." *Ibid.* The provision of rations was to be conditioned, however, on the attendance at school by Indian children, and on the labor of those who resided on lands suitable for farming. The Government also promised to assist the Sioux in finding markets for their crops and in obtaining employment in the performance of government work on the reservation. *Ibid.*

Later congressional actions having the effect of further reducing the domain of the Great Sioux Reservation are described in *Rosebud Sioux Tribe* v. *Kneip,* 430 U. S. 584, 589 (1977).

*We omit here a history of fifty-five years of litigation [Eds.].

(1979).[5] . . . The court thus held that the Sioux were entitled to an award of interest, at the annual rate of 5%, on the principal sum of $17.1 million, dating from 1877.

We granted the Government's petition for a writ of certiorari . . . in order to review the important constitutional questions presented by this case, questions not only of long-standing concern to the Sioux, but also of significant economic import to the Government.

• • •

In reaching its conclusion that the 1877 Act effected a taking of the Black Hills for which just compensation was due the Sioux under the Fifth Amendment, the Court of Claims relied upon the "good faith effort" test developed in its earlier decision in *Three Tribes of Fort Berthold Reservation* v. *United States,* 182, Ct. Cl. 543, 390 F. 2d 686 (1968). The *Fort Berthold* test had been designed to reconcile two lines of cases decided by this Court that seemingly were in conflict. The first line, exemplified by *Lone Wolf* v. *Hitchcock,* 187 U. S. 553 (1903), recognizes "that Congress possesse[s] a paramount power over the property of the Indians, by reason of its exercise of guardianship over their interests, and that such authority might be implied, even though opposed to the strict letter of a treaty with the Indians." *Id.,* at 565. The second line, exemplified by the more recent decision in *Shoshone Tribe* v. *United States,* 299 U. S. 476 (1937), concedes Congress' paramount power over Indian property, but holds, nonetheless, that "[t]he power does not extend so far as to enable the Government 'to give the tribal lands to others, or to appropriate them to its own purposes, without rendering, or assuming an obligation to render, just compensation.'" *Id.,* at 497 (quoting *United States* v. *Creek Nation,* 295 U. S. 103, 110 (1935)). In *Shoshone Tribe,* Mr. Justice Cardozo, in speaking for the Court, expressed the distinction between the conflicting principles in a characteristically pithy phrase: "Spoliation is not management." 299 U. S., at 498.

The *Fort Berthold* test distinguishes between cases in which one or the other principle is applicable:

> "It is obvious that Congress cannot simultaneously (1) act as trustee for the benefit of the Indians, exercising its plenary powers over the Indians and their property, as it thinks is in their best interests, and (2) exercise its sovereign power of eminent domain, taking the Indians' property within the meaning of the Fifth Amendment to the Constitution. In any given situation in which Congress has acted with regard to Indian people, it must have acted either in one capacity or the other. Congress can own two hats, but it cannot wear them both at the same time.

[5]While affirming the Indian Claims Commission's determination that the acquisition of the Black Hills and the rights-of-way across the reservation constituted takings, the court reversed the Commission's determination that the mining of gold from the Black Hills by prospectors prior to 1877 also constituted a taking. The value of the gold, therefore, could not be considered as part of the principal on which interest would be paid to the Sioux.**

"Some guideline must be established so that a court can identify in which capacity Congress is acting. The following guideline would best give recognition to the basic distinction between the two types of congressional action: Where Congress makes a good faith effort to give the Indians the full value of the land and thus merely transmutes the property from land to money, there is no taking. This is a mere substitution of assets or change of form and is a traditional function of a trustee." 182 Ct. Cl., at 553, 390 F. 2d, at 691.

Applying the *Fort Berthold* test to the facts of this case, the Court of Claims concluded that, in passing the 1877 Act, Congress had not made a good faith effort to give the Sioux the full value of the Black Hills.

• • •

[T]he Court found that "[t]he only item of 'consideration' that possibly could be viewed as showing an attempt by Congress to give the Sioux the 'full value' of the land the government took from them was the requirement to furnish them with rations until they became self-sufficient."** This finding is fully supported by the record, and the Government does not seriously contend otherwise. . . .

Second, the court found, after engaging in an exhaustive review of the historical record, that neither the Manypenny Commission, nor the congressional committees that approved the 1877 Act, nor the individual legislators who spoke on its behalf on the floor of Congress, ever indicated a belief that the Government's obligation to provide the Sioux with rations constituted a fair equivalent for the value of the Black Hills and the additional property rights the Indians were forced to surrender.** This finding is unchallenged by the Government.

A third finding lending some weight to the Court's legal conclusion was that the conditions placed by the Government on the Sioux' entitlement to rations,** "further show that the government's undertaking to furnish rations to the Indians until they could support themselves did not reflect a congressional decision that the value of the rations was the equivalent of the land the Indians were giving up, but instead was an attempt to coerce the Sioux into capitulating to congressional demands."** We might add only that this finding is fully consistent with similar observations made by this Court nearly a century ago in an analogous case. . . . *Choctaw Nation v. United States*, 119 U. S. 1, 35 (1886).

• • •

Finally, the Court of Claims rejected the Government's contention that the fact that it subsequently had spent at least $43 million on rations for the Sioux (over the course of three quarters of a century) established that the 1877 Act was an act of guardianship taken in the Sioux' best interest. The court concluded: "The critical inquiry is what Congress did—and how it viewed the obligation it was assuming—at the time it acquired the land, and not how much it ultimately cost the United States to fulfill the obligation." 220 Ct. Cl., at ––, 601 F. 2d, at 1168. It found no basis for believing that Congress, in 1877, anticipated that it would take the Sioux such a lengthy period of time to become self-sufficient, or that the fulfillment of the Government's obligation to feed the Sioux would entail the large expenditures ultimately made on their behalf. *Ibid*. We find no basis on which to question the legal standard applied by the Court of Claims, or the findings it reached, concerning Congress' decision to provide the Sioux with rations.

• • •

In sum, we conclude that the legal analysis and factual findings of the Court of Claims fully support its conclusions that the terms of the 1877 Act did not effect "a mere change in the form of investment of Indian tribal property." *Lone Wolf* v. *Hitchcock*, 187 U. S., at 568. Rather, the 1877 Act effected a taking of tribal property, property which had been set aside for the exclusive occupation of the Sioux by the Fort Laramie Treaty of 1868. That taking implied an obligation on the part of the Government to make just compensation to the Sioux Nation, and that obligation, including an award of interest, must now, at last, be paid.

The judgment of the Court of Claims is affirmed.

It is so ordered.

Kaiser Aetna v. United States

UNITED STATES SUPREME COURT

Mr. Justice Rehnquist delivered the opinion of the Court.

The Hawaii Kai Marina was developed by the dredging and filling of Kuapa Pond, which was a shallow lagoon separated from Maunalua Bay and the Pacific Ocean by a barrier beach. Although under Hawaii law Kuapa Pond was private property, the Court of Appeals for the Ninth Circuit held that when petitioners converted the pond into a marina and thereby connected it to the bay, it became subject to the "navigational servitude" of the Federal Government. Thus, the public acquired a right of access to what was once petitioners' private pond. We granted certiorari because of the importance of the issue and a conflict concerning the scope and nature of the servitude. . . .

444 U.S. 164 (1979). Footnotes renumbered and locations of deleted citations marked with double asterisk (**). [Eds.]

The Government contends that petitioners may not exclude members of the public from the Hawaii Kai Marina because "The public enjoys a federally protected right of navigation over the navigable waters of the United States." Brief of the United States, p. 13. It claims the issue in dispute is whether Kuapa Pond is presently a "navigable water of the United States." *Ibid.* When petitioners dredged and improved Kuapa Pond, the government continues, the pond—although it may once have qualified as fast land—became navigable water of the United States.[1] The public thereby acquired a right to use Kuapa Pond as a continuous highway for navigation, and the Corps of Engineers may consequently obtain an injunction to prevent petitioners from attempting to reserve the waterway to themselves. . . .

Reference to the navigability of a waterway adds little if anything to the breadth of Congress' regulatory power over interstate commerce. It has long been settled that Congress has extensive authority over this Nation's waters under the Commerce Clause. Early in our history this Court held that the power to regulate commerce necessarily includes power over navigation. *Gibbons* v. *Ogden,* 22 U. S. (9 Wheat.) 1, 189 (1824). As stated in *Gilman* v. *Philadelphia,* 70 U. S. (3 Wall.) 713, 724–725:

> "Commerce includes navigation. The power to regulate Commerce comprehends the control for that purpose, and to the extent necessary, of all the navigable waters of the United States which are accessible from a state other than those in which they lie. For this purpose, they are the public property of the nation, and subject to all the requisite legislation by Congress."

In light of its expansive authority under the Commerce Clause, there is no question but that Congress could assure the public a free right of access to the Hawaii Kai Marina if it so chose. Whether a statute or regulation that went so far amounted to a "taking," however, is an entirely separate question.[2]** As was recently pointed out,** this Court has generally "been unable to develop any 'set formula' for determining when 'justice and fairness' require that economic injuries caused by public action be compensated by the Government, rather than remain disproportionately concentrated on a few persons."** Rather, it has examined the "taking" question by engaging in essentially ad hoc, factual inquiries that have identified several factors—such as the economic impact of the regulation, its interference with reasonable investment backed expectations,

---

[1]The Government further argues that:

"The fact that the conversion was accomplished at private expense does not exempt Kuapa Pond from the navigable waters of the United States. To allow landowners to dredge their fast lands and reshape the navigable waters of the United States to more conveniently serve their land, and then to exclude the public from the navigable portions flowing over the site of former fast lands, would unduly burden navigation and commerce. The states lack the power under the Commerce Clause to sanction any such form of private property. . . ." Brief for the United States, pp. 14–15.

[2]Thus, this Court has observed that "Confiscation may result from a taking of the use of property without compensation quite as well as from the taking of title."**

and the character of the governmental action—that have particular signifi-cance.** When the "taking" question has involved the exercise of the public right of navigation over interstate waters that constitute highways for com-merce, however, this Court has held in many cases that compensation may not be required as a result of the federal navigational servitude.**

• • •

The navigational servitude is an expression of the notion that the determination whether a taking has occurred must take into considera-tion the important public interest in the flow of interstate waters that in their natural condition are in fact capable of supporting public naviga-tion. See *United States* v. *Cress,* 243 U. S. 316 (1917). Thus, in *United States* v. *Chandler-Dunbar Co., supra,* 229 U. S., at 66, this Court stated "that the running water in a great navigable stream is [in]capable of private ownership. . . . " And, in holding that a riparian landowner was not entitled to compensation when the construction of a pier cut off his access to navigable water, this Court observed:

> "The primary use of the waters and the lands under them is for purposes of navigation, and the erection of the piers in them to improve navigation for the public is entirely consistent with such use, and infringes no right of the riparian owner. Whatever the nature of the interest of a riparian owner in the submerged lands in front of his upland bordering on a public navigable water, his title is not as full and complete as his title to fast land which has no direct connection with the navigation of such water. It is a qualified title, a mere technical title, not at his disposal, as is his upland, but to be held at all times subordinate to such use of the submerged lands and of the waters flowing over them as may be consistent with or demanded by the public right of navigation." *Scranton* v. *Wheeler,* 179 U. S. 141, 163 (1900).

For over a century, a long line of cases decided by this Court involv-ing government condemnation of "fast lands'" delineated the elements of compensable damages that the government was required to pay because the lands were riparian to navigable streams. The Court was often deeply divided, and the results frequently turned on what could fairly be de-scribed as quite narrow distinctions. But this is not a case in which the government recognizes any obligation whatever to condemn "fast lands" and pay just compensation under the Eminent Domain Clause of the Fifth Amendment to the Bill of Rights of the United States Constitution. It is instead a case in which the owner of what was once a private pond, separated from concededly navigable water by a barrier beach and used for aquatic agriculture, has invested substantial amounts of money in making improvements. The government contends that as a result of one of these improvements, the pond's connection to the navigable water in a manner approved by the Corps of Engineers, the owner has somehow lost one of the most essential sticks in the bundle of rights that are commonly characterized as property—the right to exclude others.

Because the factual situation in this case is so different from typical ones involved in riparian condemnation cases we see little point in tracing the historical development of that doctrine here. Indeed, since this Court's decision in *United States* v. *Rands,* 389 U. S. 121, 123 (1967), closely following its decisions in *United States* v. *Virginia Electric & Power Co.,* 365 U. S. 624, 628 (1961), and *United States* v. *Twin City Power Co.,* 350 U. S. 222, 226 (1956), the elements of compensation for which the Government must pay when it condemns fast lands riparian to a navigable stream have remained largely settled. Distinctions between cases such as these, on the one hand, and *United States* v. *Kansas City Insurance Co.,* 399 U. S. 799, 808 (1950), may seem fine, indeed, in the light of hindsight, but perhaps for the very reason that it *is* hindsight which we now exercise, the shifting back and forth of the Court in this area until the most recent decisions bears the sound of "Old, unhappy, far off things, and battles long ago."

There is no denying that the strict logic of the more recent cases limiting the Government's liability to pay damages for riparian access, if carried to its ultimate conclusion, might completely swallow up any private claim for "just compensation" under the Fifth Amendment even in a situation as different from the riparian condemnation cases as this one. But, as Mr. Justice Holmes observed in a very different context, the life of the law has not been logic, it has been experience. The navigational servitude, which exists by virtue of the Commerce Clause in navigable streams, gives rise to an authority in the Government to assure that such streams retain their capacity to serve as continuous highways for the purpose of navigation in interstate commerce. Thus, when the Government acquires fast lands to improve navigation, it is not required under the Eminent Domain Clause to compensate land owners for certain elements of damage attributable to riparian location, such as the land's value as a hydroelectric site, *Twin City Power Co., supra,* or a port site, *United States* v. *Rands, supra.* But none of these cases ever doubted that when the Government wished to acquire fast lands, it was required by the Eminent Domain Clause of the Fifth Amendment to condemn and pay fair value for that interest. See *United States* v. *Kansas City Life Insurance Co., supra,* at 800 (1950); *United States* v. *Virginia Electric & Power Co.,* 365 U. S., at 628 (1961); *United States* v. *Rands,* 389 U. S., at 123 (1967). The nature of the navigational servitude when invoked by the Government in condemnation cases is summarized as well as anywhere in *United States* v. *Willow River Co.,* 324 U. S. 499, 502:

> "It is clear, of course, that a head of water has value and that the Company has an economic interest in keeping the St. Croix at the lower level. But not all economic interests are 'property rights'; only those economic advantages are 'rights' which have the law back of them, and only when they are so recognized may courts compel others to forbear from interfering with them or to compensate for their invasion."

We think, however, that when the Government makes the naked assertion it does here, that assertion collides with not merely an "economic advantage" but an "economic advantage" that has the law back of it to such an extent that courts may "compel others to forbear from interfering with [it] or to compensate for [its] invasion." *United States* v. *Willow River Co., supra,* 502.

Here the Government's attempt to create a public right of access to the improved pond goes so far beyond ordinary regulation or improvement for navigation as to amount to a taking under the logic of *Pennsylvania Coal Co.* v. *Mahon, supra.* More than one factor contributes to this result.[3] It is clear that prior to its improvement, Kuapa Pond was incapable of being used as a continuous highway for the purpose of navigation in interstate commerce. Its maximum depth at high tide was a mere two feet, it was separated from the adjacent bay and ocean by a natural barrier beach, and its principal commercial value was limited to fishing.[4] It consequently is not the sort of "great navigable stream" that this Court has previously recognized as being "[in]capable of private ownership."** And, as previously noted, Kuapa Pond has always been considered to be private property under Hawaiian law. Thus, the interest of petitioners in the now dredged marina is strikingly similar to that of owners of fast land adjacent to navigable water.

We have not the slightest doubt that the Government could have refused to allow such a dredging on the ground that it would have impaired navigation in the bay, or could have conditioned its approval of the dredging on petitioners' agreement to comply with various measures that it deemed appropriate for the promotion of navigation. But what petitioners now have is a body of water that was private property under Hawaiian law, linked to navigable water by a channel dredged by them with the consent of the respondent. While the consent of individual officials representing the United States cannot "estop" the United States,** it can lead to the fruition of a number of expectancies embodied in the concept of "property,"—expectancies that, if sufficiently important, the Government must condemn and pay for before it takes over the management of the land owner's property. In this case, we hold that the "right to exclude," so universally held to be a fundamental element of the property right,[5] falls within this category of interests that the Government cannot take without compensation. This is not a case in which the Government is exercising its regulatory power in a manner that will cause insubstantial devaluation of petitioners' private property; rather, the imposition of the navigational servitude in this context will result in an actual physical invasion of the privately owned marina. . . . Thus, if the Government wishes to make what was formerly Kuapa Pond into a public aquatic park after petitioners have proceeded as far as they have here, it may not, without

---

[3]We do not decide, however, whether in some circumstances one of these factors by itself may be dispositive.

[4]While it was still a fish pond, a few flat-bottomed shallow draft boats were operated by the fishermen in their work. There is no evidence, however, that even these boats could acquire access to the adjacent bay and ocean from the pond. . . .

[5]See, *e.g., United States* v. *Pueblo of San Ildefonso,* 513 F. 2d 1383, 1394 (U. S. Ct. Cl. 1975); *United States* v. *Lutz,* 295 F. 2d 736, 740 (CA5 1961). As stated by Justice Brandeis, "An essential element of individual property is the legal right to exclude others from enjoying it." *International News Serv.* v. *Associated Press,* 248 U. S. 215, 250 (dissenting opinion).

invoking its eminent domain power and paying just compensation, require them to allow free access to the dredged pond while petitioners'
agreement with their customers calls for an annual $72 regular fee.

Accordingly the judgment of the Court of Appeals is

Reversed.

Robins v. Pruneyard Shopping Center

CALIFORNIA SUPREME COURT

NEWMAN, Justice.

In this appeal from a judgment denying an injunction we hold that
the soliciting at a shopping center of signatures for a petition to the
government is an activity protected by the California Constitution.

Pruneyard Shopping Center is a privately owned center that consists
of approximately 21 acres—5 devoted to parking and 16 occupied by
walkways, plazas, and buildings that contain 65 shops, 10 restaurants, and
a cinema. The public is invited to visit for the purpose of patronizing the
many businesses. Pruneyard's policy is not to permit any tenant or visitor
to engage in publicly expressive activity, including the circulating of petitions, that is not directly related to the commercial purposes. The policy
seems to have been strictly and disinterestedly enforced.

Appellants are high school students who attempted one Saturday
afternoon to solicit support for their opposition to a United Nations resolution against "Zionism." They set up a cardtable in a corner of Pruneyard's central courtyard and sought to discuss their concerns with shoppers and to solicit signatures for a petition to be sent to the White House
in Washington. Their activity was peaceful and apparently well-received
by Pruneyard patrons.

Soon after they had begun their soliciting they were approached by
a security guard who informed them that their conduct violated Pruneyard regulations. They spoke to the guard's superior, who informed them
they would have to leave because they did not have permission to solicit.
The officers suggested that appellants continue their activities on the
public sidewalk at the center's perimeter.[1]

---

23 Cal. 3d 899 (1979). Footnotes renumbered and locations of deleted citations
marked with double asterisk (**). [Eds.]

[1]Pruneyard is bordered on two sides by private property, on its other sides by public
sidewalks and streets.

Appellants immediately left the premises and later brought suit. The trial court rejected their request that Pruneyard be enjoined from denying them access.

Our main questions are: (1) Did *Lloyd v. Tanner* (1972) 407 U.S. 551, 92 S.Ct. 2219, 33 L.Ed.2d 131 recognize federally protected property rights of such a nature that we now are barred from ruling that the California Constitution creates broader speech rights as to private property than does the federal Constitution? (2) If not, does the California Constitution protect speech and petitioning at shopping centers?

This court last faced those issues in *Diamond v. Bland* (1974) 11 Cal.3d 331, 113 Cal.Rptr. 468, 521 P.2d 460 (*Diamond II*), wherein *Diamond v. Bland* (1970) 3 Cal.3d 653, 91 Cal.Rptr. 501, 477 P.2d 733 (*Diamond I*) was reversed because of *Lloyd v. Tanner, supra*. The *Diamond* cases involved facts much like those of the instant case. *Diamond II* stated: "*Lloyd's* rationale is controlling here. In this case, as in *Lloyd*, plaintiffs have alternative, effective channels of communication, for the customers and employees of the center may be solicited on any public sidewalks, parks and streets adjacent to the Center and in the communities in which such persons reside." (11 Cal.3d at p. 335, 113 Cal.Rptr. at p. 471, 521 P.2d at p. 463) . . .

Appellants argue that *Lloyd* merely defined federal speech rights and did not prescribe federal property rights. Even if it did prescribe such rights, appellants contend that, since states generally may regulate shopping centers for proper state purposes, California is free to impose public-interest restrictions on the centers in order to safeguard the right of petition. That right, they assert, surely reflects a public interest that equals in importance the interests that justify restrictions designed to ensure health and safety, a natural environment, aesthetics, property values, and other accepted goals. Such restrictions on property routinely are enacted or declared and enforced.

Appellants ask us to overrule *Diamond II* and to hold that the California Constitution does guarantee the right to seek signatures at shopping centers.

• • •

Lloyd held that a shopping center owner could prohibit distribution of leaflets when they communicated no information relating to the center's business and when there was an adequate, alternate means of communication. The court stated, "We hold that there has been no such dedication of Lloyd's privately owned and operated shopping center to public use as to entitle respondents to exercise therein the asserted First Amendment rights." (407 U.S. at p. 570, 92 S.Ct. at p. 2229.)

• • •

To protect free speech and petitioning is a goal that surely matches the protecting of health and safety, the environment, aesthetics, property values and other societal goals that have been held to justify reasonable restrictions on private property rights.

• • •

No California statute prescribes that shopping center owners provide public forums. But article I, section 2 of the state Constitution reads: "Every person may freely speak, write and publish his or her sentiments on all subjects, being responsible for the abuse of this right. A law may not restrain or abridge liberty of speech or press." Though the framers could have adopted the words of the federal Bill of Rights they chose not to do so. (See Note, *Rediscovering the California Declaration of Rights* (1974) 26 Hastings L.J. 481.) Special protections thus accorded speech are marked in this court's opinions. *Wilson v. Superior Court* (1975) 13 Cal.3d 652, 658, 119 Cal.Rptr. 468, 472, 532 P.2d 116, 120, for instance, noted that "[a] protective provision more definitive and inclusive than the First Amendment is contained in our state constitutional guarantee of the right of free speech and press." . . .

Members of the public are rightfully on Pruneyard's premises because the premises are open to the public during shopping hours. *Lloyd* . . . does not preclude law-making in California which requires that shopping center owners permit expressive activity on their property. To hold otherwise would flout the whole development of law regarding states' power to regulate uses of property and would place a state's interest in strengthening First Amendment rights in an inferior rather than a preferred position. "[A]ll private property is held subject to the power of the government to regulate its use for the public welfare."**

Property rights must yield to the public interest served by zoning laws (*Village of Euclid v. Ambler Realty Co.* (1926) 272 U.S. 365, 47 S.Ct. 114, 71 L.Ed. 303), to environmental needs (Pub.Resources Code, § 21000 et seq.), and to many other public concerns. (See, e. g., the California Coastal Act (*id.*, § 30000 et seq.), the California Water Quality Control Act (Wat.Code, § 13000 et seq.), the Subdivision Map Act (Gov.Code, § 66410 et seq.), and the Subdivision Lands Act (Bus. & Prof.Code, § 11000 et seq. See also Powell, *The Relationship Between Property Rights and Civil Rights* (1963) 15 Hastings L.J. 135, 148–149.)

"We do not minimize the importance of the constitutional guarantees attaching to private ownership of property; but as long as 50 years ago it was already 'thoroughly established in this country that the rights preserved to the individual by these constitutional provisions are held in subordination to the rights of society. Although one owns property, he may not do with it as he pleases, any more than he may act in accordance with his personal desires. As the interest of society justifies restraints upon individual conduct, so also does it justify restraints upon the use to which property may be devoted. It was not intended by these constitutional provisions to so far protect the individual in the use of his property as to enable him to use it to the detriment of society. By thus protecting individual rights, society did not part with the power to protect itself or to promote its general well-being. Where the interest of the individual conflicts with the interest of society, such individual interest is subordinated to the general welfare.' "** . . .

[T]he power to regulate property is not static; rather it is capable of expansion to meet new conditions of modern life. Property rights must be "redefined in response to a swelling demand that ownership be responsible and responsive to the needs of the social whole. Property rights cannot be used as a shibboleth to cloak conduct which adversely affects the health, safety, the morals, or the welfare of others." (16 Cal.3d at p. 404, 128 Cal.Rptr. at pp. 190, 191, 546 P.2d at pp. 694–695, quoting Powell, *The Relationship Between Property Rights and Civil Rights, supra,* 15 Hastings L.J. at pp. 149–150.)

Several years have passed since this court decided *Diamond II.* Since that time central business districts apparently have continued to yield their functions more and more to suburban centers. Evidence submitted by appellants in this case helps dramatize the potential impact of the public forums sought here:

(1) As of 1970, 92.2 percent of the country's population lived outside the central San Jose planning area in suburban or rural communities.

(2) From 1960 to 1970 central San Jose experienced a 4.7 percent decrease in population as compared with an overall 67 percent increase for the 19 north county planning areas.

(3) Retail sales in the central business district declined to such an extent that statistics have not been kept since 1973. In 1972 that district accounted for only 4.67 percent of the county's total retail sales.

(4) In a given 30-day period between October 1974 and July 1975 adults making one or more shopping trips to the 15 largest shopping centers in the metropolitan San Jose statistical area totaled 685,000 out of 788,000 adults living within that area.

(5) The largest segment of the county's population is likely to spend the most significant amount of its time in suburban areas where its needs and wants are satisfied; and shopping centers provide the location, goods, and services to satisfy those needs and wants.

In assessing the significance of the growing importance of the shopping center we stress also that to prohibit expressive activity in the centers would impinge on constitutional rights beyond speech rights. Courts have long protected the right to petition as an essential attribute of governing. (*United States v. Cruikshank* (1875) 92 U.S. 542–52, 23 L.Ed. 588.) The California Constitution declares that "people have the right to . . . petition government for redress of grievances. . . ." (Art. I, § 3.) That right in California is, moreover, vital to a basic process in the state's constitutional scheme—direct initiation of change by the citizenry through initiative, referendum, and recall. (Cal.Const., art. II, §§ 8, 9, and 13.)*

Past decisions on speech and private property testify to the strength of "liberty of speech" in this state. . . .

Schwartz-Torrance . . . held that a labor union has the right to picket a

*Footnote omitted [Eds.].

bakery located in a shopping center. The opinion noted that the basic problem is one of "accommodating conflicting interests: plaintiff's assertion of its right to the exclusive use of the shopping center premises to which the public in general has been invited as against the union's right of communication of its position which, it asserts, rests upon public policy and constitutional protection." (61 Cal.2d at p. 768, 40 Cal.Rptr. at p. 234, 394 P.2d at p. 922.)

The issue arose too in *In re Hoffman* (1967) 67 Cal.2d 845, 64 Cal.Rptr. 97, 434 P.2d 353, where Vietnam War protesters had attempted to distribute leaflets in the Los Angeles Union Station, owned by three private companies. It housed a restaurant, snack bar, cocktail lounge, and magazine stand in addition to facilities directly related to transporting passengers. The public was free to use the whole station. Chief Justice Traynor's opinion made it clear that property owners as well as government may regulate speech as to time, place, and manner. (*Id.* at pp. 852–853, 64 Cal.Rptr. 97, 434 P.2d 353.) Nonetheless, "a railway station is like a public street or park." (*Id.* at p. 851, 64 Cal.Rptr. at p. 100, 434 P.2d at p. 356.) Further, "the test is not whether petitioners' use of the station was a railway use but whether it interfered with that use." (*Id.*) The opinion thus affirms that the public interest in peaceful speech outweighs the desire of property owners for control over their property. (See too *In re Cox* (1970) 3 Cal.3d 205, 217–218, 90 Cal. Rptr. 24, 32, 474 P.2d 992, 1000. "The shopping center may no more exclude individuals who wear long hair . . . who are black, who are members of the John Birch Society, or who belong to the American Civil Liberties Union, merely because of these characteristics or associations, than may the City of San Rafael.")

Diamond I quoting *Schwartz-Torrance, supra,* stated: "[T]he countervailing interest which [the owner] endeavors to vindicate emanates from the exclusive possession and enjoyment of private property. Because of the public character of the shopping center, however, the impairment of [the owner's] interest must be largely theoretical. [The owner] has fully opened his [*sic*] property to the public. . . ."(*Diamond I, supra,* 3 Cal.3d at p. 662, 91 Cal.Rptr, at p. 507, 477 P.2d at p. 739, bracketed material in original.)

In his *Diamond II* dissent Justice Mosk described the extensive use of private shopping centers.[2] His observations on the role of the centers in our society are even more forceful now than when he wrote. The California Constitution broadly proclaims speech and petition rights. Shopping

[2]"The importance assumed by the shopping center as a place for large groups of citizens to congregate is revealed by statistics: in 21 of the largest metropolitan areas of the country shopping centers account for 50 percent of the retail trade; in some communities the figure is even higher, such as St. Louis (67 percent) and Boston (70 percent). (Note, (1973) Wis.L.Rev. 612, 618 and fn. 51.) Increasingly, such centers are becoming 'miniature downtowns'; some contain major department stores, hotels, apartment houses, office buildings, theatres and churches. (Business Week, Sept. 4, 1971, pp. 34–38; Chain Store Age, Sept. 1971, p. 4.) It has been predicted that there will be 25,000 shopping centers in the United States by 1985. (Publishers Weekly, Feb. 1, 1971, pp. 54–55.) Their significance to shoppers who by choice or necessity avoid travel to the central city is certain to become accentuated in this period of gasoline and energy shortage." (11 Cal.3d at p. 342, 113 Cal.Rptr. at p. 476, 521 P.2d at p. 468 (dis. opn. of Mosk, J.).)

centers to which the public is invited can provide an essential and invaluable forum for exercising those rights.

We therefore hold that *Diamond II* must be overruled. (See particularly 11 Cal.3d at p. 335, fn. 4, 113 Cal.Rptr. 468, 521 P.2d 460.) A closer look at *Lloyd, supra,* 407 U.S. 551, 92 S.Ct. 2219, 33 L.Ed.2d 131, has revealed that it does not prevent California's providing greater protection than the First Amendment now seems to provide. We conclude that sections 2 and 3 of article 1 of the California Constitution protect speech and petitioning, reasonably exercised, in shopping centers even when the centers are privately owned.

By no means do we imply that those who wish to disseminate ideas have free rein. We noted above Chief Justice Traynor's endorsement of time, place, and manner rules. (*In re Hoffman, supra,* 67 Cal.2d at pp. 852–853, 64 Cal.Rptr. 97, 434 P.2d 353.) Further, as Justice Mosk stated in *Diamond II,* "It bears repeated emphasis that we do not have under consideration the property or privacy rights of an individual homeowner or the proprietor of a modest retail establishment. As a result of advertising and the lure of a congenial environment, 25,000 persons are induced to congregate daily to take advantage of the numerous amenities offered by the [shopping center there]. A handful of additional orderly persons soliciting signatures and distributing handbills in connection therewith, under reasonable regulations adopted by defendant to assure that these activities do not interfere with normal business operations (see *Diamond* [I] 3 Cal.3d at p. 665, 91 Cal.Rptr. 501, 477 P.2d 733) would not markedly dilute defendant's property rights." (11 Cal.3d at p. 345, 113 Cal.Rptr. at p. 478, 521 P.2d at p. 470 (dis. opn. of Mosk, J.).)

The judgment rejecting appellants' request that Pruneyard be enjoined from denying access to circulate the petition is reversed.

BIRD, C.J., and TOBRINER and MOSK, JJ., concur.

RICHARDSON, Justice, dissenting.

I respectfully dissent. The majority relegates the private property rights of the shopping center owner to a secondary, disfavored, and subservient position vis-a-vis the "free speech" claims of the plaintiffs. Such a holding clearly violates *federal* constitutional guarantees announced in *Lloyd Corp. v. Tanner* (1972) 407 U.S. 551, 92 S.Ct. 2219, 33 L.Ed.2d 131. . . .

In brief, following a full evidentiary hearing, the trial court specifically found as follows: The Pruneyard Shopping Center is located entirely on private property, and its owner had adopted a nondiscriminatory policy of prohibiting all handbilling and circulation of petitions by anyone and regardless of content. Plaintiffs entered on Pruneyard property and sought to obtain signatures to petitions entirely unrelated to any activities occurring at the center. (The petitions were to the President of the United States and the Congress opposing a United Nations resolution which condemned Zionism and attacking Syria's emigration policy.) Pruneyard is located in Santa Clara County which contains numerous forums for distributing handbills or gathering signatures, including "many shopping centers, public shopping and business areas, public buildings, parks, stadia, universities, colleges, schools, post offices and similar public areas where large numbers of people congregate." The court further found that numerous alternative public sites were available to plaintiffs for their purposes. Nonetheless, plaintiffs made no attempt whatever to obtain signatures on their petition in these alternative public areas, whether situated nearby or otherwise.

From the foregoing findings of fact the trial court expressly concluded as matters of law that there had been no dedication of the center's property to public use, that the center is not the "functional equivalent" of a municipality, and that "There are adequate, effective channels of communication for plaintiffs other than soliciting on the private property of the Center." On the basis of these findings of fact and conclusions of law, the trial court denied plaintiffs the injunctive relief which they sought.

• • •

Recognizing the "special solicitude" owed to the First Amendment guarantees, the high court in *Lloyd* nonetheless noted that "this Court has never held that a trespasser or an uninvited guest may exercise general rights of free speech on property privately owned and used non-discriminatorily for private purposes only." (p. 568, 92 S.Ct. p. 2228.) Moreover, the court determined that although a *shopping center* is open to the public, "property [does not] lose its private character merely because the public is generally invited to use it for designated purposes." (p. 569, 92 S.Ct. p. 2229.) It is self-evident that the *federally* protected property rights are the same whether the shopping center is in *Oregon,* as in *Lloyd,* or in *California,* as in the present case.

. . . The United States Supreme Court, interpreting the United States Constitution, has declared that an owner of a private shopping center "when adequate, alternative avenues of communication exist," has a property right protected by the Fifth and Fourteenth Amendments which is superior to the First Amendment right of those who come upon the shopping center premises for purposes unrelated to the center. In such cases, no state court, interpreting a state Constitution, including this court interpreting the California Constitution, can contravene such a federal constitutionally protected right. Thus, in this case, the majority is prevented from relying on the California Constitution to impair or interfere with those property rights. We are bound by the United States Supreme Court interpretations of the United States Constitution. More specifically, in a confrontation between federal and state constitutional interests federally protected property rights recognized by the United States Supreme Court will prevail against state protected free speech interests where alternative means of free expression are available.

• • •

Because, as the trial court expressly found, plaintiffs had adequate public forums in which to conduct their activities, their unauthorized entries on Pruneyard property manifestly cannot be excused on the basis of any state policy or goal "to protect free speech and petitioning." (*Ante*, p. 859 of 153 Cal.Rptr., p. 346 of 592 P.2d.) The *Lloyd* rationale is applicable and unanswerable. The majority may not evade it by resort, in this instance, to the California Constitution, which must yield to a paramount federal constitutional imperative.

The judgment should be affirmed.

CLARK and MANUEL, JJ., concur.

PruneYard Shopping Center v. Robins

UNITED STATES SUPREME COURT

MR. JUSTICE REHNQUIST delivered the opinion of the Court.

We postponed jurisdiction of this appeal from the Supreme Court of California to decide the important federal constitutional questions it presented. Those are whether state constitutional provisions, which permit individuals to exercise free speech and petition rights on the property of a privately owned shopping center to which the public is invited, violate the shopping center owner's property rights under the Fifth and Fourteenth Amendments.

Appellant PruneYard is a privately owned shopping center in the city of Campbell, Cal. It covers approximately 21 acres—five devoted to parking and 16 occupied by walkways, plazas, sidewalks, and buildings that contain more than 65 specialty shops, 10 restaurants, and a movie theater. The PruneYard is open to the public for the purpose of encouraging the patronizing of its commercial establishments. It has a policy not to permit any visitor or tenant to engage in any publicly expressive activity, including the circulation of petitions, that is not directly related to its commercial purposes. This policy has been strictly enforced in a nondiscriminatory fashion. The PruneYard is owned by appellant Fred Sahadi.

Appellees are high school students who sought to solicit support for their opposition to a United Nations resolution against "Zionism." On a Saturday afternoon they set up a card table in a corner of PruneYard's

447 U.S. 74 (1979). Footnotes renumbered. [Eds.]

central courtyard. They distributed pamphlets and asked passersby to sign petitions, which were to be sent to the President and Members of Congress. Their activity was peaceful and orderly and so far as the record indicates was not objected to by PruneYard's patrons.

Soon after appellees had begun soliciting signatures, a security guard informed them that they would have to leave because their activity violated PruneYard regulations. The guard suggested that they move to the public sidewalk at PruneYard's perimeter. Appellees immediately left the premises and later filed this lawsuit in the California Superior Court of Santa Clara County. They sought to enjoin appellants from denying them access to the PruneYard for the purpose of circulating their petitions.

The Superior Court held that appellees were not entitled under either the Federal or California Constitution to exercise their asserted rights on the shopping center property. Jurisdictional Statement, p. A-2. It concluded that there were "adequate, effective channels of communication for [appellees] other than soliciting on the private property of the [PruneYard]." Jurisdictional Statement, p. A-3. The California Court of Appeal affirmed.

The California Supreme Court reversed, holding that the California Constitution protects "speech and petitioning, reasonably exercised, in shopping centers even when the centers are privately owned." 23 Cal. 3d 899, 910 (1979). It concluded that appellees are entitled to conduct their activity on PruneYard property. In rejecting appellants' contention that such a result infringed property rights protected by the Federal Constitution, the California Supreme Court observed:

> " 'It bears repeated emphasis that we do not have under consideration the property or privacy rights of an individual homeowner or the proprietor of a modest retail establishment. As a result of advertising and the lure of a congenial environment, 25,000 persons are induced to congregate daily to take advantage of the numerous amenities offered by the [shopping center there]. A handful of additional orderly persons soliciting signatures and distributing handbills in connection therewith, under reasonable regulations adopted by defendant to assure that these activities do not interfere with normal business operations (see *Diamond* [v. *Bland*, 3 Cal. 3d 653, 665 (1970) (*Diamond I*)]) would not markedly dilute defendant's property rights." ([*Diamond* v. *Bland*, 11 Cal. 3d 331, 345 (1974) (*Diamond II*)] (dis. opn. of Mosk, J.).)" *Id.*, at 910–911.

The California Supreme Court thus expressly overruled its earlier decision in *Diamond II*, which had reached an opposite conclusion. *Id.*, 910.[1]

[1]The California Supreme Court in *Diamond II* had reasoned:

"In this case, as in *Lloyd* [v. *Tanner*, 407 U. S. 551 (1972)], plaintiffs have alternative, effective channels of communication, for the customers and employees of the center may be solicited on any public sidewalks, parks and streets adjacent to the Center and in the communities in which such persons reside. Unlike the situation in *Marsh* [v. *Alabama*, 326 U. S. 501 (1946)] and [*Amalgamated Food Employees Union* v. *Logan Valley Plaza*, 391 U. S. 308 (1968)], no reason appears why such alternative means of communication would be ineffective, and

Before this Court, appellants contend that their "constitutionally established rights under the Fourteenth Amendment to exclude appellees from adverse use of appellants' private property cannot be denied by invocation of a state constitutional provision or by judicial reconstruction of a state's laws of private property." Jurisdictional Statement, p. 10. We postponed consideration of the question of jurisdiction until the hearing of the case on the merits. We now affirm. . . .

Appellants . . . contend that a right to exclude others underlies the Fifth Amendment guarantee against the taking of property without just compensation and the Fourteenth Amendment guarantee against the deprivation of property without due process of law.*

It is true that one of the essential sticks in the bundle of property rights is the right to exclude others. *Kaiser Aetna* v. *United States*, 48 U. S. L. W. 4045, 4049 (1979). And here there has literally been a "taking" of that right to the extent that the California Supreme Court has interpreted the state constitution to entitle its citizens to exercise free expression and petition rights on shopping center property.[2] But it is well-established that "not every destruction or injury to property by governmental action has been held to be a 'taking' in the constitutional sense." *Armstrong* v. *United States*, 364 U. S. 40, 48 (1960). Rather, the determination whether a state law unlawfully infringes a land owner's property in violation of the Taking Clause requires an examination of whether the restriction on private property "forc[es] some people alone to bear public burdens which, in all fairness and justice, should be borne by the public as a whole." *Id.*, at 49.[3] This examination entails inquiry into such factors as the character of the governmental action, its economic impact, and its interference with reasonable investment backed expectations. *Kaiser Aetna* v. *United States*, 48 U. S. L. W., at 4048. When "regulation goes too far it will be recognized as a taking." *Pennsylvania Coal Co.* v. *Mahon*, 260 U. S., at 415.

---

plaintiffs concede that, unlike *Logan*, their initiative petition bears no particular relation to the shopping center, its individual stores or patrons." 11 Cal. 3d, at 335. *Diamond II* thus held that the shopping center owner's property rights outweighed the rights of free expression and petition asserted by the plaintiffs. *Ibid.*

*Footnote omitted [Eds.].

[2]The term "property" as used in the Taking Clause includes the entire "group of rights inhering in the citizen's [ownership]." *United States* v. *General Motors Corp.*, 323 U.S. 373 (1945). It is not used in the "vulgar and untechnical sense of the physical thing with respect to which the citizen exercises rights recognized by law. [Instead, it] . . . denote[s] the group of rights inhering in the citizen's relation to the physical thing, as the right to possess, use and dispose of it. . . . The constitutional provision is addressed to every sort of interest the citizen may possess." *Id.*, at 377–378.

[3]Thus, as this Court stated in *Monongahela Navigation Co.* v. *United States*, 148 U. S. 312, 325 (1893), a case which has since been characterized as resting primarily on "estoppel," see, *e.g.*, *United States* v. *Rands*, 380 U. S. 121, 126 (1967), the Fifth Amendment "prevents the public from loading upon one individual more than his just share of the burdens of government, and says that when he surrenders to the public something more and different from that which is exacted from other members of the public, a full and just equivalent shall be returned to him." See also *Penn. Central Transportation Co.* v. *New York City*, 438 U. S. 104, 123–125 (1978); *Pennsylvania Coal Co.* v. *Mahon*, 260 U. S. 393, 416 (1922).

Here the requirement that appellants permit appellees to exercise state-protected rights of free expression and petition on shopping center property clearly does not amount to an unconstitutional infringement of appellants' property rights under the Taking Clause. There is nothing to suggest that preventing appellants from prohibiting this sort of activity will unreasonably impair the value or use of their property as a shopping center. The PruneYard is a large commercial complex that covers several city blocks, contains numerous separate business establishments, and is open to the public at large. The decision of the California Supreme Court makes it clear that the PruneYard may restrict expressive activity by adopting time, place and manner regulations that will minimize any interference with its commercial functions. Appellees were orderly, and they limited their activity to the common areas of the shopping center. In these circumstances, the fact that they may have "physically invaded" appellants' property cannot be viewed as determinative.

This case is quite different from *Kaiser Aetna* v. *United States, supra.* *Kaiser Aetna* was a case in which the owners of a private pond had invested substantial amounts of money in dredging the pond, developing it into an exclusive marina, and building a surrounding marina community. The marina was open only to fee-paying members, and the fees were paid in part "to maintain the privacy and security of the pond." *Id.,* at 4046. The Federal Government sought to compel free public use of the private marina on the ground that the marina became subject to the federal navigational servitude because the owners had dredged a channel connecting it to "navigable water."

The Government's attempt to create a public right of access to the improved pond interfered with *Kaiser Aetna's* "reasonable investment backed expectations." We held that it went "so far beyond ordinary regulation or improvement for navigation as to amount to a taking. . . ." *Id.,* at 4049. Nor as a general proposition is the United States, as opposed to the several States, possessed of residual authority that enables it to define "property" in the first instance. A State is, of course, bound by the Just Compensation Clause of the Fifth Amendment, *Chicago, Burlington & Quincy Railroad Co.* v. *Chicago,* 166 U. S. 226, 233, 236–237 (1897), but here appellants have failed to demonstrate that the "right to exclude others" is so essential to the use or economic value of their property that the State-authorized limitation of it amounted to a "taking."

There is also little merit to appellants' argument that they have been denied their property without due process of law. In *Nebbia* v. *New York,* 291 U. S. 502 (1934), this Court stated that

"[Neither] property rights nor contract rights are absolute; . . . . Equally fundamental with the private right is that of the public to regulate it in the common interest. . . . [¶] [T]he guaranty of due process, as has often been held, demands only that the law shall not be unreasonable, arbitrary or capricious, and that the means selected shall have a real and substantial relation to the objective sought to be obtained." *Id.,* at 523, 525. See also *Railway Express Agency* v. *New York,* 336 U. S. 106 (1949); *Exxon Corp.* v. *Governor of Maryland,* 437 U. S. 117, 124–125 (1978).

Appellants have failed to provide sufficient justification for concluding that this test is not satisfied by the State's asserted interest in promoting more expansive rights of free speech and petition than conferred by the Federal Constitution.[4]

• • •

We conclude that . . . appellants' federally recognized property rights have [not] been infringed by the California Supreme Court's decision recognizing a right of appellees to exercise state protected rights of expression and petition on appellants' property. The judgment of the Supreme Court of California is therefore

Affirmed.

MR. JUSTICE BLACKMUN joins the opinion of the Court except that sentence thereof, *ante*, at 8–9, which reads "Nor as a general proposition is the United States, as opposed to the several States, possessed of residual authority that enables it to define 'property' in the first instance."

Suggestions for Further Reading

In addition to the cases cited in *Sioux Nation*, the reader may find it useful to consider R. H. Lowie, "Property Rights and Coercive Powers of Plains Indian Military Societies," *Journal of Legal and Political Sociology* 1 (1943), which traces the use of Locke's labor theory of property (considered below in Section One of Part Three) in justifying the expropriation of Indian lands. On the more abstract question of whether the original nomadic Indian inhabitants of land have legal title to it, see J. C. Smith, "The Concept of Native Title," 24 *University of Toronto Law Journal* 1 (1974).

On the theory of takings and the issue of fair compensation, consult Frank I. Michelman, "Property, Utility and Fairness," 80 *Harvard Law Review* 1165 (1968); and Joseph L. Sax, "Takings, Private Property and Public Rights," 81 *Yale Law Journal* 149 (1971). On issues more directly related to zoning, see Bernard H. Siegan, "Non-Zoning in Houston," 13 *Journal of Law and Economics* 71 (1970); and Robert C. Ellickson, "Alternatives to Zoning," 40 *University of Chicago Law Review* 681 (1973). Portions

---

[4]Although appellants contend there are adequate alternative avenues of communication available for appellees, it does not violate the United States Constitution for the State Supreme Court to conclude that access to appellants' property in the manner required here is necessary to the promotion of state-protected rights of free speech and petition.

of these four articles are reprinted in Bruce A. Ackerman, ed., *Economic Foundations of Property Law* (Boston: Little Brown, 1975). A relevant case-book here is Jacob H. Beuscher and Robert R. Wright, eds., *Cases and Materials on Land Use* (St. Paul: West, 1969). Many of the issues raised by zoning may be explored by reading *Village of Belle Terre* v. *Boraas*, 416 U.S. 1 (1974), and following out the references given there.

On the issue of free speech versus property rights, the reader is referred to the many cases cited in *PruneYard*. For convenience, we list some of the leading ones here: *Marsh* v. *Alabama*, 326 U.S. 501 (1946); *Amalgamated Food Employees* v. *Logan Valley Plaza*, 391 U.S. 308 (1968); and *Lloyd Corp.* v. *Tanner*, 407 U.S. 551 (1972). Picketing by labor unions raises some similar issues. See *International Brotherhood of Teamsters Union* v. *Vogt, Inc.*, 354 U.S. 284 (1957).

PART TWO
CONCEPTS

When in very good spirits [Wittgenstein] would jest in a delightful manner. This took the form of deliberately absurd or extravagant remarks uttered in a tone, and with a mien, of affected seriousness. On one walk he "gave" to me each tree that we passed, with the reservation that I was not to cut it down or do anything to it, or prevent the previous owners from doing anything to it: with those reservations it was henceforth *mine.*

> Norman Malcolm,
> *Ludwig Wittgenstein: A Memoir*

It is incorrect to say that the judiciary protected property; rather they called that property to which they accorded protection.

> Hamilton and Till, "Property,"
> *Encyclopedia of Social Science*

"Get off this estate."
"What for?"
"Because it's mine."
"Where did you get it?"
"From my father."
"Where did he get it?"
"From his father."
"And where did he get it?"
"He fought for it."
"Well, I'll fight you for it."

> Carl Sandburg,
> *The People, Yes*

Property: That which is peculiar or proper to any person; that which belongs exclusively to one; in the strict legal sense, an aggregate of rights which are guaranteed and protected by the government. . . . More specifically, ownership; the unrestricted and exclusive right to a thing; the right to dispose of a thing in every legal way, to possess it, to use it, and to exclude everyone else from interfering with it. . . . The highest right a man can have to anything . . . .

> *Black's Law Dictionary*

OVERVIEW

As the legal materials of Part One make plain, the concepts of "property right" and "ownership" are immensely controversial. When one asks whether job security is or ought to be a property right, whether the news is owned, or whether government limitations on the use of private property can constitute a "taking" of that property, one is driven rapidly to questions of definition. What do we mean, what have we meant, what are we coming to mean by "property"? To progress with these questions it is necessary to pay careful attention to the meanings of terms, to the history of changing concepts of ownership, and to attempts to interpret trends in both the practical and theoretical treatment of property. In the two sections that follow we offer materials intended to open up these inquiries. In Section One we examine various attempts to understand the basic nature of property. The differences here can heighten our sensitivity to the issues that will arise in connection with the critiques of Part Three. In Section Two we consider changes in property. We look at efforts to extend our understanding of property and to appreciate how our ideas of property are changing.

SECTION ONE
ANALYSES OF PROPERTY

How are we to understand and appreciate the nature of property rights? The three selections here provide glimpses of the directions in which investigation might proceed. The first selection deals with the moral status of rights as such, and property rights in particular. The second analyzes the legal concept of ownership, and the third reminds us to look carefully at the economic context of moral and legal rights.

Lawrence Becker, in an excerpt from his article "Individual Rights," focuses attention on the nature of rights per se. He explores the various positions on the place of rights in moral argument generally, and discusses the differences between various types of rights—claim-rights, liberties, powers, immunities, natural and conventional rights. This discussion describes the theoretical context in terms of which the discussion of property rights is carried on. In the full article, Becker goes on to examine the justification and scope of rights.

A. M. Honoré, a legal philosopher at Oxford, gives in his article "Ownership" a lucid account of the "liberal concept of ownership" to be found in "mature legal systems." While his list of eleven "incidents" recalls the "bundle of rights" model of property (found, for example, in Justice Rehnquist's opinions in *Kaiser Aetna* and *PruneYard*), Honoré notes that at least two of the incidents do not involve rights that owners can be said to have. Also, in Honoré's view, ownership may be present though some of the incidents are absent. His list includes the rights to possess, use, and manage; the rights to income, capital, and security; transmissibility, absence of term, and prohibition of harmful use; liability to execution (for debt) and residuarity (rules governing the reversion of lapsed ownership rights).

For Karl Marx (1818–1883), the basic conceptual problem in the theory of property is that of achieving a thoroughgoing transformation of the way we think about it. It is beside the point to ask who is entitled to property. What must be attended to is the history of the actual socioeconomic function of property rights. This history, as Marx sees it, is largely the history of expropriation—the taking of wealth by force, fraud, or systematic exploitation. Marx holds that the basic economic structure of society determines the form given to property rights by society's legal superstructure; it determines even the general way in which people think about property. That structure may be at the stage of petty industry, where the artisan and the farmer own the means of their own labor. Land and tools would here represent "scattered private property." From this primitive arrangement evolves an ever more concentrated system of ownership until, eventually, the artisan or farmer has become a "wage-laborer," working with tools, land, and institutions that belong to a small class of capitalists. This is "capitalist private property." From this second stage of economic development, in which production has become "socialized" as laborers work communally rather than individually, Marx thought it was an inevitable and relatively simple step to a third stage of economic development in which property becomes "socialized" as land and the means of production come to be held in common. In these excerpts from *Capital,* we can do little more than suggest Marx's thinking on property. His views are complex, extensive, and difficult to extract from the vast body of his writings.

Rights: An Introduction

LAWRENCE C. BECKER

Moral arguments produce a bewildering array of claims and counterclaims. . . . Duties are pitted against desires, rights against consequences, ideals against practicality, social welfare against individual welfare, cost-benefit analysis against obligations.

From "Individual Rights" by Lawrence C. Becker, first published in Tom Regan and Donald Van De Veer, eds., *And Justice for All* (Totowa, N.J.: Rowman and Littlefield, 1982).

Rights . . . have a special prominence in popular rhetoric, in political debate, in legal argument, and in moral philosophy. The most poignant claims of oppressed people are put in terms of rights to freedom and equality. Counterclaims from people in power are put in terms of rights to liberty and property. Pro- anti-abortion battles are waged over the right to life and a woman's right to control her body. All sorts of political action groups form around rights: civil rights, women's rights, prisoners' rights, children's rights, gay rights, the rights of the handicapped. The list is long and familiar.

What is not so familiar is the difficulty of getting a satisfactory account of the *place* of rights in moral arguments. Consider property rights. If I own some land, I have a bundle of rights with respect to it. But what rights? And how are they related to other important considerations? Suppose, due to a drought, my land now contains the only source of water for hundreds of miles. Do I have the right to withhold that water from my neighbors, or from travellers? Do I have the right to sell it at an exorbitant price? Do I have the right to sell it at all? Perhaps life-threatening emergencies override my rights. (Or perhaps those in need have rights to life that override my property rights.) And what about zoning? Suppose I want to develop my land, but my neighbors think a development would lessen the value of their own property, disturb their peace and quiet, and generally degrade the quality of their environment. Should I have the right, because I own the land, to do what I choose? Or should the interests, desires and welfare of my neighbors prevent me? These questions illustrate the problem of establishing the proper place of rights in moral argument. Are rights the most important kind of moral considerations? Or just one of many? Do rights automatically take priority over everything else? Or must they always be balanced against other factors?

Here is an instructive conceit—instructive, that is, if you can study it with a straight face. The basic metaphor comes from the contemporary legal theorist Ronald Dworkin,[1] but he had the good taste not to elaborate it.

Think of a card game called Moral Argument. The cards—sometimes called "considerations"—are divided into four suits: Rights, Consequences, Ideals, and Desires. (In real moral arguments, of course, the considerations are more numerous and divided somewhat differently. There is normally a place for Needs, for example, as well as for Duties, Social Goals, Social Welfare, and so on. But this is a simplified game.)

In this game, Rights is the most powerful suit, analogous to Spades in an ordinary deck of playing cards. Consequences, Ideals, and Desires follow in descending order.

Each suit is double, however. Each positive consideration—Ace, King, Queen, and so on—is matched by a negative one in the same suit. So there is a +10 of Desires, but also a −10. Each suit thus has 26 cards, and there are 104 in the full deck.

[1]Ronald Dworkin, *Taking Rights Seriously* (Cambridge, Mass.: Harvard University Press, 1977), xi.

Moral Argument is a four-handed game. There is no bidding. The players merely "make arguments" (tricks) by laying down considerations (cards) in turn. The Dealer leads, and positive and negative considerations are played in turn. (If the Dealer plays a negative, West must play a positive, North must respond with a negative, and East ends the argument with a positive consideration.)

The object of the game is to take arguments (take tricks) by either nullifying or besting the considerations already on the table. You nullify a 3 with the other 3 of the same suit, for example. You best a 3 with a 4 or better of the same suit—or with a 3 or better of a more powerful suit. (Remember that the weakest suit is Desires, followed up the scale by Ideals, Consequences, and Rights.)

Here is a sample of play. Dealer leads with a small negative Desire—say a −4. West nullifies it with a +4 of the same suit. North bests both of those considerations with a −10 Ideal, and East takes the argument with a +10 Consequence. Simple game.

Now imagine that there are two radically different ways of playing Moral Argument. The standard "weak" game is the one I just described. It is played by most competitors. But certain hard-nosed tournament players favor a "strong" game in which one or more of the suits can be trump. And there are disputes about this, too. Hedonists make Desires trump. Utilitarians favor Consequences. And Intuitionists play a rather messy game in which any one of the suits—or none at all—may be trump depending on the circumstances in which the game is being played.

The toughest game of all is played by a few hardy Rights Theorists. (Detractors call this version Social Suicide.) In this game Rights are always trump. They take any argument constructed from considerations of Consequences, Ideals, and Desires. In such a game the following scenario is common: Dealer leads with a positive ideal—not a particularly high one, perhaps. Something like "Write good letters to your lover." West counters with a big negative desire: "I hate writing letters." North bests both of those with a big consequence: "What would the world be like if everyone were so selfish?" And then East takes the argument with the lowest right in the deck: "I don't have to if I don't want to." Not a game for the faint of heart.

The metaphor points to the problem of deciding how important rights are going to be in moral argument. And the different versions of the game correspond roughly to the various logical possibilities.

It is unlikely that anyone actually favors the strict "Rights are trump" rule, even though some writers occasionally speak as though they do. Dworkin says:

> Individual rights are political trumps. . . . Individuals have rights, when, for some reason, a collective goal is not a sufficient justification for denying them what they wish.[2]

[2]Ibid.

Harvard philosopher Robert Nozick opens his book this way:

> Individuals have rights, and there are things no person or group may do to them (without violating their rights). So strong and far-reaching are these rights that they raise the question of what, if anything, the state and its officials may do. How much room do individual rights leave for the state?[3]

Alan Gewirth, a philosopher at the University of Chicago, says:

> Whatever else may be demanded of moral rules and principles, they cannot be held to fulfill even their minimal point if they do not require that persons be protected in their rights. . . .[4]

And Harvard law professor Charles Fried says that "the violation of a right is always wrong."[5]

But in fact all of these writers would reject the view that just any right must be honored regardless of the consequences. If I have a right to the last bit of sugar in the vicinity (because I just bought it, though the shopkeeper has not yet handed it over), and it is suddenly needed to save the life of a diabetic who has collapsed on the floor next to me, does my right to the sugar trump her desperate need for it? No serious rights theorist would say so. Most acknowledge that rights can be overridden in emergencies—at least those rights that are not essential for one's health or survival. Furthermore, even basic rights may conflict to produce difficult cases. Nozick raises the case of the "innocent shield"—an innocent person used as a shield by an attacker. May you kill the shield to save your life?[6] It is unclear.

The fact is, however, that most rights are thought of as having built-in exceptions. John Locke, for example, in Chapter V of his *Second Treatise of Government*, argued that people were entitled to property rights in whatever they acquired through their labor—but only if they left as much and as good for others. Current discussions of Locke's "labor theory" of property rights agree that this qualification is necessary. And yet another qualification is introduced by those who divide rights into strong or basic ones (such as rights to life and well-being) and weak or non-basic ones, and then hold that only the basic ones are trumps. Some of what Dworkin says can be understood this way.[7]

In any case, most rights theorists take a position roughly equivalent to the standard game—the game in which rights are merely the most powerful considerations in moral arguments rather than trumps. The Ace of Rights beats any other Ace, but the 2 of Rights doesn't.

---

[3]Robert Nozick, *Anarchy, State and Utopia* (New York: Basic Books, 1974), ix.

[4]Alan Gewirth, *Reason and Morality* (Chicago: University of Chicago Press, 1978), 327.

[5]Charles Fried, *Right and Wrong* (Cambridge, Mass.: Harvard University Press, 1978), 108.

[6]Nozick, *Anarchy*, 34–35.

[7]Dworkin, *Takings Rights Seriously*, 191.

Alternatives

Even this position gets strong opposition, however. Some people want to think of rights simply as rules of thumb which place the burden of proof on anyone who wants to go against them. Such a conception of rights amounts to this: If I want to do something and you don't want me to do it, so far we have a standoff. But if I have a right to do it, there is no standoff. Unless you come forward with a good argument against my plan, I may disregard your wishes and go ahead. On this view, rights amount to something more than ordinary moral considerations, but not very much more.

We leave rights theory altogether if we hold that rights are actually subordinate to other considerations. This corresponds to playing the Moral Argument game with Consequences, or Ideals, or even Desires on top. And if we play the "messy" version—letting intuitions decide when to treat Rights as trump and when to treat some other suit (or none) as trump, we have also abandoned rights theory.

The choice we make about the place of rights in moral argument is a crucial one. Our political system differs from Great Britain's on this issue. They do not have a bill of rights which is immune from repeal through the ordinary legislative process. We do. And the Western liberal democracies generally differ from revolutionary socialist regimes on the importance of individual rights. The philosophical basis for this important choice ultimately depends on the definitions of various types of rights, and on the sorts of justification we can give for them.

TYPES OF RIGHTS

What is a right? Everyone agrees that there is no simple answer to that question because there are so many radically different types of rights. The word "right" is multiply ambiguous.

One important thing to get straight from the outset is the difference between the specialized and the unspecialized use of the term "right." In the unspecialized use, "I have a right to do it" may mean no more than "I am justified in doing it." A right in this sense is not a separate sort of moral consideration at all. It is simply any sort of consideration that is sufficient to justify a course of action. But here we are concerned with the other category—the specialized use of "right"—in which "I have a right to do it" means "I have a special sort of moral claim to do it." But what "special sort"? Again, there isn't just one.

Claim-Rights, Liberties, Powers and Immunities

Wesley Hohfeld, an American legal theorist working in the early part of this century, distinguished four sorts,[8] and his distinctions are

---

[8]W. N. Hohfeld, *Fundamental Legal Conceptions* (New Haven: Yale University Press, 1919).

enormously useful. The idea is to think about what is on "the other side" of a right. If *you* have a right of some sort, what does that mean for *my* situation?

Claim-rights. One thing it might mean is that I have a duty to you. If you have a right not to be tortured, that means I have a duty not to do it. If you have a right to get pay for your work, your employer has a duty to pay for it. When rights correlate with duties in this way they are called claims, or claim-rights, or sometimes rights in the strict sense.

Liberties. But sometimes there is not a duty on the other side. Sometimes there is just a kind of moral or legal vacuum. If you have a right to run in the race, that doesn't mean that the other runners have a duty to let you win. It simply means that they have no claim-right to the victory—no claim-right that you not win. Such rights are called liberties, or liberty-rights, or (less accurately) privileges. The United States Supreme Court has made it clear that a woman's legal right to an abortion is at present a liberty-right, not a claim-right. Women are simply at liberty to have abortions; no particular person has a duty to perform them, and states have no duty to pay for them.

Powers. A third sort of right is a power. If you have the right to make a will, that means that you have the power to change some of the rights and duties of those around you. You can make me your executor, for example, which imposes duties on me. Or, as I would much prefer, you can make me your beneficiary. When you have a power, or power-right, people on the other side of it have a liability. They are, in effect, at your mercy.

Immunities. A fourth sort of right is an immunity. The other side of this is a disability or lack of power. If you have the right to remain silent, then I lack the power-right to make you speak.

Schematically, Hohfeld's distinctions look like this:

CLAIM RIGHTS	LIBERTIES	POWERS	IMMUNITIES
↑	↑	↑	↑
correlate with	correlate with	correlate with	correlate with
↓	↓	↓	↓
DUTIES	"NO-RIGHTS"	LIABILITIES	DISABILITIES

Careful attention to these distinctions is important. Rights are often compounds of two or more types, but until the elements of the compound have been identified, it is hard to make much progress in a moral argument about it.

Consider, for example, how you would deal with the following argument: "All rights, if they are genuine legal rights, have to be enforceable. If they are enforceable, that means the law can require people to respect them. If people are required to respect them, then duties are being imposed. So it is just a fraud to say in one breath that women have the right to have abortions and in the next breath to say that no one has a duty to provide or perform abortions. Either women have the right or they don't. If they do, then we have the duty to provide them."

There are several mistakes in this argument, but the fundamental one is its failure to see that the law might enforce (with appropriate duties) Hohfeldian "no-rights," liabilities and disabilities. The law might make sure, for example, that no one interferes with doctors who decide to perform abortions or women who decide to have them. The law might insist that hospitals permit staff doctors to schedule abortions in just the same way they schedule other elective surgery. The liberty-right to an abortion, then, would be buttressed by a duty on the part of hospitals not to put obstacles in the way. Doctors and their patients would then have correlative claim-rights against their hospitals, but those claim-rights would be for the enforcement of liberties.

Negative and Positive, General and Special Rights

Just two other distinctions are of crucial importance here. (For the moment I shall leave aside "natural," "conventional," "moral" and "legal" rights because those categories have to do with how a right is justified. Similarly, "human" rights, "women's" rights and so forth refer to scope— to those who are in the class of right-holders.)

One distinction is between *negative* and *positive rights*. Negative rights are rights to be free from interference. Criminal law defines many of these rights by imposing duties of restraint on people. We have duties to refrain from murder, mayhem, rape, pillage, and theft, and others have the corresponding negative rights against us. Positive rights, on the other hand, are rights to assistance of some sort. Rights to food, to health care, and to an equal share of the world's resources would be positive rights. One of the most fundamental disagreements in political theory is between advocates of the minimal or "nightwatchman" state (who hold that the government has no business enforcing any [non-contractual] positive rights at all) and advocates of the welfare state (who insist that the government must enforce some positive rights).

The other important distinction is between general and special rights. In law, general rights are sometimes referred to as rights *in rem*— rights "against the world." Special rights are rights *in personam*—rights "against (specific) persons." My right not to be murdered is a general one: I have that right "against" everyone—against the world. But my right to compensation for my work is a special one. It comes from a special relationship between me and my employer. This distinction brings out the importance of identifying who is on the other side of a right. Until that is settled, it is hard to get very far with a moral argument about the right.

Getting a General Definition

Now with all that said, are we any closer to a general answer to the question of what a right is? Is there a general answer? Not a very useful one, I think. The various types of rights are different enough so that anything true of them all will be very general indeed. Wittgenstein liked to use the example of the problem of defining the concept of a game. There are so many different kinds of games that it is hard to find any interesting feature common to them all. Some are played alone (solitaire), and others are not. Some are played to win, and others are not (Spin the Bottle). Some are played just for fun; others are serious business for professionals. Some have fixed rules; others (like impromptu children's games) do not. And so on. Rights are a bit like that.

Even so, rights have a few common elements which are important. One is that rights are more than just norms, or expectations, or standards of conduct. They are rules which define the boundaries of what is "owed" to a specified group of people (the right holders) by another group (the right respecters). Consider the statement, "When Americans greet strangers, they typically smile and shake hands." Imagine this being given as a piece of advice to foreigners. Would it state a rule defining what is "owed" to strangers by Americans? No. It would merely define a general practice, or expectation. The statement, "Keep your promises," however, is quite different. It does state a ruling defining what is owed. And the people who are owed—that is, the promisees—are often said to have a right to what was promised.

This feature of rights accounts for two other general characteristics. One has to do with gratitude and indebtedness. When you respect my rights, you haven't done me a favor. I don't "owe" you anything for it—not even gratitude. (Though civility is not out of place.) . . . The other characteristic is that rights are supposed to be enforceable in a way that mere ideals or desires are not. If I simply want you to do something for me and you do not, that is too bad for me. Depending on the circumstance, it might not be good of you to refuse, but if all I have on my side is the fact that I want your help, I do not have any business twisting your arm for it. If I have a right to your help, however, and you refuse it, some sort of arm-twisting is presumably in order. I say some sort because of course the extent of it depends on the sort of right involved. If the right is a moral but not a legal one, verbal demands are frequently as far as one can go. But the general principle is important: If I have a right to it I can justifiably take steps to extract it from you if you fail to hand it over.

If rights are to be enforceable, however, they must be specific. They must indicate *who* has the right against whom, what the *content* of the right is, and what *kind of enforcement* is appropriate. Some claims of right are criticized on just this ground. What could "Everyone has a right to an education" mean? If it means that everyone has a right to go to school, then we can readily understand how it could be enforced. If it means more than that (say, for example, that the state has a duty to see to it that everyone actually learns calculus), could it be enforced at all? If it cannot be enforced, is it really a "right"?

Finally, there is *compensation*. The violation of rights—unlike other moral considerations—always at least raises a presumption that the victims should be compensated. If our desires conflict, and mine must be sacrificed, I am just unfortunate. But if my rights conflict with your desires, and for some reason my rights must (or just are) sacrificed, I am presumably "owed" something. Often this takes the form of compensation for my loss. Sometimes it merely means that I am owed an apology. But always, when rights are involved, a violation leaves unfinished business.

So to summarize: Rights are rules that define what is owed to some (the right holders) by others. Rights may be demanded and enforced. They are therefore part of our system of permissions and requirements.

Beyond that, because rights are so various, there is not much else one can usefully say about their general nature.

Ownership

A. M. HONORÉ

Ownership is one of the characteristic institutions of human society. A people to whom ownership was unknown, or who accorded it a minor place in their arrangements, who meant by *meum* and *tuum* no more than 'what I (or you) presently hold' would live in a world that is not our world. Yet to see why their world would be different, and to assess the plausibility of vaguely conceived schemes to replace 'ownership' by 'public administration', or of vaguely stated claims that the importance of ownership has declined or its character changed in the twentieth century, we need first to have a clear idea of what ownership is.

I propose, therefore, to begin by giving an account of the standard incidents of ownership: *i.e.* those legal rights, duties and other incidents which apply, in the ordinary case, to the person who has the greatest interest in a thing admitted by a mature legal system. To do so will be to analyse the concept of ownership, by which I mean the 'liberal' concept of 'full' individual ownership, rather than any more restricted notion to which the same label may be attached in certain contexts. . . .

If ownership is provisionally defined as the *greatest possible interest in a thing which a mature system of law recognizes,* then it follows that, since all

From *Oxford Essays in Jurisprudence*, edited by A. G. Guest, © Oxford University Press 1961. Reprinted by permission of Oxford University Press and the author. Footnotes renumbered.

mature systems admit the existence of 'interests' in 'things', all mature systems have, in a sense, a concept of ownership. Indeed, even primitive systems, like that of the Trobriand islanders, have rules by which certain persons, such as the 'owners' of canoes, have greater interests in certain things than anyone else.[1]

For mature legal systems it is possible to make a larger claim. In them certain important legal incidents are found, which are common to different systems. If it were not so, 'He owns that umbrella', said in a purely English context, would mean something different from 'He owns that umbrella', proferred as a translation of 'Ce parapluie est à lui'. Yet, as we know, they mean the same. There is indeed, a substantial similarity in the position of one who 'owns' an umbrella in England, France, Russia, China, and any other modern country one may care to mention. Everywhere the 'owner' can, in the simple uncomplicated case, in which no other person has an interest in the thing, use it, stop others using it, lend it, sell it or leave it by will. Nowhere may he use it to poke his neighbour in the ribs or to knock over his vase. Ownership, *dominium, propriété, Eigentum* and similar words stand not merely for the greatest interest in things in particular systems but for a type of interest with common features transcending particular systems. It must surely be important to know what these common features are?

· · ·

I now list what appear to be the standard incidents of ownership. They may be regarded as necessary ingredients in the notion of ownership, in the sense that, if a system did not admit them, and did not provide for them to be united in a single person, we would conclude that it did not know the liberal concept of ownership, though it might still have a modified version of ownership, either of a primitive or sophisticated sort. But the listed incidents are not individually necessary, though they may be together sufficient, conditions for the person of inherence to be designated 'owner' of a particular thing in a given system. As we have seen, the use of 'owner' will extend to cases in which not all the listed incidents are present.

Ownership comprises the right to possess, the right to use, the right to manage, the right to the income of the thing, the right to the capital, the right to security, the rights or incidents of transmissibility and absence of term, the prohibition of harmful use, liability to execution, and the incident of residuarity: this makes eleven leading incidents. Obviously, there are alternative ways of classifying the incidents; moreover, it is fashionable to speak of ownership as if it were just a bundle of rights, in which case at least two items in the list would have to be omitted.

No doubt the concentration in the same person of the right (liberty)[2]

---

[1] Malinowsky, *Crime and Custom in Savage Society*, p. 18.

[2] In this article I identify rights with claims, liberties etc. For a criticism of this identification see (1960), 34 Tulane L.R. 453.

of using as one wishes, the right to exclude others, the power of alienating and an immunity from expropriation is a cardinal feature of the institution. Yet it would be a distortion—and one of which the eighteenth century, with its over-emphasis on subjective rights, was patently guilty—to speak as if this concentration of patiently garnered rights was the only legally or socially important characteristic of the owner's position. The present analysis, by emphasizing that the owner is subject to characteristic prohibitions and limitations, and that ownership comprises at least one important incident independent of the owner's choice, is an attempt to redress the balance.

(1) THE RIGHT TO POSSESS

The right to possess, *viz.* to have exclusive physical control of a thing, or to have such control as the nature of the thing admits, is the foundation on which the whole superstructure of ownership rests. It may be divided into two aspects, the right (claim) to be put in exclusive control of a thing and the right to remain in control, *viz.* the claim that others should not without permission, interfere. Unless a legal system provides some rules and procedures for attaining these ends it cannot be said to protect ownership.

It is of the essence of the right to possess that it is *in rem* in the sense of availing against persons generally. This does not, of course, mean that an owner is necessarily entitled to exclude everyone from his property. We happily speak of the ownership of land, yet a largish number of officials have the right of entering on private land without the owner's consent, for some limited period and purpose. On the other hand, a general licence so to enter on the 'property' of others would put an end to the institution of landowning as we now know it.

The protection of the right to possess (still using 'possess' in the convenient, though over-simple, sense of 'have exclusive physical control') should be sharply marked off from the protection of mere present possession. To exclude others from what one presently holds is an instinct found in babies and even, as Holmes points out,[3] in animals, of which the seal gives a striking example. To sustain this instinct by legal rules is to protect possession but not, as such, to protect the right to possess and so not to protect ownership. If dispossession without the possessor's consent is, in general, forbidden, the possessor is given a right *in rem,* valid against persons generally, to remain undisturbed, but he has no *right to possess in rem* unless he is entitled to recover from persons generally what he has lost or had taken from him, and to obtain from them what is due to him but not yet handed over. . . .

To have worked out the notion of 'having a right to' as distinct from merely 'having', or, if that is too subjective a way of putting it, of rules allocating things to people as opposed to rules merely forbidding forcible taking, was a major intellectual achievement. Without it society would

---

[3]*The Common Law,* p. 213.

have been impossible. Yet the distinction is apt to be overlooked by English lawyers, who are accustomed to the rule that every adverse possession is a root of title, *i.e.* gives rise to a right to possess,[4] or at least that '*de facto* possession is *prima facie* evidence of seisin in fee and right to possession'.[5]

The owner, then, has characteristically a battery of remedies in order to obtain, keep and, if necessary, get back the thing owned. Remedies such as the actions for ejectment and wrongful detention and the *vindicatio* are designed to enable the plaintiff either to obtain or to get back a thing, or at least to put some pressure on the defendant to hand it over. Others, such as the actions for trespass to land and goods, the Roman possessory interdicts and their modern counterparts are primarily directed towards enabling a present possessor to keep possession. Few of the remedies mentioned are confined to the owner; most of them are available also to persons with a right to possess falling short of ownership, and some to mere possessors. Conversely, there will be cases in which they are not available to the owner, for instance because he has voluntarily parted with possession for a temporary purpose, as by hiring the thing out. The availability of such remedies is clearly not a necessary and sufficient condition of owning a thing; what is necessary, in order that there may be ownership of things at all, is that such remedies shall be available to the owner in the usual case in which no other person has a right to exclude him from the thing.

(2) THE RIGHT TO USE

The present incident and the next two overlap. On a wide interpretation of 'use', management and income fall within use. On a narrow interpretation, 'use' refers to the owner's personal use and enjoyment of the thing owned. On this interpretation it excludes management and income.

The right (liberty) to use at one's discretion has rightly been recognized as a cardinal feature of ownership, and the fact that, as we shall see, certain limitations on use also fall within the standard incidents of ownership does not detract from its importance, since the standard limitations are, in general, rather precisely defined, while the permissible types of use constitute an open list.

(3) THE RIGHT TO MANAGE

The right to manage is the right to decide how and by whom the thing owned shall be used. This right depends, legally, on a cluster of powers, chiefly powers of licensing acts which would otherwise be unlawful and powers of contracting: the power to admit others to one's land, to permit

[4]Pollock & Wright, *Possession in the Common Law* (1888), pp. 91, 95; Wade and Megarry, *The Law of Real Property* (2nd ed.), p. 955.

[5]*N.R.M.A. Insurance, Ltd.* v. *B. & B. Shipping and Marine Salvage Co. (Pty.), Ltd.* (1947), 47 S.C.R. (N.S.W.) 273.

others to use one's things, to define the limits of such permission, and to contract effectively in regard to the use (in the literal sense) and exploitation of the thing owned. An owner may not merely sit in his own deck chair but may validly license others to sit in it, lend it, impose conditions on the borrower, direct how it is to be painted or cleaned, contract for it to be mended in a particular way. This is the sphere of management in relation to a simple object like a deck chair. When we consider more complex cases, like the ownership of a business, the complex of powers which make up the right to manage seems still more prominent. The power to direct how resources are to be used and exploited is one of the cardinal types of economic and political power; the owner's legal powers of management are one, but only one possible basis for it. Many observers have drawn attention to the growth of managerial power divorced from legal ownership; in such cases it may be that we should speak of split ownership or redefine our notion of the thing owned. This does not affect the fact that the right to manage is an important element in the notion of ownership; indeed, the fact that we feel doubts in these cases whether the 'legal owner' *really* owns is a testimony to its importance. . . .

(4) THE RIGHT TO THE INCOME

To use or occupy a thing may be regarded as the simplest way of deriving an income from it, of enjoying it. It is, for instance, expressly contemplated by the English income tax legislation that the rent-free use or occupation of a house is a form of income, and only the inconvenience of assessing and collecting the tax presumably prevents the extension of this principle to movables.

Income in the more ordinary sense (fruits, rents, profits) may be thought of as a surrogate of use, a benefit derived from forgoing personal use of a thing and allowing others to use it for reward; as a reward for work done in exploiting the thing; or as the brute product of a thing, made by nature or by other persons. Obviously the line to be drawn between the earned and unearned income from a thing cannot be firmly drawn. . . .

(5) THE RIGHT TO THE CAPITAL

The right to the capital consists in the power to alienate the thing and the liberty to consume, waste or destroy the whole or part of it: clearly it has an important economic aspect. The latter liberty need not be regarded as unrestricted; but a general provision requiring things to be conserved in the public interest, so far as not consumed by use in the ordinary way, would perhaps be inconsistent with the liberal idea of ownership. . . .

An owner normally has both the power of disposition and the power of transferring title. Disposition on death is not permitted in many primitive societies but seems to form an essential element in the mature notion of ownership. The tenacity of the right of testation once it has been recognized is shown by the Soviet experience. The earliest writers were hostile to inheritance, but gradually Soviet law has come to admit that citizens may dispose freely of their 'personal property' on death, subject to limits not unlike those known elsewhere.[6]

(6) THE RIGHT TO SECURITY

An important aspect of the owner's position is that he should be able to look forward to remaining owner indefinitely if he so chooses and he remains solvent. His right to do so may be called the right to security. Legally, this is in effect an immunity from expropriation, based on rules which provide that, apart from bankruptcy and execution for debt, the transmission of ownership is consensual.

However, a general right to security, availing against others, is consistent with the existence of a power to expropriate or divest in the state or public authorities. From the point of view of security of property, it is important that when expropriation takes place, adequate compensation should be paid; but a general power to expropriate subject to paying compensation would be fatal to the institution of ownership as we know it. Holmes' paradox, that where specific restitution of goods is not a normal remedy,[7] expropriation and wrongful conversion are equivalent, obscures the vital distinction between acts which a legal system permits as rightful and those which it reprobates as wrongful: but if wrongful conversion were general and went unchecked, ownership as we know it would disappear, though damages were regularly paid.

In some systems, as (*semble*) English law, a private individual may destroy another's property without compensation when this is necessary in order to protect his own person or property from a greater danger.[8] Such a rule is consistent with security of property only because of its exceptional character. Again, the state's (or local authority's) power of expropriation is usually limited to certain classes of thing and certain limited purposes. A general power to expropriate any property for any purpose would be inconsistent with the institution of ownership. If, under such a system, compensation were regularly paid, we might say either that ownership was not recognized in that system, or that money alone could be owned, 'money' here meaning a strictly fungible claim on the resources of the community. As we shall see, 'ownership' of such claims is not identical with the ownership of material objects and simple claims.

---

[6]Constitution of the U.S.S.R., 1936, s. 10; Gsovski, *op. cit.*, p. 620.
[7]Holmes (1897), 10 Harv. L.R. 457, 461.
[8]*Cope* v. *Sharpe.* [1912] 1 K.B. 496; *Cresswell* v. *Sirl*, [1948] 1 K.B. 241.

(7) THE INCIDENT OF TRANSMISSIBILITY

It is often said that one of the main characteristics of the owner's interest is its 'duration'. In England, at least, the doctrine of estates made lawyers familiar with the notion of the 'duration' of an interest and Maitland, in a luminous metaphor, spoke of estates as 'projected upon the plane of time'.[9]

Yet this notion is by no means as simple as it seems. What is called 'unlimited' duration (*perpétuité*)[10] comprises at least two elements (i) that the interest can be transmitted to the holder's successors and so on *ad infinitum* (The fact that in medieval land law all interests were considered 'temporary'[11] is one reason why the terminology of ownership failed to take root, with consequences which have endured long after the cause has disappeared); (ii) that it is not certain to determine at a future date. These two elements may be called 'transmissibility' and 'absence of term' respectively. We are here concerned with the former.

No one, as Austin points out,[12] can enjoy a thing after he is dead (except vicariously) so that, in a sense, no interest can outlast death. But an interest which is transmissible to the holder's successors (persons designated by or closely related to the holder who obtain the property after him) is more valuable than one which stops with his death. This is so both because on alienation the alienee or, if transmissibility is generally recognized, the alienee's successors, are thereby enabled to enjoy the thing after the alienor's death so that a better price can be obtained for the thing, and because, even if alienation were not recognized, the present holder would by the very fact of transmissibility be dispensed *pro tanto* from making provision for his intestate heirs. Hence, for example, the moment when the tenant in fee acquired a heritable (though not yet fully alienable) right was a crucial moment in the evolution of the fee simple. Heritability by the state would not, of course, amount to transmissibility in the present sense: it is assumed that the transmission is in some sense *advantageous* to the transmitter.

Transmissibility can, of course, be admitted, yet stop short at the first, second or third generation of transmittees. The owner's interest is characterized by *indefinite* transmissibility, no limit being placed on the possible number of transmissions, though the nature of the thing may well limit the actual number.

In deference to the conventional view that the exercise of a right must depend on the choice of the holder,[13] I have refrained from calling transmissibility a right. It is, however, clearly something in which the holder has an economic interest, and it may be that the notion of a right requires revision in order to take account of incidents not depending on the holder's choice which are nevertheless of value to him.

[9]Pollock & Maitland, *op. cit.*, Vol. II, p. 10.

[10]Planiol-Ripert-Esmein, *Traité pratique de droit civil français* (1952), Vol. II, p. 220.

[11]Hargreaves, *Introduction to the Principles of Land Law* (1952), p. 47.

[12]Austin, *Jurisprudence*, 4th ed., (1873), p. 817.

[13]Hart, *Definition and Theory in Jurisprudence* (1953), p. 16; (1954), 70 L.Q.R. 49.

(8) THE INCIDENT OF ABSENCE OF TERM

This is the second part of what is vaguely called 'duration.' The rules of a legal system usually seem to provide for determinate, indeterminate and determinable interests. The first are certain to determine at a future date or on the occurrence of a future event which is certain to occur. In this class come leases for however long a term, copyrights, etc. Indeterminate interests are those, such as ownership and easements, to which no term is set. Should the holder live for ever, he would, in the ordinary way, be able to continue in the enjoyment of them for ever. Since human beings are mortal, he will in practice only be able to enjoy them for a limited period, after which the fate of his interest depends on its transmissibility. Again, since human beings are mortal, interests for life, whether of the holder or another, must be regarded as determinate. The notion of an indeterminate interest, in the full sense, therefore requires the notion of transmissibility, but if the latter were not recognized, there would still be value to the holder in the fact that his interest was not due to determine on a fixed date or on the occurrence of some contingency, like a general election, which is certain to occur sooner or later. . . .

(9) THE PROHIBITION OF HARMFUL USE

An owner's liberty to use and manage the thing owned as he chooses is in mature systems of law, as in primitive systems, subject to the condition that uses harmful to other members of society are forbidden. There may, indeed, be much dispute over what is to count as 'harm' and to what extent give and take demands that minor inconvenience between neighbours shall be tolerated. Nevertheless, at least for material objects, one can always point to abuses which a legal system will not allow.

I may use my car freely but not in order to run my neighbour down, or to demolish his gate, or even to go on his land if he protests; nor may I drive uninsured. I may build on my land as I choose, but not in such a way that my building collapses on my neighbour's land. I may let off fireworks on Guy Fawkes night, but not in such a way as to set fire to my neighbour's house. These and similar limitations on the use of things are so familiar and so obviously essential to the existence of an orderly community that they are not often thought of as incidents of ownership; yet, without them 'ownership' would be a destructive force.

(10) LIABILITY TO EXECUTION

Of a somewhat similar character is the liability of the owner's interest to be taken away from him for debt, either by execution of a judgment debt or on insolvency. Without such a general liability the growth of credit would be impeded and ownership would, again, be an instrument by which the owner could defraud his creditors. This incident, therefore, which may be called *executability,* seems to constitute one of the standard ingredients of the liberal idea of ownership. . . .

(11) RESIDUARY CHARACTER

A legal system might recognize interests in things less than ownership and might have a rule that, on the determination of such interests, the rights in question lapsed and could be exercised by no one, or by the first person to exercise them after their lapse. There might be leases and easements; yet, on their extinction, no one would be entitled to exercise rights similar to those of the former lessee or of the holder of the easement. This would be unlike any system known to us and I think we should be driven to say that in such a system the institution of ownership did not extend to any thing in which limited interests existed. In such things there would, paradoxically, be interests less than ownership but no ownership.

This fantasy is intended to bring out the point that it is characteristic of ownership that an owner has a residuary right in the thing owned. In practice, legal systems have rules providing that on the lapse of an interest rights, including liberties, analogous to the rights formerly vested in the holder of the interest, vest in or are exercisable by someone else, who may be said to acquire the 'corresponding rights.' Of course, the 'corresponding rights' are not the same rights as were formerly vested in the holder of the interest. The easement holder had a right to exclude the owner; now the owner has a right to exclude the easement holder. The latter right is not identical with, but corresponds to, the former.

It is true that corresponding rights do not always arise when an interest is determined. Sometimes, when ownership is abandoned, no corresponding right vests in another; the thing is simply *res derelicta.* Sometimes, on the other hand, when ownership is abandoned, a new ownership vests in the state, as is the case in South Africa when land has been abandoned.

It seems, however, a safe generalization that, whenever an interest less than ownership terminates, legal systems always provide for corresponding rights to vest in another. When easements terminate, the 'owner' can exercise the corresponding rights, and when bailments terminate, the same is true. It looks as if we have found a simple explanation of the usage we are investigating, but this turns out to be but another deceptive short cut. For it is not a sufficient condition of *A*'s being the owner of a thing that, on the determination of *B*'s interests in it, corresponding rights vest in or are exercisable by *A*. On the determination of a sub-lease, the rights in question become exercisable by the lessee, not by the 'owner' of the property.

Can we then say that the 'owner' is the ultimate residuary? When the sub-lessee's interest determines the lessee acquires the corresponding rights; but when the lessee's right determines the 'owner' acquires these rights. Hence the 'owner' appears to be identified as the ultimate residuary. The difficulty is that the series may be continued, for on the determination of the 'owner's' interest the state may acquire the corresponding rights; is the state's interest ownership or a mere expectancy?

A warning is here necessary. We are approaching the troubled waters of split ownership. Puzzles about the location of ownership are often generated by the fact that an ultimate residuary right is not coupled with present alienability or with the other standard incidents we have listed. . . .

We are of course here concerned not with the puzzles of split ownership but with simple cases in which the existence of *B*'s lesser interest in a thing is clearly consistent with *A*'s owning it. To explain the usage in such cases it is helpful to point out that it is a necessary but not sufficient condition of *A*'s being owner that, either immediately or ultimately, the extinction of other interests would enure for his benefit. In the end, it turns out that residuarity is merely one of the standard incidents of ownership, important no doubt, but not entitled to any special status. . . .

From Capital

KARL MARX

[P]rimitive accumulation plays in Political Economy about the same part as original sin in theology. Adam bit the apple, and thereupon sin fell on the human race. Its origin is supposed to be explained when it is told as an anecdote of the past. In times long gone by there were two sorts of people; one, the diligent, intelligent, and, above all, frugal élite; the other, lazy rascals, spending their substance, and more, in riotous living. The legend of theological original sin tells us certainly how man came to be condemned to eat his bread in the sweat of his brow; but the history of economic original sin reveals to us that there are people to whom this is by no means essential. Never mind! Thus it came to pass that the former sort accumulated wealth, and the latter sort had at last nothing to sell except their own skins. And from this original sin dates the poverty of the great majority that, despite all its labour, has up to now nothing to sell but itself, and the wealth of the few that increases constantly although they have long ceased to work. Such insipid childishness is every day preached to us in the defence of property. M. Thiers, *e.g.*, had the assurance to

From Chapters XXVI and XXXII of Karl Marx, *Capital*, Volume I, first published in 1867. The version here is a translation by Samuel Moore and Edward Aveling of the Third German Edition, edited by Friedrich Engels.

repeat it with all the solemnity of a statesman, to the French people, once so *spirituel*. But as soon as the question of property crops up, it becomes a sacred duty to proclaim the intellectual food of the infant as the one thing fit for all ages and for all stages of development. In actual history it is notorious that conquest, enslavement, robbery, murder, briefly force, play the great part. In the tender annals of Political Economy, the idyllic reigns from time immemorial. Right and "labour" were from all time the sole means of enrichment, the present year of course always excepted. As a matter of fact, the methods of primitive accumulation are anything but idyllic.

• • •

The capitalist system presupposes the complete separation of the labourers from all property in the means by which they can realise their labour. As soon as capitalist production is once on its own legs, it not only maintains this separation, but reproduces it on a continually extending scale. The process, therefore, that clears the way for the capitalist system, can be none other than the process which takes away from the labourer the possession of his means of production; a process that transforms, on the one hand, the social means of subsistence and of production into capital, on the other, the immediate producers into wage-labourers. The so-called primitive accumulation, therefore, is nothing else than the historical process of divorcing the producer from the means of production.

• • •

What does the primitive accumulation of capital, *i.e.*, its historical genesis, resolve itself into? In so far as it is not immediate transformation of slaves and serfs into wage-labourers, and therefore a mere change of form, it only means the expropriation of the immediate producers, *i.e.*, the dissolution of private property based on the labour of its owner. Private property, as the antithesis to social, collective property, exists only where the means of labour and the external conditions of labour belong to private individuals. But according as these private individuals are labourers or not labourers, private property has a different character. The numberless shades, that it at first sight presents, correspond to the intermediate stages lying between these two extremes. The private property of the labourer in his means of production is the foundation of petty industry, whether agricultural, manufacturing or both; petty industry, again, is an essential condition for the development of social production and of the free individuality of the labourer himself. Of course, this petty mode of production exists also under slavery, serfdom, and other states of dependence. But it flourishes, it lets loose its whole energy, it attains its adequate classical form, only where the labourer is the private owner of his own means of labour set in action by himself: the peasant of the land which he cultivates, the artizan of the tool which he handles as a virtuoso. This mode of production pre-supposes parcelling of the soil, and scattering of the other means of production. As it excludes the concentration of these means of production, so also it excludes cooperation, division of labour within each separate process of production, the control over, and the productive application of the forces of Nature by society, and the free development of the social productive powers. It is compatible only with a system of production, and a society, moving within narrow and more or less primitive bounds. To perpetuate it would be, as Pecqueur rightly says, "to decree universal mediocrity." At a certain stage of development it brings forth the material agencies for its own dissolution. From that moment new forces and new passions spring up in the bosom of society; but the old social organization fetters them and keeps them down. It must be annihilated; it is annihilated. Its annihilation, the transformation of the individualised and scattered means of production into socially concentrated ones, of the pigmy property of the many into the huge property of the few, the expropriation of the great mass of the people from the soil, from the means of subsistence, and from the means of labour, this fearful and painful expropriation of the mass of the people forms the prelude to the history of capital. It comprises a series of forcible methods, of which we have passed in review only those that have been epoch-making as methods of the primitive accumulation of capital. The expropriation of the immediate producers was accomplished with merciless Vandalism, and under the stimulus of passions the most infamous, the most sordid, the pettiest, the most meanly odious. Self-earned private property, that is based, so to say, on the fusing together of the isolated, independent labouring-individual with the conditions of his labour, is supplanted by capitalistic private property, which rests on exploitation of the nominally free labour of others, *i.e.,* on wages-labour.*

As soon as this process of transformation has sufficiently decomposed the old society from top to bottom, as soon as the labourers are turned into proletarians, their means of labour into capital, as soon as the capitalist mode of production stands on its own feet, then the further socialisation of labour and further transformation of the land and other means of production into socially exploited and, therefore, common means of production, as well as the further expropriation of private proprietors, takes a new form. That which is now to be expropriated is no longer the labourer working for himself, but the capitalist exploiting many labourers. This expropriation is accomplished by the action of the immanent laws of capitalistic production itself, by the centralisation of capital. One capitalist always kills many. Hand in hand with this centralisation, or this expropriation of many capitalists by few, develop, on an ever extending scale, the co-operative form of the labour-process, the

*Footnote omitted [Eds.].

conscious technical application of science, the methodical cultivation of the soil, the transformation of the instruments of labour into instruments of labour only usable in common, the economising of all means of production by their use as the means of production of combined, socialised labour, the entanglement of all peoples in the net of the world-market, and this, the international character of the capitalistic régime. Along with the constantly diminishing number of the magnates of capital, who usurp and monopolise all advantages of this process of transformation, grows the mass of misery, oppression, slavery, degradation, exploitation; but with this too grows the revolt of the working-class, a class always increasing in numbers, and disciplined, united, organised by the very mechanism of the process of capitalist production itself. The monopoly of capital becomes a fetter upon the mode of production, which has sprung up and flourished along with, and under it. Centralisation of the means of production and socialisation of labour at last reach a point where they become incompatible with their capitalist integument. This integument is burst asunder. The knell of capitalist private property sounds. The expropriators are expropriated.

The capitalist mode of appropriation, the result of the capitalist mode of production, produces capitalist private property. This is the first negation of individual private property, as founded on the labour of the proprietor. But capitalist production begets, with the inexorability of a law of Nature, its own negation. It is the negation of negation. This does not re-establish private property for the producer, but gives him individual property based on the acquisitions of the capitalist era: *i.e.*, on co-operation and the possession in common of the land and of the means of production.

The transformation of scattered private property, arising from individual labour, into capitalist private property is, naturally, a process, incomparably more protracted, violent, and difficult, than the transformation of capitalistic private property, already practically resting on socialized production, into socialised property. In the former case, we had the expropriation of the mass of the people by a few usurpers; in the latter, we have the expropriation of a few usurpers by the mass of the people.[1]

---

[1]The advance of industry, whose involuntary promoter is the bourgeoisie, replaces the isolation of the labourers, due to competition, by their revolutionary combination, due to association. The development of Modern Industry, therefore, cuts from under its feet, the very foundation on which the bourgeoisie produces and appropriates products. What the bourgeoisie, therefore, produces, above all, are its own grave-diggers. Its fall and the victory of the proletariat are equally inevitable . . . Of all the classes, that stand face to face with the bourgeoisie to-day, the proletariat alone is a really revolutionary class. The other classes perish and disappear in the face of Modern Industry, the proletariat is its special and essential product . . . The lower middle-classes, the small manufacturers, the shopkeepers, the artisan, the peasant, all these fight against the bourgeoisie, to save from extinction their existence as fractions of the middle-class . . . they are reactionary, for they try to roll back the wheel of history. Karl Marx und Friedrich Engels, "Manifest der Kommunistischen Partei," London, 1848, pp. 9, 11.

Suggestions for Further Reading

For other aspects of Marx's views, see his "Critique of the Gotha Programme" in Lewis S. Feuer, ed., *Marx and Engels: Basic Writings on Politics and Philosophy* (New York: Doubleday/Anchor, 1959), 112–132. "The Communist Manifesto" is also reprinted there, pages 1–41. Friedrich Engels's *The Origin of the Family, Private Property, and the State* (Moscow: Foreign Language Publishing House, n.d.) is also relevant, as is Marx and Engels's jointly authored *The German Ideology*, ed. R. Pascal (London: Lawrence and Wishart, Ltd., 1939). Compare the economic analysis given by Karl Polanyi in George Dalton, ed., *Primitive, Archaic and Modern Economics: Essays of Karl Polanyi* (New York: Doubleday/Anchor, 1968). Polanyi's views are summarized nicely by Helen Codere in the article on "Exchange and Display" in the *International Encyclopedia of the Social Sciences* (1968).

Legal scholars have produced much material that is useful in analyzing concepts of property. Two works that are especially worth noting are Guido Calabresi and A. Douglas Melamed, "Property Rules, Liability Rules, and Inalienability: One View of the Cathedral," 85 *Harvard Law Review* 1089 (1972); and Bruce A. Ackerman, ed., *Economic Foundations of Property Law* (Boston: Little, Brown, 1975).

Philosophic material on rights is abundant. Helpful anthologies include David Lyons, ed., *Rights* (Belmont, Calif: Wadsworth, 1979); and Tom Regan and Donald Van De Veer, eds. *And Justice for All* (Totowa, N.J.: Rowman and Littlefield, 1982). James W. Nickel and Rex Martin have published an extensive bibliography, "A Bibliography on the Nature and Foundations of Rights, 1947–1977," *Political Theory* 6 (1978): 395–415; and a survey article, "Recent Work on the Concept of Rights," *American Philosophical Quarterly* 17 (1980): 165–180.

Not surprisingly, economic anthropology provides a wealth of important material against which to test the modern conception of property. Honoré suggests that the elements of his analysis make a useful framework for understanding property arrangements in primitive and ancient societies as well as in our own. Becker has used it to survey some of the questions about property raised in anthropology, economics, and political theory in J. Roland Pennock and John W. Chapman, eds., *Property*, NOMOS XXII (New York: New York University Press, 1980). For a summary of relevant anthropological data, see Melville J. Herskovits, *Economic Anthropology* (New York: Alfred A. Knopf, 1952). Both Becker and Honoré employ Hohfeld's analysis of rights. See Wesley Newcomb Hohfeld, *Fundamental Legal Conceptions* (New Haven: Yale University Press, 1919). But for a concise, clear presentation of the basic ideas, consult *Salmond on Jurisprudence*, 12th ed. (London: Sweet & Maxwell, 1966), section 42.

SECTION TWO
EXTENSIONS OF
PROPERTY

While the materials in the last section reviewed some of the most basic issues in understanding the nature of property rights, the materials in this section focus upon property as a dynamic concept. We now consider how the concept of property has changed and how it might continue to change.

In the first selection here, C. B. Macpherson, a political scientist at the University of Toronto, urges that we attend to the history of the concept of property and see human rights (e.g., the right to a certain quality of life), not as opposed to property rights, but as property rights themselves. Macpherson describes four ways in which, historically, the modern concept of property represents a "drastic narrowing" of earlier concepts. Property in one's person, one's capabilities, one's rights and liberties, gradually gave way to property in material things. The right not to be excluded gave way to the right to exclude. The right to enjoy things gave way to the right to enjoy and dispose of things. And the right to revenue gave way to the right to the things that produce revenue. Hence the modern concept of property—an exclusive right to use and dispose of material things—emerged from a very different earlier idea. Attributing these important changes to the demands of market capitalism, Macpherson argues that we now need and are experiencing a widening of the concept of private property to meet the demands of democracy and managerial capitalism, to reflect our concerns for the environment, and to address the problems of depletable resources and welfare rights. Macpherson urges us to recapture "on a higher level, the idea that individual property is much more a matter of property in life and liberty, in the use and development and enjoyment of human capacities, than it is merely a matter of rights in things or revenues."

The second selection is Charles Reich's well-known "The New Property," written while he was a professor at Yale Law School. Reich maintains that the concept of property must be systematically enlarged to protect wealth dispensed in the form of government "largess." This largess includes such things as professional licenses, government contracts, welfare and social security payments, communication channels, and access to transportation facilities. He sees property as drawing a circle of privacy, with greater freedom within and greater accountability without. It is "not a natural right but a deliberate construction by society." According to Reich, property rights can enhance liberty or erode it, depending upon the conditions we attach. If government can lift licenses, suspend welfare benefits, deny contracts, and terminate access to facilities, on any grounds that serve the "public interest," then those who must rely upon largess— licensed professionals, welfare recipients, etc.—may become unreasonably subservient to government, excessively willing to trade away constitutional guarantees to avoid jeopardizing their claims to government-dispensed goods. What is required is "a new property."

While Macpherson and Reich are concerned with rather general ways in which the concept of property might be extended, the authors of the next two selections are concerned with more specific extensions of the concept. In the brief excerpt from a Comment in the *Buffalo Law Review*, Philip J. Levine proposes that employees be accorded a property interest in their jobs, the right not to be fired without "just cause." Like governments, private organizations can unreasonably encroach upon the liberties and fundamental rights of those who work within them. Following Reich, Levine maintains that the concept of property "must be expanded to encompass the employment relationship, to protect against wrongful discharge."

Thomas D. Schaefer, in the excerpt from his Comment in the *California Western Law Review*, considers whether professional education is property. The issue arises in a striking way in states that have "community property" laws providing that, with some exceptions, all property acquired during a marriage must be divided equally between the spouses in the event of divorce: Husband and wife are each presumed to own half. But suppose one spouse takes a job in order to put the other through professional school. Immediately after entry into the profession there is a divorce. Is the nonstudent somehow entitled to half of the professional education? Two questions are raised. Ought the law to consider the professional education as "community property?" Schaefer's answer here is yes. And second, since professional education is not divisible or transferable in any ordinary sense, how is its value to be determined? We have omitted Schaefer's extensive discussion of this second issue but, in brief, he suggests two answers. The first is based on a calculation of "purchase price" and the second on an estimation of the economic difference that a professional education makes for lifetime earnings.

The final piece in the section, a selection of materials on copyright and fair use, illustrates how technology can force a redefinition of property rights and how legislation and negotiation can play roles in the process. Owners of copyrights have an exclusive right to reproduce, adapt, publish, perform, and display their works. But the widespread use of photocopying technology has posed difficult questions concerning the conditions under which copyright is infringed. This is especially so in educational institutions, where photoduplication of copyrighted works has become routine. Sections 106 and 107 of Title 17 of the U.S. Code, reprinted here, are intended to set out the owner's rights in copyrighted works and the "fair use" limitations on those rights. But the letter of the law must be understood in terms of the intention of the legislature. Some sense of what this intention was (and how it was formed) can be gathered in the excerpts reprinted here from the 1976 Report of the House of Representatives Judiciary Committee. Of particular interest is the "Agreement on Guidelines for Classroom Copying in Not-For-Profit Educational Institutions," negotiated by representatives of educational institutions, authors, and publishers.

Human Rights as Property Rights

C. B. MACPHERSON

In these days, when we are all becoming more concerned about the way we are using up our natural resources, polluting our environment, and destroying the ecological balance of nature, it still seems to some that there is an insuperable difficulty in doing anything effective about it. The difficulty is that any effective action about it seems to contradict one of the central concepts, and to undermine one of the basic institutions, on which all the advanced Western or liberal democratic societies are based: the concept and institution of individual property.

This contradiction, of course, will have to be resolved, or compromised or patched up or papered over, by our politicians. That is what we elect politicians to do.

But can the political theorist make any contribution to the resolu-

From pp. 72–77 of *Dissent,* vol. 24 (Winter 1977). © 1977 by Dissent Publishing Company. Reprinted by permission of the author and publisher.

tion, beyond the papering over of this contradiction? He can perhaps say something useful by drawing attention to some demonstrable facts: to the fact that the concept of property has changed in several ways, not only as between ancient and medieval and modern societies but also within the span of modern market society; and to the fact that it is now again perceptibly changing and may be expected to change still further. He may also inquire whether changes are now needed, in order to make the concept of property consistent with a democratic society, and if so, whether such changes are impossibly difficult. I shall suggest that they are needed, and that they are not impossibly difficult.

I shall only try to deal with a few of the changes that have in fact occurred; only with those whose implications for the present and future seem to be most worth looking at. I shall look at four changes.

- *(1)* The first change I want to notice may appear to be only a lexicographical or dictionary change in the usage of the word "property," but I think it goes deeper. As late as the 17th century, it was quite usual for writers to use the word in what seems to us an extraordinarily wide sense. John Locke repeatedly and explicitly defined men's properties as their lives, liberties, and estates. For Hobbes, the things in which a man had property included "his own life and limbs; and in the next degree, (in most men), those that concern conjugal affection; and after them riches and means of living.* One's own person, one's capacities, one's rights and liberties were regarded as individual property. They were even more important than individual property in material things and revenues, partly because they were seen as the source and justification of individual material property.

That broad meaning of property was lost in the measure that modern societies became fully market societies. Property soon came to have only the narrower meaning it generally has today: property in material things or revenues. The reason is fairly obvious: with the predominance of the market, every individual's effective rights and liberties, their effective ability to develop their own persons and exercise their capacities, came to depend so much on what material property they had that the very idea of property was easily reduced to the idea of material property.

- *(2)* A second change in the concept of property, which came at about the same time, was even more striking. It was, like the other, a drastic narrowing of the concept: this was a narrowing even of the concept of material property.

From the earliest ideas of property, say from Aristotle down to the 17th century, property was seen to include both of two kinds of individual rights: both an individual right to exclude others from some use or enjoyment of some thing, and an individual right not to be excluded from the use or enjoyment of things the society had declared to be for common use—common lands, parks, roads, waters. Both were rights of individu-

---

*Leviathan, chap. 30, pp. 382–83 (Pelican Classics edition, C. B. Macpherson, ed.).

als. Both rights were created and maintained by society or the state. Both therefore were individual property.

From the 17th century to our own time, the idea of property has generally been much narrower. It has largely been narrowed to the first right—the right to exclude others.

True, we do have such things as national parks. But it is not usual to think of these as property at all. It is more usual to think of them as something set aside from the property arena. The only time we treat any part of them as property is when the state does turn some part of them into property in the narrow sense, by giving some person or corporation the right to exclude others from some use of them, as when its sells or leases logging or mining rights. Certainly we don't ordinarily think of every citizen's right of using a national park as part of each citizen's individual property. So it seems accurate to say that the modern concept of property is pretty well confined to the right of an individual or corporation—a natural or artificial person—to exclude others from some use or enjoyment of some thing.

- *(3)*   A third, related change is a further narrowing—from property as an exclusive right merely to use and enjoy some thing, to property as an exclusive right both to use and to dispose of the thing: a right to sell it to somebody else, or to alienate it. This is now taken so much as a matter of course that it may seem surprising to say that it came as a change a few centuries ago. I shall postpone a description of this change till I come to look at the causes of this and all the other changes.

- *(4)*   A fourth change in the concept of property is also a narrowing, and also dates from about the same time. It is not as important as the others, but it is worth noticing. It is a change from property as a right to a revenue to property as a right to things (including the things that produce revenue). A further description of this change I shall also postpone until I look at causes.

- To sum up these changes, we are left with a modern concept of property as an exclusive individual right to use and dispose of material things.

Obviously, some further change now is needed to make our narrow concept of property consistent with a democratic society. Property as an exclusive right of a natural or artificial person to use and dispose of material things (including land and resources) leads necessarily, in any kind of market society (from the freeest, most perfectly competitive one, to a highly monopolistic one), to an inequality of wealth and power that denies a lot of people the possibility of a reasonably human life.

The narrow institution of property is bound to result in such inequality, in any society short of a genetically engineered one that would have ironed out all differences in skill and energy. Even if you started from complete equality of property, the operation of exclusive and disposable property rights would soon lead to some getting more than others; and the more one gets, the easier it is to get still more, so that, at least after free land runs out, a relatively few people get the exclusive right to the bulk of the land and working capital. Those who are left without any, or without enough to work on or work with on their own, then have to pay the others for access to it. There is then a continuous net transfer of part of the powers of the nonowners to the owners.

This is an inevitable consequence of turning everything into exclusive property and throwing everything into the market. This is clearly inconsistent with one of the first principles of a democratic society, which I take to be the maintenance of equal opportunity to use and develop and enjoy whatever capacities each person has. Those who have to pay for access to the means of using their capacities and exerting their energies, and pay by making over to others both the control of their capacities and some of the product of their energies—those people are denied equality in the use and development and enjoyment of their own capacities. And in a modern market society, that amounts to most people: almost everybody except the fortunate few who are, as professional people, more or less independent and more or less exempt from that transfer of powers.

This kind of inequality is not only inconsistent with the democratic principle: it also contradicts one of the basic justifications of the very institution of individual property, namely, that human needs cannot be met without that institution. It can easily be demonstrated that, granted an equal right to life, everyone needs such an amount of individual property, in the means of life and in access to the means of labor, as will ensure the continuance of his or her life. And on any acceptable notion of human rights, this requires more than a right to bare physical subsistence. It requires an equal right to such means of life and means of labor as any society, at its given level of command of Nature, can provide.

The very nature of human beings, then, requires individual property of two kinds. One kind, some property in the means of life, is a property in consumable things. This must be an *exclusive* property: I must have the right to exclude you from my shirt, from my dinner, from my toothbrush, and from my bed.

The other, a property in the means of labor—that is, in the resources, the land and capital, access to which I need in order to exert my energies and utilize my capacities—this does not need to be an exclusive property. It can, equally well, be the other kind of individual property—the right *not to be excluded from* some use or enjoyment of something.

The validity of the case for property as a necessary human right depends, then, on whether we take property in the modern narrow sense, or in the more extended and more natural sense of an individual right both to some exclusive property and to some nonexclusive right of access to the remaining natural resources and the accumulated capital of a given society. If we continue to take it in the modern narrow sense, the property right contradicts democratic human rights. If we take it in the broader sense, it does not contradict a democratic concept of human rights: indeed, it then may bring us back to something like the old concept of individual property in one's life, liberty, and capacities.

So it becomes important to consider what are the chances of our moving away from the narrow concept of property to the broader one that seems required by any concept of human rights. And to do this we must look at the causes of the narrowing, and see if, or to what extent, they still operate.

Each of the four narrowings that I singled out can be shown to be a pretty direct result of the rise of the competitive capitalist market economy, which, as it became predominant, brought within its sway things, and people, and the values that are embodied in concepts.

• I have mentioned the obvious source of the first narrowing (the narrowing from an individual property in one's life, one's person, capacities, rights and liberties, as well as in the material means of life, to merely property in the material means of life). This, I said, was an evident result of the fact that, with the predominance of the market, all individuals' effective rights, liberties, ability to develop their own persons and exercise their own capacities came to depend so much on the amount of their material property that it was not unrealistic to equate their individual property with their material property.

• What about the second narrowing, from an individual property in both the individual right *to exclude others* from the use or enjoyment of some thing and an individual right *not to be excluded from* the use or enjoyment of some thing, to merely the right to exclude others?

This also was required by the full market economy. To the extent that the whole job of deciding what was to be produced, and how the whole product was to be divided between people, was to be done by the market, rather than by custom or prescription or political authority—to that extent, all rights in material things, including land and other natural resources, not to mention rights in one's capacity to work, had to be made marketable and brought into the market. And clearly only the exclusive rights can be marketed. The right not to be excluded from some use or enjoyment of some thing cannot, by its very nature, be marketed. So, of the two earlier kinds of individual property—the right to exclude others, and the right not to be excluded by others—the second virtually dropped out of sight with the predominance of this market, and the very idea of property was narrowed to cover only the right to exclude others.

• Much the same explanation applies to the third narrowing of the concept of property, which was a further narrowing even of the notion of property as an exclusive right in material things. Before the full market society came to prevail, a great deal of property in land and other material things was a right to exclude others from some use or enjoyment of the thing, but not a right to dispose of it. The right to use, or enjoy the revenue from, a parcel of land or a corporate charter or a monopoly granted by the state did not always carry with it the right to sell that property. But a full market economy requires that everything be marketable. If the market is to do the whole job of allocating resources and labor between possible uses, then all resources and labor have to become marketable. Individual rights in them all must include the right to buy and sell, the right to dispose of or alienate. As the capitalist market economy grew, it was expected to do, and did do, most of the whole job of allocation. So it was not surprising that the very concept of property was narrowed to property as exclusive alienable rights.

• The fourth narrowing, less important than the others but worth noticing, dates from the same period and can be seen to have come about for similar reasons. It is the change from property as rights in things and in revenues to property as rights in things, or, if you like to sharpen the contrast, a change from rights in revenues to rights in things. This change in the concept reflected a change in the facts. Until the emergence of the capitalist market economy, most individual property had in fact been a right to a revenue rather than a right to a thing. The great bulk of property had been property in land, and, at least in the case of substantial estates, that property was seen as a right to a revenue rather than a right to the land itself, the more so because, as we have noticed, the land itself was often not in the owner's power to sell. Another large segment of individual property was the right to a revenue from such things as corporate charters, monopolies, and various political and ecclesiastic offices. Whether these properties were salable or not, they were obviously rights to a revenue rather than rights to any specific material things.

Then, with the rise of the capitalist market economy, the bulk of actual property shifted from often nontransferable rights to a revenue from land, charters, monopolies, and offices, to transferable rights in freehold land, salable leases, physical plant, and money. Property became predominantly a right to things.

Now let us recall that the point of looking at the causes of the various narrowings of the concept of property was to enable us to consider the chances of the concept of property being broadened again. What are the chances of any such broadening? In considering this, it will be convenient to treat the four narrowings in reverse order.

• *(Re 4)* Property is already being reconceived as a right to a revenue. As capitalism has matured and has become subject to much regulation, and as the distribution of its whole annual product has become subject to some redistribution by welfare-state measures, the most realistic description of most people's property is coming to be a right to a revenue: either (a) the right to earn an income, or (b) the right to an income not currently earned. Category (b) comprises all investment income, including pension rights (which are increasingly widespread in blue-collar as well as white-collar sectors); and all the many kinds of income provided by the state, in money or in services, such as family allowances, unemployment benefits, health services, and old-age benefits. Category (a) comprises (i), for self-employed people, from doctors to independent taxi operators, the right to earn an income from the practice of their skills. This often comes down to the need for a license: the license itself is a property, sometimes (as with taxi licenses) a salable property. And (ii), for wage earners, it comes down to a right to a job. This right is increasingly being asserted by organized labor. It is an assertion of a right of access to the means of labor, no matter by whom owned. That right is increasingly seen as a property. The perception of it as a property is quite a big change in the concept of property.

• *(Re 3* and 2, which we may take together)   The concept of property as an *exclusive, alienable* right (in things and revenues) is already beginning to change. The right to a job that is now being asserted is clearly not an alienable right; and it is also not, at least in principle, a right to exclude others, so much as it is a right not to be excluded from something, namely, from access to society's accumulated means of labor (although it may be, in the immediate short-run, a right of organized labor to exclude unorganized labor from that access).

Another form of individual property, which by now is well over the horizon, is also neither an exclusive nor an alienable right: this is the "guaranteed annual income," or the income provided by a "negative in- come tax." One or other of these schemes is almost certainly going to become increasingly implemented, both for technical economic reasons and because of democratic political pressures.

Besides these two factors that are now perceptible in our society, there is a reason to expect more change away from the idea of property as merely exclusive alienable rights. The reason is that this concept was necessary only to the extent that the market was expected to do the whole work of allocation of resources and labor and products and rewards. But in our age of regulated and managed capitalism (regulated by the state, and managed by corporations engaged in less than perfect competition), the market is no longer expected to do this work. The state now does, and in future will increasingly do, much of the work of allocation. As it does so, there will be less and less need of the concept of property as nothing but exclusive alienable rights. So there is now some prospect of our break- ing out of the second and third narrowings.

• *(Re 1)*   What are the chances of reversing the first narrowing: of recapturing, on a higher level, the idea that individual property is much more a matter of property in life and liberty, in the use and development and enjoyment of human capacities, than it is merely a matter of rights in things or revenues? What makes this now possible is the inevitability of increasing productivity, with less need for current compulsory labor, through technological advance. Technological advance is inherent in capi- talism: it is virtually the only means of survival of the oligopolistic firm within the capitalist economy, and the only means of the survival of that economy as a whole in its competition with the Communist economies. It is bound to make current labor less and less necessary to provide an acceptable standard of life, always provided that we opt for less work rather than more things.

As current labor becomes less needed, individual property in the means of labor becomes less important, and individual property in the means of a full and free life becomes more important. The important thing becomes individual property in the means of a life of using and developing and exerting our capacities and energies.

I think it is probable, or at least possible, that there will be more demand for this kind of property. There is no certainty about this. We may just go on behaving as insatiable consumers. Our demand for the means of a full life may just be a demand for more consumer goods. But it need not be so. We may pick up again what is a very old idea, the idea that used to prevail before the market economy converted us all into consumers: the idea that life is for *doing* rather than just *getting*. You may ask, can the right to such a full and free life of action and enjoyment be made an individual property, i.e., a legally enforceable claim that society will enforce in favor of each individual? There is no intrinsic difficulty about this. It may seem surprising, but the historical record bears me out.

All societies that preceded the market society did establish and maintain legal rights not only to life but to a certain quality of life. I am thinking of the rights of different orders or ranks—guild masters, journeymen, apprentices, servants and laborers; serfs, freemen and noblemen; members of the first and second and third estates. All of these were rights, enforced by law or custom, to a certain standard of life, not just of material means of life, but also of liberties, privileges, honor, and status. And these rights could be seen as *properties*.

Of course these were very unequal rights: they adhered to rank or class. They had to be unequal, since there was never enough to go around. But the point is that there was no difficulty in having the right to a certain quality of life made into a legally enforceable claim of the individual, i.e., an individual property.

And now, in the 20th century, one factor has changed: there is enough to go around, or will be if we make intelligent use of our knowledge of Nature, i.e., of our presently possible productive technology. So it now becomes possible to assert an equal right, for everyone, to a certain quality of life, certain liberties to develop and enjoy the use of our capacities. And it becomes possible to treat these rights, just as the earlier unequal rights were treated—as property, i.e., enforceable claims of the individual.

If you have followed me so far, you may still wonder what is the point of treating the right to a quality of life as a property right? Why not just put it forward as a human right? The reason seems to me quite compelling. If it is asserted as a human right separate from the property right, the whole prestige of property will work against it rather than for it. We have made property so central to our society that any thing and any rights that are not property are very apt to take second place. So I think that, given our present scale of values, it is only if the human right to a full life is seen as a property right that it will stand much chance of general realization.

Moralists and reformers, and writers of declarations of human rights, have often played up human rights as opposed to property rights. I am suggesting that this is a mistake, and that we will get further if we treat human rights as property rights.

Obviously, this does not solve all problems, perhaps not any problems. But it does remove a mental barrier that is no longer justified or required, and so opens the way to a shift in public opinion, the sort of shift that is needed if we are to make much headway with human rights.

The New Property

CHARLES A. REICH

The institution called property guards the troubled boundary between individual man and the state. It is not the only guardian; many other institutions, laws, and practices serve as well. But in a society that chiefly values material well-being, the power to control a particular portion of that well-being is the very foundation of individuality.

One of the most important developments in the United States during the past decade has been the emergence of government as a major source of wealth. Government is a gigantic syphon. It draws in revenue and power, and pours forth wealth: money, benefits, services, contracts, franchises, and licenses. Government has always had this function. But while in early times it was minor, today's distribution of largess is on a vast, imperial scale.

The valuables dispensed by government take many forms, but they all share one characteristic. They are steadily taking the place of traditional forms of wealth—forms which are held as private property. Social insurance substitutes for savings; a government contract replaces a businessman's customers and goodwill. The wealth of more and more Americans depends upon a relationship to government. Increasingly, Americans live on government largess—allocated by government on its own terms, and held by recipients subject to conditions which express "the public interest." . . .

The significance of government largess is increased by certain underlying changes in the forms of private wealth in the United States. Changes in the forms of wealth are not remarkable in themselves; the forms are constantly changing and differ in every culture. But today more and more of our wealth takes the form of rights or status rather than of tangible goods. An individual's profession or occupation is a prime example. To many others, a job with a particular employer is the principal form of wealth. A profession or a job is frequently far more valuable than a house or bank account, for a new house can be bought, and a new bank account created, once a profession or job is secure. For the jobless, their status as governmentally assisted or insured persons may be the main source of subsistence. . . .

Wealth or value is created by culture and by society; it is culture that makes a diamond valuable and a pebble worthless. Property, on the other hand, is the creation of law. A man who has property has certain legal rights with respect to an item of wealth; property represents a relationship between wealth and its "owner." Government largess is plainly "wealth," but it is not necessarily "property." . . .

From the beginning, individual rights in largess have been greatly affected by several traditional legal concepts, each of which has had lasting significance:

Right vs. privilege. The early law is marked by courts' attempts to distinguish which forms of largess were "rights" and which were "privileges." Legal protection of the former was by far the greater. If the holder of a license had a "right," he might be entitled to a hearing before the license could be revoked; a "mere privilege" might be revoked without notice or hearing.[1]

The gratuity principle. Government largess has often been considered a "gratuity" furnished by the state.[2] Hence it is said that the state can withhold, grant, or revoke the largess at its pleasure.[3] Under this theory, government is considered to be in somewhat the same position as a private giver.

The whole and the parts. Related to the gratuity theory is the idea that, since government may completely withhold a benefit, it may grant it subject to any terms or conditions whatever. This theory is essentially an exercise in logic: the whole power must include all of its parts.[4]

Internal management. Particularly in relation to its own contracts, government has been permitted extensive power on the theory that it should have control over its own housekeeping or internal management func-

---

[1]See generally GELLHORN [INDIVIDUAL FREEDOM AND GOVERNMENTAL RESTRAINTS (1956)], at 105–51.

[2]For example, the District of Columbia Court of Appeals declared that veterans' disability benefits "fall within the legal principles respecting gratuities." Thompson v. Gleason, 317 F.2d 901, 906 (1962).

[3]See, *e.g.,* Lynch v. United States, 292 U.S. 571, 577 (1934).

[4]See Note, *Unconstitutional Conditions*, 73 HARV. L. REV. 1595, 1609 (1960), which rejects the theory and states that the imposition of such conditions is "a distinct exercise of power which must find its own justification."

tions. Under this theory, government is treated like a private business. In its dealings with outsiders it is permitted much of the freedom to grant contracts and licenses that a private business would have.[5]

Quite often these four theories are blurred in a single statement of judicial attitude. The following illustrations are typical:

> It is an elementary rule of law that the right to operate a motor vehicle upon a public street or highway is not a natural or unrestrained right, but a *privilege* which is subject to reasonable regulation under the police power of the state in the interest of public safety and welfare.[6]

> A taxicab is a common carrier and use by it of the public streets is not a right but a privilege or license which can be granted on such conditions as the Legislature may impose.[7]

> The practice of medicine is lawfully prohibited by the State except upon the conditions it imposes. Such practice is a privilege granted by the State under its substantially plenary power to fix the terms of admission.[8]

One court put the idea in somewhat more pithy form: ". . . in accepting charity, the appellant has consented to the provisions of the law under which the charity is bestowed."[9] . . .

The recipient of largess, whether an organization or an individual, feels the government's power. The company that is heavily subsidized or dependent on government contracts is subjected to an added amount of regulation and inspection, sometimes to the point of having resident government officials in its plant.[10] And it is subject to added government pressures. The well known episode when the large steel companies were forced to rescind a price rise, partly by the threat of loss of government contracts, illustrates this. Perhaps the most elaborate and onerous regulation of businesses with government contracts is the industrial security system, which places all employees in defense industries under government scrutiny, and subjects them, even high executives, to dismissal if they fail to win government approval.[11]

Individuals are also subject to great pressures. Dr. Edward K. Barsky, a New York physician and surgeon since 1919, was for a time

[5]Perkins v. Lukens Steel Co., 310 U.S. 113, 127 (1940):

Like private individuals and businesses, the Government enjoys the unrestricted power to produce its own supplies, to determine those with whom it will deal, and to fix the terms and conditions upon which it will make needed purchases.

[6]Lee v. State, 187 Kan. 566, 570, 358 P.2d 765 (1961).

[7]Stewart v. District of Columbia, 35 A.2d 247, 248 (D.C. Munic. Ct. App. 1943).

[8]Barsky v. Board of Regents, 347 U.S. 442, 451 (1954).

[9]Wilkie v. O'Connor, 261 App. Div. 373, 25 N.Y.S.2d 617, 620 (Sup. Ct. 1941).

[10]PECK & SCHERER, THE WEAPONS ACQUISITION PROCESS: AN ECONOMIC ANALYSIS 85 (1962).

[11]See, *e.g.*, Kanarck v. United States, 314 F.2d 802 (Ct. Cl. 1963).

chairman of the Joint Anti-Fascist Refugee Committee.[12] In 1946 he was summoned before the House Committee on Un-American Activities. In the course of his examination he refused, on constitutional grounds, to produce records of the organization's contributions and expenditures. For this refusal he served six months in jail for contempt of Congress. Thereafter the New York State Education Department filed a complaint against him, under a provision of law making any doctor convicted of a crime subject to discipline. Although there was no evidence in any way touching Dr. Barsky's activities as a physician, The Department's Medical Grievance Committee suspended his medical license for six months. The New York courts upheld the suspension. The New York Court of Appeals answered as follows the argument that its holding would subject individuals to arbitrary governmental power:

> Appellants suggest that a literal construction of section 6514 (subd. 2, par. [b]) will empower the Board of Regents to destroy a person, professionally, solely on a showing of the commission by him in some other State (or country) of an act which we in New York consider noncriminal, or even meritorious. Two answers are available to that: first, some reliance must be placed on the good sense and judgment of our Board of Regents, in handling any such theoretically possible cases; and, second, the offense here committed, contempt of Congress, is no mere trivial transgression of an arbitrary statute.[13]

On appeal, the suspension was upheld by the United States Supreme Court.[14] The Court declared that New York had "substantially plenary power" to fix conditions for the practice of medicine,[15] and concluded that the state's action was reasonable, especially "in a field so permeated with public responsibility as that of health."[16] . . .

The chief legal bulwark of the individual against oppressive government power is the Bill of Rights. But government largess may impair the individual's enjoyment of those rights.

The Appellate Division of the Supreme Court of New York instituted an inquiry into improper solicitation and handling of contingent retainers in personal injury cases in Brooklyn. Solicitation of legal business is a crime in New York. In the course of the inquiry Albert Martin Cohen, an attorney for thirty-nine years, was called to testify. In reply to approximately sixty questions, he pleaded his privilege against self-incrimination, guaranteed by the state constitution. The unanswered questions related to such matters as his records in contingent retainer cases, the activities of his associates, and whether he had paid others for referring cases to him. After warnings, disciplinary proceedings were instituted against Cohen for refusing to cooperate with the inquest, and he

[12]Barsky v. Board of Regents, 347 U.S. 442 (1954).

[13]Barsky v. Board of Regents, 305 N.Y. 89, 97–98, 111 N.E.2d 222, 225–26 (1953).

[14]347 U.S. 442 (1954).

[15]*Id.* at 451.

[16]*Id.* at 453.

was disbarred by the Appellate Division.[17] On review, the United States Supreme Court upheld the disbarment.[18] The Court quoted with approval the following from the opinion of the New York Court of Appeals:

> Of course [petitioner] had the right to assert the privilege and to withhold the criminating answers. That right was his as it would be the right of any citizen and it was not denied to him. He could not be forced to waive his immunity. . . . But the question still remained as to whether he had broken the "condition" on which depended the "privilege" of membership in the Bar. . . . "Whenever the condition is broken, the privilege is lost. . . ."[19]

Thus the effect of the holding in *Cohen* is that a lawyer may lose his profession if he exercises his constitutional privilege, or may have to relinquish his privilege in order to keep his profession. . . .

It takes a brave man to stand firm against the power that can be exerted through government largess. This is nowhere better shown than by the case of George Anastaplo. In the fall of 1950, Anastaplo passed the Illinois bar examination, and applied for approval to the Committee on Character and Fitness, which in Illinois has the duty "to examine applicants who appear before them for moral character, general fitness to practice law and good citizenship."[20] Anastaplo came from a small town in Illinois, served honorably in the Air Force during World War II, and graduated from the University of Chicago. In his written application, Anastaplo was asked to state his understanding of American constitutional principles. After mentioning such fundamentals as the separation of powers, and protection of life, liberty, and the pursuit of happiness, Anastaplo added this sentence: "And, of course, whenever the particular government in power becomes destructive of these ends, it is the right of the people to alter or abolish it and thereupon to establish a new government."[21] When Anastaplo appeared before a subcommittee of the Character Committee, the members showed great concern about the quoted sentence—despite the fact that it is taken almost word for word from the Declaration of Independence. Anastaplo was questioned in detail about his "views on revolution." In the course of that questioning one member asked him whether he was a member of any organization on the Attorney General's list, or of the Communist Party. Anastaplo refused to answer these questions on the ground that they were political questions which he was privileged not to answer under the first amendment. After further hearings during which Anastaplo stuck to his position, he was notified by the Committee that, solely because of his failure to reply, he

---

[17]In the Matter of Cohen, 9 App. Div. 2d 436, 195 N.Y.S.2d 990 (1959), *aff'd*, 7 N.Y.2d 488, 166 N.E.2d 672 (1960).

[18]Cohen v. Hurley, 366 U.S. 117 (1961).

[19]*Id.* at 125–26 (brackets and deletions by the Court), quoting from 7 N.Y.2d at 495, 166 N.E.2d at 675.

[20]*In re* Anastaplo, 366 U.S. 82, 83 n.1 (1961).

[21]*Id.* at 99 (Black, J., dissenting).

had failed to prove such qualifications as to character and general fitness as would justify his admission to the bar of Illinois.[22]

The U. S. Supreme Court upheld the denial of admission, resting its decision on the refusal to answer the question concerning Communist Party membership. It held this question to be material to the issue of the applicant's fitness, contending that the questions were material because of their "bearing upon the likelihood that a bar applicant would observe as a lawyer the orderly processes that lie at the roots of this country's legal and political systems. . . ."[23] As for the first amendment, the Court held that "the State's interest in enforcing such a rule as applied to refusals to answer questions about membership in the Communist Party outweighs any deterrent effect upon freedom of speech and association. . . ."[24] Justice Black, dissenting, said that the decision would "humiliate and degrade" the Bar by forcing it "to become a group of thoroughly orthodox, time-serving, government-fearing individuals." . . .[25]

The characteristics of the public interest state are varied, but there is an underlying philosophy that unites them. This is the doctrine that the wealth that flows from government is held by its recipients conditionally, subject to confiscation in the interest of the paramount state. This philosophy is epitomized in the most important of all judicial decisions concerning government largess, the case of *Flemming v. Nestor*.[26]

Ephram Nestor, an alien, came to this country in 1913, and after a long working life became eligible in 1955 for old-age benefits under the Social Security Act. From 1936 to 1955 Nestor and his employers had contributed payments to the government which went into a special old-age and survivors insurance trust fund. From 1933 to 1939 Nestor was a member of the Communist Party. Long after his membership ceased, Congress passed a law retroactively making such membership cause for deportation, and a second law, also retroactive, making such deportation for having been a member of the Party grounds for loss of retirement benefits. In 1956 Nestor was deported, leaving his wife here. Soon after his deportation, payment of benefits to Nestor's wife was terminated.

In a five to four decision, the Supreme Court held that cutting off Nestor's retirement insurance, although based on conduct completely lawful at the time, was not unconstitutional. Specifically, it was not a taking of property without due process of law; Nestor's benefits were not an "accrued property right."[27] The Court recognized that each worker's benefits flow "from the contributions be made to the national economy while actively employed," but it held that his interest is "noncontractual" and

---

[22]*In re* Anastaplo, 3 Ill. 2d 471, 121 N.E.2d 826 (1954), *cert. denied*, 348 U.S. 946 (1955); 18 Ill. 2d 182, 163 N.E.2d 429 (1959), *cert. granted*, 362 U.S. 968 (1960).

[23]366 U.S. at 89 n.10.

[24]*Id*. at 89.

[25]*Id*. at 115–16.

[26]363 U.S. 603 (1960).

[27]*Id*. at 608.

"cannot be soundly analogized to that of the holder of an annuity."[28] The Court continued:

> To engraft upon the Social Security system a concept of "accrued property rights" would deprive it of the flexibility and boldness in adjustment of ever-changing conditions which it demands. . . . It was doubtless out of an awareness of the need for such flexibility that Congress included . . . a clause expressly reserving to it "[t]he right to alter, amend or repeal any provision" of the Act. . . . That provision makes express what is implicit in the institutional needs of the program.[29]

The Court stated further that, in any case where Congress "modified" social security rights, the Court should interfere only if the action is "utterly lacking in rational justification."[30] This, the Court said, "is not the case here." As the Court saw it, it might be deemed reasonable for Congress to limit payments to those living in this country; moreover, the Court thought it would not have been "irrational for Congress to have concluded that the public purse should not be utilized to contribute to the support of those deported on the grounds specified in the statute."[31]

The implications of *Flemming v. Nestor* are profound. No form of government largess is more personal or individual than an old age pension. No form is more clearly earned by the recipient, who, together with his employer, contributes to the Social Security fund during the years of his employment. No form is more obviously a compulsory substitute for private property; the tax on wage earner and employer might readily have gone to higher pay and higher private savings instead. No form is more relied on, and more often thought of as property. No form is more vital to the independence and dignity of the individual. Yet under the philosophy of Congress and the Court, a man or woman, after a lifetime of work, has no rights which may not be taken away to serve some public policy. The Court makes no effort to balance the interests at stake. The public policy that justifies cutting off benefits need not even be an important one or a wise one—so long as it is not utterly irrational, the Court will not interfere. In any clash between individual rights and public policy, the latter is automatically held to be superior.

The philosophy of *Flemming v. Nestor*, of *Barsky, In Re Anastaplo,* and *Cohen v. Hurley,* resembles the philosophy of feudal tenure. Wealth is not "owned," or "vested" in the holders. Instead, it is held conditionally, the conditions being ones which seek to ensure the fulfillment of obligations imposed by the state. Just as the feudal system linked lord and vassal through a system of mutual dependence, obligation, and loyalty, so gov-

---

[28]*Id.* at 609–10.
[29]*Id.* at 610–11.
[30]*Id.* at 611.
[31]*Id.* at 612.

ernment largess binds man to the state.[32] And, it may be added, loyalty or fealty to the state is often one of the essential conditions of modern tenure. In the many decisions taking away government largess for refusal to sign loyalty oaths, belonging to "subversive" organizations, or other similar grounds, there is more than a suggestion of the condition of fealty demanded in older times. . . .

Property is a legal institution the essence of which is the creation and protection of certain private rights in wealth of any kind. The institution performs many different functions. One of these functions is to draw a boundary between public and private power. Property draws a circle around the activities of each private individual or organization. Within that circle, the owner has a greater degree of freedom than without. Outside, he must justify or explain his actions, and show his authority. Within, he is master, and the state must explain and justify any interference. It is as if property shifted the burden of proof; outside, the individual has the burden; inside, the burden is on government to demonstrate that something the owner wishes to do should not be done.

Thus, property performs the function of maintaining independence, dignity and pluralism in society by creating zones within which the majority has to yield to the owner. Whim, caprice, irrationality and "antisocial" activities are given the protection of law; the owner may do what all or most of his neighbors decry. The Bill of Rights also serves this function, but while the Bill of Rights comes into play at extraordinary moments of conflict or crisis, property affords day-to-day protection in the ordinary affairs of life. Indeed, in the final analysis the Bill of Rights depends upon the existence of private property. Political rights presuppose that individuals and private groups have the will and the means to act independently. But so long as individuals are motivated largely by self-interest, their well-being must first be independent. Civil liberties must have a basis in property; or bills of rights will not preserve them.

Property is not a natural right but a deliberate construction by society. If such an institution did not exist, it would be necessary to create it, in order to have the kind of society we wish. The majority cannot be expected, on specific issues, to yield its power to a minority. Only if the minority's will is established as a general principle can it keep the majority at bay in a given instance. Like the Bill of Rights, property represents a general, long range protection of individual and private interests, created by the majority for the ultimate good of all.

Today, however, it is widely thought that property and liberty are separable things; that there may, in fact, be conflicts between "property rights" and "personal rights." Why has this view been accepted? The explanation is found at least partly in the transformations which have taken place in property.

---

[32]See generally BLOCH, FEUDAL SOCIETY (1961). Personal dependence was a fundamental element of feudalism, expressed in the concept of being the "man" of another man. *Id.* at 145.

During the industrial revolution, when property was liberated from feudal restraints, philosophers hailed property as the basis of liberty, and argued that it must be free from the demands of government or society.[33] But as private property grew, so did abuses resulting from its use. In a crowded world, a man's use of his property increasingly affected his neighbor, and one man's exercise of a right might seriously impair the rights of others. Property became power over others; the farm landowner, the city landlord, and the working man's boss were able to oppress their tenants or employees. Great aggregations of property resulted in private control of entire industries and basic services capable of affecting a whole area or even a nation. At the same time, much private property lost its individuality and in effect became socialized. Multiple ownership of corporations helped to separate personality from property, and property from power.[34] When the corporations began to stop competing, to merge, agree, and make mutual plans, they became private governments. Finally, they sought the aid and partnership of the state, and thus by their own volition became part of public government.

These changes led to a movement for reform, which sought to limit arbitrary private power and protect the common man. Property rights were considered more the enemy than the friend of liberty. The reformers argued that property must be separated from personality.[35] Walton Hamilton wrote:

> As late as the turn of the last century justices were not yet distinguishing between liberty and property; in the universes beneath their hats liberty was still the opportunity to acquire property.

> . . . the property of the Reports is not a proprietary thing; it is rather a shibboleth in whose name the domain of business enterprises has enjoyed a limited immunity from the supervision of the state.

> In the annals of the law property is still a vestigial expression of personality and owes its current constitutional position to its former association with liberty.[36]

During the first half of the twentieth century, the reformers enacted into law their conviction that private power was a chief enemy of society and of individual liberty. Property was subjected to "reasonable" limitations in the interests of society. The regulatory agencies, federal and state, were

---

[33]See generally Philbrick, *Changing Conceptions of Property in Law*, 86 U. PA. L. REV. 691 (1938); Hamilton & Till, *Property*, 12 ENCYC. SOC. SCI. 528 (1934); FREUND, THE SUPREME COURT OF THE UNITED STATES 31–40 (1961).

[34]See generally BERLE & MEANS, THE MODERN CORPORATION AND PRIVATE PROPERTY (1932); and BERLE, POWER WITHOUT PROPERTY (1957).

[35]Philbrick, *Changing Conceptions of Property in Law*, 86 U. PA. L. REV. 691, 732 (1938).

[36]Hamilton, *Property—According to Locke*, 41 YALE L.J. 864, 877–78 (1932); see also Hamilton & Till, *supra* note 133, at 528.

born of the reform. In sustaining these major inroads on private property, the Supreme Court rejected the older idea that property and liberty
were one, and wrote a series of classic opinions upholding the power of
the people to regulate and limit private rights.

The struggle between abuse and reform made it easy to forget the
basic importance of individual private property. The defense of private
property was almost entirely a defense of its abuses—an attempt to defend not individual property but arbitrary private power over other
human beings. Since this defense was cloaked in a defense of private
property, it was natural for the reformers to attack too broadly. Walter
Lippmann saw this in 1934:

> But the issue between the giant corporation and the public should not be
> allowed to obscure the truth that the only dependable foundation of per-
> sonal liberty is the economic security of private property.

> For we must not expect to find in ordinary men the stuff of martyrs, and we
> must, therefore, secure their freedom by their normal motives. There is no
> surer way to give men the courage to be free than to insure them a com-
> petence upon which they can rely.[37]

The reform took away some of the power of the corporations and
transferred it to government. In this transfer there was much good, for
power was made responsive to the majority rather than to the arbitrary
and selfish few. But the reform did not restore the individual to his
domain. What the corporation had taken from him, the reform simply
handed on to government. And government carried further the powers
formerly exercised by the corporation. Government as an employer, or as
a dispenser of wealth, has used the theory that it was handing out gratuities to claim a managerial power as great as that which the capitalists
claimed. Moreover, the corporations allied themselves with, or actually
took over, part of government's system of power. Today it is the combined power of government and the corporations that presses against the
individual.

From the individual's point of view, it is not any particular kind of
power, but all kinds of power, that are to be feared. This is the lesson of
the public interest state. The mere fact that power is derived from the
majority does not necessarily make it less oppressive. Liberty is more than
the right to do what the majority wants, or to do what is "reasonable."

---

[37]LIPPMANN, THE METHOD OF FREEDOM 101 (1934). See also Philbrick, *Changing Conceptions of Property in Law*, 86 U. PA. L. REV. 691 (1938):

> It is not, however, the *use* of ordinary property, nor the property of ordinary or
> "natural" persons that presents today serious problems of adjusting law to new social
> conditions. Those problems arise in connection with property for *power*, and therefore
> primarily in connection with industrial property.

Id. at 726.

Liberty is the right to defy the majority, and to do what is unreasonable. The great error of the public interest state is that it assumes an identity between the public interest and the interest of the majority.

The reform, then, has not done away with the importance of private property. More than ever the individual needs to possess, in whatever form, a small but sovereign island of his own. . . .

The chief obstacle to the creation of private rights in largess has been the fact that it is originally public property, comes from the state, and may be withheld completely. But this need not be an obstacle. Traditional property also comes from the state, and in much the same way. Land, for example, traces back to grants from the sovereign. In the United States, some was the gift of the King of England, some that of the King of Spain. The sovereign extinguished Indian title by conquest, became the new owner, and then granted title to a private individual or group.[38] Some land was the gift of the sovereign under laws such as the Homestead and Preemption Acts.[39] Many other natural resources—water, minerals and timber, passed into private ownership under similar grants. In America, land and resources all were originally government largess. In a less obvious sense, personal property also stems from government. Personal property is created by law; it owes its origin and continuance to laws supported by the people as a whole. These laws "give" the property to one who performs certain actions. Even the man who catches a wild animal "owns" the animal only as a gift from the sovereign, having fulfilled the terms of an offer to transfer ownership.[40]

Like largess, real and personal property were also originally dispensed on conditions, and were subject to forfeiture if the conditions failed. The conditions in the sovereign grants, such as colonization, were generally made explicit, and so was the forfeiture resulting from failure to fulfill them. In the case of the Preemption and Homestead Acts, there were also specific conditions.[41] Even now land is subject to forfeiture for neglect; if it is unused it may be deemed abandoned to the state or forfeited to an adverse possessor. In a very similar way, personal property may be forfeited by abandonment or loss.[42] Hence, all property might be described as government largess, given on condition and subject to loss.

If all property is government largess, why is it not regulated to the same degree as present-day largess? Regulation of property has been limited, not because society had no interest in property, but because it was in the interest of society that property be free. Once property is seen not as a natural right but as a construction designed to serve certain func-

[38]Johnson v. McIntosh, 21 U.S. (8 Wheat.) 543 (1823).

[39]5 Stat. 453, 455 (Sept. 4, 1841), 12 Stat. 392 (May 20, 1862).

[40]Pierson v. Post, 3 Cai. R. 175 (1805).

[41]The Homestead Act had conditions of age, citizenship, intention to settle [what] was cultivated, and loyalty to the United States. 12 Stat. 392 (1862).

[42]Mullett v. Bradley, 24 Misc. 695, 53 N.Y. Supp. 781 (1898); Bridges v. Hawkesworth, 21 L.J. Rep. 75 (Q.B. 1851).

tions, then its origin ceases to be decisive in determining how much regulation should be imposed. The conditions that can be attached to receipt, ownership, and use depend not on where property came from, but on what job it should be expected to perform. Thus in the case of government largess, nothing turns on the fact that it originated in government. The real issue is how it functions and how it should function.

To create an institution, or to make an existing institution function in a new way, is an undertaking far too ambitious for the present article. But it is possible to begin a search for guiding principles. Such principles must grow out of what we know about how government largess has functioned up to the present time. And while principles must remain at the level of generality, it should be kept in mind that not every principle is equally applicable to all forms of largess. Our primary focus must be those forms of largess which chiefly control the rights and status of the individual. . . .

The most clearly defined problem posed by government largess is the way it can be used to apply pressure against the exercise of constitutional rights. A first principle should be that government must have no power to "buy up" rights guaranteed by the Constitution.[43] It should not be able to impose any condition on largess that would be invalid if imposed on something other than a "gratuity."[44] Thus, for example, government should not be able to deny largess because of invocation of the privilege against self-incrimination.[45]

This principle is in a sense a revival of the old but neglected rule against unconstitutional conditions, as enunciated by the Supreme Court:

> Broadly stated, the rule is that the right to continue the exercise of a privilege granted by the state cannot be made to depend upon the grantee's submission to a condition prescribed by the state which is hostile to the provisions of the federal constitution.[46]

> If the state may compel the surrender of one constitutional right as a condition of its favor, it may in like manner, compel a surrender of all. It is

---

[43]Note, *Unconstitutional Conditions*, 73 HARV. L. REV. 1595, 1599 (1960).

[44]Compare Calabresi, *Retroactivity: Paramount Powers and Contractual Changes*, 71 YALE L.J. 1191 (1962). In the context of legislation dealing with government obligations, Professor Calabresi argues that certain regulation can only be justified by a "paramount power of government" (*e.g.*, the commerce power) rather than power incidental to the obligation itself.

[45]Judge Curtis Bok wrote:

We are unwilling to engraft upon our law the notion, nowhere so decided, that unemployment benefits may be denied because of raising the bar of the [Fifth] Amendment against rumor or report of disloyalty or because of refusing to answer such rumor or report. The possible abuses of such a doctrine are shocking to imagine. . . .

Ault Unemployment Compensation Case, 398 Pa. 250, 259, 157 A.2d 375, 380 (1960).

[46]United States v. Chicago, M., St. P. & P.R.R., 282 U.S. 311, 328–29 (1931).

inconceivable that guaranties embedded in the Constitution of the United States thus be manipulated out of existence.[47]

• • •

Beyond the limits deriving from the Constitution, what limits should be imposed on governmental power over largess? Such limits, whatever they may be, must be largely self-imposed and self-policed by legislatures; the Constitution sets only a bare minimum of limitations on legislative policy. The first type of limit should be on relevance. It has proven possible to argue that practically anything in the way of regulation is relevant to some legitimate legislative purpose. But this does not mean that it is desirable for legislatures to make such use of their powers. As Justice Douglas said in the *Barsky* case:

> So far as I know, nothing in a man's political beliefs disables him from setting broken bones or removing ruptured appendixes, safely and efficiently. A practicing surgeon is unlikely to uncover many state secrets in the course of his professional activities.[48] . . .

Besides relevance, a second important limit on substantive power might be concerned with discretion. To the extent possible, delegated power to make rules ought to be confined within ascertainable limits, and regulating agencies should not be assigned the task of enforcing conflicting policies. Also, agencies should be enjoined to use their powers only for the purposes for which they were designed.[49] . . .

A final limit on substantive power, one that should be of growing importance, might be a principle that policy making authority ought not to be delegated to essentially private organizations. The increasing practice of giving professional associations and occupational organizations authority in areas of government largess tends to make an individual subject to a guild of his fellows. A guild system, when attached to government largess, adds to the feudal characteristics of the system. . . .

Because it is so hard to confine relevance and discretion, procedure offers a valuable means for restraining arbitrary action. This was recognized in the strong procedural emphasis of the Bill of Rights, and it is being recognized in the increasingly procedural emphasis of administra-

---

[47]Frost & Frost Co. v. Railroad Comm'n, 271 U.S. 583, 594 (1926); Note, *Unconstitutional Conditions*, 73 HARV. L. REV. 1595 (1960); Hale, *Unconstitutional Conditions and Constitutional Rights*, 35 COLUM. L. REV. 321 (1935). The latter is an elaborate study of the older cases on the Federal conditioning power.

[48]Barsky v. Board of Regents, 347 U.S. 442, 472, 474 (1954) (Douglas, J., dissenting).

[49]Compare Housing Authority v. Cordova, 130 Cal. App. 2d 883, 889, 279 P.2d 215, 218 (1955):

> [W]e fail to find in the act, pursuant to which the plaintiff Housing Authority was created, anything to suggest that it is authorized to use the powers conferred upon it to punish subversives or discourage persons from entertaining subversive ideas by denying to such the right of occupying its facilities. . . .

tive law. The law of government largess has developed with little regard for procedure. Reversal of this trend is long overdue.

The grant, denial, revocation, and administration of all types of government largess should be subject to scrupulous observance of fair procedures. Action should be open to hearing and contest, and based upon a record subject to judicial review. The denial of any form of privilege or benefit on the basis of undisclosed reasons should no longer be tolerated.[50] Nor should the same person sit as legislator, prosecutor, judge and jury, combining all the functions of government in such a way as to make fairness virtually impossible. There is no justification for the survival of arbitrary methods where valuable rights are at stake. . . .

At the very least, it is time to reconsider the theories under which new forms of wealth are regulated, and by which governmental power over them is measured. It is time to recognize that "the public interest" is all too often a reassuring platitude that covers up sharp clashes of conflicting values, and hides fundamental choices. It is time to see that the "privilege" or "gratuity" concept, as applied to wealth dispensed by government, is not much different from the absolute right of ownership that private capital once invoked to justify arbitrary power over employees and the public.

Above all, the time has come for us to remember what the framers of the Constitution knew so well—that "a power over a man's subsistence amounts to a power over his will." We cannot safely entrust our livelihoods and our rights to the discretion of authorities, examiners, boards of control, character committees, regents, or license commissioners. We cannot permit any official or agency to pretend to sole knowledge of the public good. We cannot put the independence of any man—least of all our Barskys and our Anastaplos—wholly in the power of other men.

If the individual is to survive in a collective society, he must have protection against its ruthless pressures. There must be sanctuaries or enclaves where no majority can reach. To shelter the solitary human spirit does not merely make possible the fulfillment of individuals; it also gives society the power to change, to grow, and to regenerate, and hence to endure. These were the objects which property sought to achieve, and can no longer achieve. The challenge of the future will be to construct, for the society that is coming, institutions and laws to carry on this work. Just as the Homestead Act was a deliberate effort to foster individual values at an earlier time, so we must try to build an economic basis for liberty today—a Homestead Act for rootless twentieth century man. We must create a new property.

[50]The Administrative Conference of the United States has recommended "drastic changes" in the procedures by which persons or firms may be debarred from government contracting. The Conference said that such action should not be taken without prior notice, which includes a statement of reasons, and a trial-type hearing before an impartial trier of facts, all within a framework of procedures. Thus, protections would surround even that form of largess which is closest to being a matter within the managerial function of government. FINAL REPORT OF THE ADMINISTRATIVE CONFERENCE OF THE UNITED STATES, p. 15 and Recommendation 'No. 29' (1962).

Towards a Property Right in Employment

PHILIP J. LEVINE

In the layman's conception, a person's "property" is limited to his ownership of "things."[1] However, the boundaries of the legal definition are far less constricting;[2] a limitation of "property" to physical objects would be rigid and static, in conflict with the flexible nature of the common law. Thus, in law, "property" may also refer to intangible concepts such as thoughts and ideas.[3]

Property, then, might be defined as a "legal institution, the essence of which is the creation and protection of certain private rights in wealth of any kind."[4] It sets a "pattern of behavior" and fixes a "zone of tolerance for some segment of human activity."[5] Property is a legal construct, of an experiential nature, its content changing in response to societal developments.[6] It took form in relation to a recognized social problem, and as the problem varied with time, the response showed "the results of new moulding."[7]

Ideally property law is a dynamic process, expanding and contracting to meet societal needs. But, like other institutions, there is a tendency for responses to harden; answers to old problems remain, long after they cease to serve a useful purpose.

> Courts have a duty to reappraise old doctrines in the light of the facts and values of contemporary life—particularly old common law doctrines which the courts themselves created and developed. . . . "[T]he continued vitality of the common law * * * depends upon its ability to reflect contemporary community values and ethics."[8]

From 22 *Buffalo Law Review* 1081. Copyright 1973 by Buffalo Law Review. Reprinted by permission of the author and publisher. Footnotes renumbered.

[1]Philbrick, *Changing Conceptions of Property in Law*, 86 U. PA. L. REV. 691 (1938).

[2]A. PORTER, JOB PROPERTY RIGHTS: A STUDY OF THE JOB CONTROLS OF THE INTERNATIONAL TYPOGRAPHICAL UNION 4 (1954).

[3]An example of this is the law of patents, copyrights and trademarks.

[4]Reich, *The New Property*, 73 YALE L.J. 733, 771 (1964).

[5]1 R. POWELL, REAL PROPERTY ¶ 6, at 7 (P. Rohan ed. 1969).

[6]*Id.* ¶ 11, at 22–24.

[7]*Id.* ¶ 6, at 7.

[8]Javins v. First Nat'l Realty Corp., 428 F.2d 1071, 1074 (D.C. Cir. 1970), *quoting* Whetzel v. Jess Fisher Management Co., 282 F.2d 943, 946 (D.C. Cir. 1960).

THE RELATION OF PROPERTY TO EMPLOYMENT

The law of master-servant exemplifies a law created for a different era, persisting today. Employment is an at will relationship where, in the absence of a specific statute or a contract for a definite term, the master may arbitrarily discharge his servant without interference from the courts.[9]

A product of laissez-faire, employment at will evolved as a reaction to early feudal status concepts. In the Middle Ages all property was held subject to the will of the king, and with possession came an obligation to serve the realm.[10] There was a static social structure, in which an individual's place was determined at birth. The legal system rested heavily on status, tending to impose rights and duties based upon the relationship of parties within the social structure.[11] If an individual neglected his service responsibilities, his property was subject to confiscation.

[9]*E.g.*, Pearson v. Youngstown Sheet & Tube Co., 332 F.2d 439 (7th Cir. 1964); Hablas v. Armour & Co., 270 F.2d 71 (8th Cir. 1959); Odell v. Humble Oil & Ref. Co., 201 F.2d 123 (10th Cir. 1953); McKinney v. Armco Steel Corp., 270 F. Supp. 360 (W.D. Pa. 1967); Electrical Workers v. General Elec. Co., 127 F. Supp. 934 (D.D.C. 1954); Patterson v. Philco Corp., 252 Cal. App. 2d 63, 60 Cal. Rptr. 110 (1st Dist. 1967); Carey v. Westinghouse Elec. Corp., 14 Misc. 2d 237, 178 N.Y.S.2d 846 (Sup. Ct. 1958). *See generally* 53 AM. JUR. 2d *Master and Servant* §§ 27–59 (1970); Blades, *Employment at Will vs. Individual Freedom: On Limiting the Abusive Exercise of Employer Power*, 67 COLUM. L. REV. 1404 (1967); Annot., 51 A.L.R.2d 742 (1957); Lecture by Ruth Weyand, Twenty-second Annual Conference on Labor, June 10, 1969, in PROCEEDINGS OF NEW YORK UNIVERSITY TWENTY-SECOND ANNUAL CONFERENCE ON LABOR 171 (T. Christensen & A. Christensen eds. 1970). *See also* Shaw v. Fisher, 113 S.C. 287, 102 S.E. 325 (1920). (While upholding the employer's right to discharge at will, the court held that any state which prevented an employee from seeking other employment would violate the thirteenth amendment prohibition of involuntary servitude.)

The title master-servant is indicative of the state of the law. The relationship is created by an expression of will by the master. Since the power is held for his benefit and subject to his control, it can continue only so long as "his expression of willingness for its continuance." W. SEAVEY, *The Rationale of Agency*, in STUDIES IN AGENCY 105 (1949).

> The essence of the agency is the agent's duty of obedience, that is, a duty not to act in the principal's affairs except in accordance with the principal's desires as he had manifested them to the agent. It follows that the principal can terminate the authority at any time, irrespective of his contractual obligations to the agent.

W. SEAVEY, LAW OF AGENCY 87 (1964).

Seavey also speculates on the rationale for the law of respondeat superior, believing it to be based on an insurance concept. The master's activity is expanded by use of the activity of others and inevitably leads to wreckage. It is therefore proper for him to pay damages for injuries tortiously caused, in return for the benefits he receives from his servant's proper conduct. The master is able to purchase liability insurance, with the burden of the premiums passed on to the consumers. Respondeat superior also fosters safety measures since it induces masters to exercise greater care in the selection of servants. *Id.* at 141 (1964); W. SEAVEY, *Speculations as to "Respondeat Superior,"* in STUDIES IN AGENCY 129–59 (1949).

It might be argued that since the master is held liable for the torts of his servants, his right to discharge should remain unrestricted. He should not be forced to retain incompetent employees. However, the creation of a job property right would not limit the employer's freedom to dismiss on the basis of poor performance, it would only prevent discharge for reasons which infringe on fundamental rights.

[10]A. PORTER, *supra* note 2, at 1–2.

[11]Tobriner & Grodin, *The Individual and the Public Service Enterprise in the Industrial State*, 55 CALIF. L. REV. 1247, 1249 (1967).

In the seventeenth century, with increasing social mobility, the status system began to break down. Property was considered to be held as a right; not subject to any limitation, or even regulation, by the sovereign.[12] It became identified with liberty, and could neither be abridged nor confiscated without due process. This conception of ownership made property one of the prime barriers to governmental encroachments, allowing individuals to act in ways which did not conform to societal norms. Thus the institution of property was instrumental in the development of new and sometimes unpopular ideas, and became one of man's most basic rights.[13]

An outgrowth of the industrial revolution, the concept of laissez-faire was a logical extension of the new property rights. This economic theory promoted free competition and discouraged governmental interference. The principle of freedom of contract became the standard governing the employment relationship. It encouraged individual initiative, allowing men to establish their own law through consent.[14] The basic premise was unlimited mobility, where there was no need to bind either party to the employment relationship. The bargaining power of the parties was believed to be approximately equal. It was assumed that employees could easily find new jobs, while the employer would have no difficulty replacing them. Under these circumstances legal intervention was considered undesirable.

One might seriously question whether the foundations of laissez-faire theory were ever realistic. But regardless of the extent of their original truth, these assumptions were gradually undercut by industrial development in the late nineteenth century. By this time businesses had grown to such an enormous size that the relative bargaining powers of employee and employer had become grossly unequal. Employment opportunity had diminished as technological advances, requiring increasing specialization, limited the employee's options to move from place to place.[15] Despite this changed environment, the courts refused to intervene in the employment relationship. The justification for continued judicial restraint was social Darwinism, a theory which applied the principles of biological evolution to societal conditions: "survival of the fittest" foreclosed interference with the process of "natural selection."[16] Although this approach is now generally discredited,[17] the at will standard still prevails in master-servant law.

The employee has thus been placed in a highly vulnerable position in which his ability to earn a living is subject to the employer's whim. He

---

[12]A. PORTER, *supra* note 2, at 2–3.

[13]Reich, *supra* note 4, at 771–72.

[14]Tobriner & Grodin, *supra* note 11, at 1251.

[15]Blades, *supra* note 9, at 1405.

[16]*See* Coppage v. Kansas, 236 U.S. 1 (1915); Adair v. United States, 208 U.S. 161 (1908); Lochner v. New York, 198 U.S. 45 (1905).

[17]*See* Justice Holmes' dissent in *Lochner*, 198 U.S. at 75: "The Fourteenth Amendment does not enact Mr. Herbert Spencer's Social Statics."

may be forced to forfeit such fundamental rights as freedom of speech in order to retain his job. The employer's power is further enhanced by the damage created by a dismissal on a worker's employment record. Future employment is far more difficult to obtain once the stigma of having been fired is attached.[18]

The notion of an absolute right to property, although originally conceived of as the basis of liberty,[19] has resulted in the subjugation of the working class. It has allowed employers to exercise dominion over their employees, without any corresponding protection of the employee's interests. This freedom from governmental restraint has enabled employers to place unconscionable conditions on employment.

The seriousness of the situation is compounded by the importance of employment to the individual employee. The essential elements of his life are all dependent on his ability to derive income.[20] His job is the basis of his position in society, and, therefore, may be the most meaningful form of wealth he possesses.[21]

Old conceptions of property limited to the protection of interests in land and physical objects will no longer serve as adequate protection for the individual. Abstractions like jobs must be protected if individual liberty is to survive. Our concept of property must be expanded to encompass the employment relationship, to protect against wrongful discharge.[22]

> If the individual is to survive in a collective society, he must have protection against its ruthless pressures. There must be sanctions or enclaves where no majority can reach. To shelter the solitary human spirit does not merely make possible the fulfillment of individuals; it also gives society the power to change, to grow, and to regenerate, and hence to endure. . . . The challenge of the future will be to construct, for the society that is coming, institutions and laws to carry on this work. Just as the Homestead Act was a deliberate effort to foster individual values at an earlier time, so we must try to build an economic basis for liberty today—a Homestead Act for rootless twentieth century man. We must create a new property.[23] . . .

[18]Blades, *supra* note 9, at 1405–06.

[19]*See* Reich, *supra* note 4, at 771–72.

[20]*I.e.*, his ability to support a family, provide food, shelter, etc.

[21]Reich, *supra* note 4, at 739.

> To men dependent for daily existence on continuous employment, the protection of this means of livelihood from confiscation or encroachment appears as fundamental a basis of the social order as it does to the owners of land. What both parties claim is security and continuity of livelihood—that maintenance of the "established expectation" which is the "condition precedent" of civilized life.

A. Porter, *supra* note 2, at 80–81, *quoting* S. Webb & B. Webb, Industrial Democracy 566 (1914).

[22]*See* Comment, *Unemployment as a Taking Without Just Compensation*, 43 S. Calif. L. Rev. 488 (1970).

[23]Reich, *supra* note 4, at 787. This new right need not be called "property." A more exact definition might be the protection of the worker's interest in his employment from discharge without just cause. Yet "property" seems to be a more convenient handle, since it implies a recognition that this right is consistent with preexisting law; that it is an adaptation of the common law to modern needs.

The Interest of the Community in a Professional Education

THOMAS D. SCHAEFER

Contemporary efforts to promote equality between the sexes in our society[1] are revealing subtle inequities that the law can no longer ignore.[2] Within the marital community a significant number of individuals, many of whom are women[3] supporting their mates through school, are viewing themselves less as dutiful spouses than economic partners hopeful of improving future community earnings. It is not surprising that a growing number of such supporting spouses feel deprived and manipulated when their marriage is dissolved upon the conclusion of their spouse's education. In most cases community earnings will have been drained to provide for educational expenses, and the likelihood of sufficient spousal support, if any, will be minimal. In short, the student spouse will walk away with a degree and the supporting spouse will depart with little more than the knowledge that he or she has substantially contributed toward the attainment of that degree.

Although this unfortunate sequence of events is becoming increasingly more common, the possibility of establishing a community interest in the education continues to be ignored by most attorneys. In truth, the relative novelty of this concept, coupled with an apparently reluctant precedent,[4] may suggest more than mere inadvertence on their part. Whatever the reasons, sound legal foundation exists for pursuing this concept. The equities are clear: When an education, acquired at the expense of the community's funds and labors, is held to be an intangible possession of the student spouse upon dissolution, unjust enrichment and unusual hardship result. In addition, the amount at stake in securing a proportionate return of the educational investment to the nonstudent spouse may make the effort very worthwhile.

This Comment espouses the position that a professional education[5]

From 10 *California Western Law Review* 590 (1974). Copyright 1974 by California Western Law Review. Reprinted by permission of the publisher. Footnotes renumbered.

[1]*See, e.g.*, CAL. CIV. CODE §§ 4800, 5125, 5127 (West Supp. 1974).

[2]Durant, *New Feminism Benefits Men in Divorce Actions*, L.A. Times, Dec. 30, 1973, § 2, at 1, col. 1.

[3]Reference throughout the text will be made to the respective spouses as student and nonstudent, or student and supporting spouse. For purposes of consistency and the utilization of pronouns, the student spouse will be assumed to be male and the nonstudent, or supporting spouse, female.

[4]*See* text accompanying note 6 *infra*.

[5]Although the arguments contained herein are not necessarily limited in application to the specific form of professional education, it is the distinguishing characteristic of this form which facilitates a discussion of education within the scheme of community transactions

is capable of classification and evaluation as community property for the purposes of dissolution or legal separation. In comparison, alternative solutions are incapable of providing the nonstudent spouse with the protection which only the law of community property can provide.* Moreover, in the context of the community, the entity "education" suffers no crisis of credibility in identifying with the concept of "property." In fact, its fundamental attributes are common to similar entities already recognized as community property.* Where an education is acquired during marriage at the expense of community assets, it too should be regarded as a community asset, subject to the underlying community property law policies which protect the community's acquisitions.* Finally, based on the assumption that an education is capable of classification as community property, two methods will be proposed for its evaluation upon dissolution of the community.*

• • •

In the California case of *Todd v. Todd,*[6] the Third District Court of Appeal questioned the validity of a nonstudent spouse's claim under the law of community property. During his marriage Mr. Todd had attended and graduated from the University of San Francisco Law School with an LL.B. degree. His wife had been employed on a full-time basis the entire time he had been in school and for several years after he had been admitted to the State Bar. Their assets in the year of his graduation had been negligible, but, by the time of their divorce thirteen years later, the community had accumulated net assets in excess of $200,000, and net income from the law practice was approximately $23,000 per year.

For the division of community property, the trial court listed Mr. Todd's legal education as a community asset,[7] but without value.[8] While not wishing to disturb the *classification* of her husband's legal education as community property, Mrs. Todd appealed on the issue of the *value* as-

---

and which provides the elements necessary for its practical evaluation. . . . Undergraduate education is generally directed less at a professional career than at a general comprehension of the liberal arts. Moreover, a professional education is likely to be sought during that period of life where marriage is more common and the spouses more likely to invest in education with an eye toward future earnings. Even where the marital relation exists in the undergraduate years many instances would be found where the direct purchase cost of the education . . . would be paid from other than community resources, for example, a gift of funds from the student's parents. Similarly, informal education or on the job training will generally lack not only a direct purchase cost but also any significant opportunity cost for purposes of evaluation. . . .

*Footnote omitted [Eds.].

[6]272 Cal. App. 2d 786, 78 Cal. Rptr. 131 (3d Dist. 1969).

[7]Clerk's Transcript, vol. 1, at 138–39, 154 line 18, 172, 176–80 item XI, and 183–85, Todd v. Todd, Civil No. 14302 (Nevada County, Cal., Jan. 31, 1966) (mem. dec.), *questioned* 272 Cal. App. 2d 786, 78 Cal. Rptr. 731 (3d Dist. 1969) (*dictum*).

[8]*Id.*

signed to it by the lower court.[9] The court of appeal, however, saw fit to voice its sentiments on both issues:

> If a spouse's education preparing him for the practice of law can be said to be "community property," a proposition which is extremely doubtful even though the education is acquired with community moneys, it manifestly is of such a character that a monetary value for division with the other spouse cannot be placed upon it.[10]

Though *Todd* does not specifically deny a professional education the status of community property, it does distinguish the two primary issues. First, it must be established that a professional education is property, at least to the extent of being within the scheme of community property law. Second, if found to be community property, a method of calculating its worth must be employed to facilitate proper division in the event of dissolution.

IS EDUCATION PROPERTY?

1. Property: A Concept Relative to Its Context.—The term "property," in both its common and legal[11] usage, has become a catch-all word covering a wide array of titles and interests.[12] It is most adequately defined when its meaning is drawn from an appropriate context.[13] For example, a chose in action will be recognized as property for the purpose of the California Civil Code,[14] but not for the purposes of California Probate Code, concerning one who conceals the property of a decedent.[15] Similarly, the right to practice a profession has been termed "property" for the purposes of due process, in that it is a right which may not be taken from a person except

[9]Brief for Appellant at 10–13, Todd v. Todd, 272 Cal. App. 2d 786, 78 Cal. Rptr. 131 (3d Dist. 1969).

[10]272 Cal. App. 2d at 791, 78 Cal. Rptr. at 134.

[11]"Property" is a generic term. *See* Ponsonby v. Suburban Fruit Lands Co., 210 Cal. 229, 232, 291 P. 167, 168 (1930). It is sufficiently comprehensive to include every species of right and interest capable of being enjoyed as such and upon which it is practicable to place a money value. *See* Yuba River Power Co. v. Nevada Irr. Dist., 207 Cal. 521, 523, 279 P. 128, 129 (1929).

[12]"Property" is commonly used to denote everything which is the subject of ownership, corporeal or incorporeal, tangible or intangible, visible or invisible, real or personal; everything that has an exchangeable value or which goes to make up wealth or estate. Jeffrey v. City of Salinas, 232 Cal. App. 2d 29, 47, 42 Cal. Rptr. 486, 499 (1st Dist. 1965); Southern Pac. Co. v. Riverside County, 35 Cal. App. 2d 380, 387, 95 P.2d 688, 692 (4th Dist. 1939).

[13]What is property under one statute may not be property under another. *See* Ponsonby v. Suburban Fruit Lands Co., 210 Cal. 229, 232, 291 P. 167, 168 (1930); Bogan v. Wiley, 90 Cal. App. 2d, 288, 293, 202 P.2d 824, 827 (1st Dist. 1949).

[14]CAL. CIV. CODE § 14 (West 1954); Seaboard Fin. Co. v. Federal Leasing Co., 247 Cal. App. 2d 444, 55 Cal. Rptr. 458 (2d Dist. 1966).

[15]CAL. PROB. CODE § 612 (West 1956); Bogan v. Wiley, 90 Cal. App. 2d 288, 202 P.2d 824 (1st Dist. 1949).

upon a clear proof that he has forfeited it.[16] However, that same right is not cognizable "property" under the California Constitution,[17] which requires that all "property" in the state, not otherwise exempt, be taxed in proportion to its value.[18]

In order to determine whether a professional education is "property" within community property law, two elements should be considered: First, whether an education is capable of such a general conceptual classification, insofar as it possesses certain attributes common to other recognized forms of property;[19] and second, does protection of the community's interest in that which is acquired during marriage[20] require an education be deemed property?[21] The weight given each of these considerations will vary with individual situations, but neither should be considered to the exclusion of the other.[22]

2. Education: Its Common Attributes.

—An education is at once intangible, nonsurvivable, and not transferable in an ordinary sense. These at-

---

[16]*See* Laisne v. California St. Bd. of Optometry, 19 Cal. 2d 831, 123 P.2d 457 (1942) (optometrist); Cavassa v. Off, 206 Cal. 307, 274 P. 523 (1929) (pharmacist).

[17]CAL. CONST. art. XIII, § 1.

[18]*See* People v. Coleman, 4 Cal. 46 (1854).

[19]*See, e.g.,* Franklin v. Franklin, 67 Cal. App. 2d 717, 725, 155 P.2d 637, 641 (2d Dist. 1945).

[20]The thrust of this consideration is evident in the following:

> The [community property law] proceeds upon the theory that the marriage, in respect to property acquired during its existence, is a community of which each spouse is a member, equally contributing by his or her industry to its prosperity. . . . To the community all acquisitions by either, whether made jointly or separately, belong.

In re Marriage of Cary, 34 Cal. App. 3d 345, 348, 109 Cal. Rptr. 862, 863 (1st Dist. 1973), *quoting from* Meyer v. Kinzer, 12 Cal. 247, 251 (1859). *See also* CAL. CIV. CODE §§ 5107–10 (West 1970).

[21]"Property" is a dynamic concept. Where justice has required the protection of rights that do not enjoy a physical actuality the term has been employed, notwithstanding. For example, choses in action, note 14 *supra* and accompanying text, a cause of action, note 25 *infra* and accompanying text, the right to take an appeal, People v. Cadman, 57 Cal. 562 (1881), and the good will of a business, Mueller v. Mueller, 144 Cal. App. 2d 245, 301 P.2d 90 (3d Dist. 1956), have all been termed "property" within the context of specific areas of the law though actually lacking in physical substance.

[22]In the case of Franklin v. Franklin, 67 Cal. App. 2d 717, 155 P.2d 637 (2d Dist. 1945), the court of appeal relied solely on the common-attributes concept of property in denying a cause of action, for personal injuries, the status of community property. The husband had sustained personal injuries in the interim period between the interlocutory and final decree of divorce. The wife successfully claimed in the trial court that the right to sue was community property. The appeal court reasoned, however, that although the right arose during the community's existence, a cause of action for personal injuries was not subject to transfer by agreement or by law and was lacking in the attributes common to the entire scheme of community property laws; it belonged "exclusively" to the person injured. The *Franklin* court, however, overlooked the strong community property policy consideration that views the community as impaired when one of its members is personally injured. *See* note 31 *infra.* A consideration of the status of the cause of action for personal injuries in this context may have led the court to the contrary conclusion subsequently made by the California Supreme Court in Zaragosa v. Craven, 33 Cal. 2d 315, 202 P.2d 73 (1949).

tributes do not, however, prevent its classification as property, for each is a characteristic common to an already recognized form of community property. The examples of intangible forms of community property are numerous: the good will of a business,[23] the interest of a spouse in a partnership,[24] and a cause of action for injury to either spouse[25] or to a minor child.[26]

An education also should not be denied the status of property merely because it is incapable of surviving the student who has acquired it. Survivability has not been the earmark of property in the past and should not be now. California courts have consistently held causes of action for personal injury to be community property,[27] both prior to[28] and after the enactment of legislation permitting their survival.[29]

Neither is transferability a prerequisite to community property status. Although the assignment of a cause of action for personal injury is conceivable in theory, the fact that the claim is purely personal in nature has prevented its transfer by either law or agreement.[30] Thus, an education has much in common with a personal injury claim, for the latter demonstrates that an intangible, nonsurvivable, nontransferable interest of a purely personal nature may nevertheless be subject to community ownership. The same policy regarding the community as impaired when an individual member is injured[31] should also consider the community as improved when an individual member is educated.

3. Education: What Is Acquired by the Community?—The underlying intent of community property law, to protect the community and its interest in that which is acquired during marriage,[32] should not be overlooked in determining whether that education is property under the California Civil

[23]Mueller v. Mueller, 144 Cal. App. 2d 245, 301 P.2d 90 (3d Dist. 1956).

[24]Wood v. Gunther, 89 Cal. App. 2d 718, 201 P.2d 874 (2d Dist. 1949).

[25]Flores v. Brown, 39 Cal. 2d 622, 248 P.2d 922 (1952). *See also* CAL. CIV. CODE § 5126 (West Supp. 1974).

[26]Emery v. Emery, 45 Cal. 2d 421, 289 P.2d 218 (1955).

[27]Sanderson v. Niemann, 17 Cal. 2d 563, 110 P.2d 1025 (1941).

[28]In early California decisions a claim for personal injury was considered the exclusive possession of the injured party and was not capable of surviving him. De la Torre v. Johnson, 200 Cal. 754, 254 P. 1105 (1927). *See also* Cort v. Steen, 36 Cal. 2d 437, 224 P.2d 723 (1950).

[29]*See* ch. 1380, § 2, [1949] Cal. Stats. 2400 (repealed 1961); CAL. PROB. CODE § 573 (West Supp. 1974).

[30]This has been recognized from the common law to the present. *See* Wikstrom v. Yolo Fliers Club, 206 Cal. 461, 274 P. 959 (1929). CAL. PROB. CODE § 573 (West Supp. 1974) specifically provides that it is not to be construed as making assignable things in action that were not assignable prior to its enactment.

[31]*See* CAL. CIV. CODE § 5126 (West Supp. 1974). A frequently cited rationale for holding a cause of action for personal injury to be community property is that the bulk of the damages award usually represents the loss of earnings (normally the largest source of community earnings). *See* Note, 37 CALIF. L. REV. 318 (1949).

[32]See note 20 *supra*.

Code.[33] To illustrate, assume that the acquiring of a professional education during marriage results in the acquisition of something other than
property. When this acquisition is compared with other transactions involving community funds or skills, a basic scheme within the community
property law becomes apparent.

(a) Community Funds.—A disposition of community funds in any manner other than in the acquiring of an education is necessarily accomplished by one of the following: Community funds may be disposed of
through waste, by gift, furnished as consideration in exchange for other
property, or used by a managing spouse in the improvement of his separate estate. Regardless of which disposition results, however, the scheme
of community property law is such that the community is protected in any
event.[34]

Where a professional education is acquired with community funds,
however, the interests sought to be protected in the scheme of community
property law are abridged. Despite its representing a valuable consideration in exchange for community funds, it innures to the sole benefit of
the student spouse. In essence a change in form—from community funds
to education—results in a change of status—from community property to
the student's separate asset.[35] Upon divorce or legal separation, the nonstudent is consequently denied both an interest in the entity acquired and
reimbursement for a pro-rata share in the community funds expended.

(b) The Efforts and Skills of the Student Spouse.—The efforts and skills
of each member of the community are regarded as community assets.[36]
Unlike a disposition of community funds, however, there is no recourse
for wasted or gratuitously rendered personal services. Nevertheless, the

[33]Cal. Civ. Code § 5110 (West Supp. 1974).

[34]Where waste is involved the injured spouse may proceed against the disposing
spouse personally. *See* People v. Schlette, 139 Cal. App. 2d 165, 293 P.2d 79 (1st Dist. 1956),
cert. denied, 352 U.S. 1012 (1957). *See also* Fields v. Michael, 91 Cal. App. 2d 443, 205 P.2d
402 (2d Dist. 1949). Where a gift of community funds is made by a donor spouse to his
separate estate, or to a third party, the written consent of the nondonor spouse is required.
See Cal. Civ. Code § 5125 (West 1970) (unaffected by amendment operative Jan. 1, 1975).
Where property is received in exchange for community funds, a change in form does not
result in a change of status. *See* Burby, Real Property § 102 at 239 (3d ed. 1965). The
acquired property is thus community property. *See* Cal. Civ. Code § 5110 (West Supp.
1974). Even where property received in the exchange for community funds is a less than
"valuable" consideration, the transaction will be treated as a gift, and the community thereby
protected. *See* Cal. Civ. Code § 5125 (West 1970) (unaffected by amendment operative Jan.
1, 1975); Winchester v. Winchester, 175 Cal. 391, 165 P. 965 (1917). Finally, where the
manager of the community uses its funds to improve his separate estate, even though such
improvements may remain a part of that estate, the community will be protected against any
unconsented to appropriation through reimbursement. *See* Provost v. Provost, 102 Cal. App.
775, 782–83, 283 P. 842, 845 (2d Dist. 1929).

[35]*Compare* note 34 *supra.*

[36]Beam v. Bank of Am., 6 Cal. 3d 12, 490 P.2d 257, 98 Cal. Rptr. 137 (1971); Pereira
v. Pereira, 156 Cal. 1, 103 P. 488 (1909).

scheme of community property law protects against the use of such services for the separate benefit of the performing spouse. If the efforts and skills of one spouse are contributed to the improvement of his separate estate, the community is to be reimbursed for the reasonable value of those services,[37] or to the extent they have contributed to the growth of the separate estate.[38] Moreover, where the services of either spouse are rendered in an exchange for property, the acquisition is community property.[39]

In the acquisition of an education, however, the community may be deprived of the ultimate fruits of its labors. If placed beyond the scope of community property law, the education becomes solely an acquisition of the student. The community is deprived of both an interest in the asset acquired and the value of the services expended in its acquisition.

Materials on Copyright and "Fair Use"

FROM TITLE 17 OF THE U.S. CODE

§ 106. Exclusive Rights in Copyrighted Works

Subject to sections 107 through 118, the owner of copyright under this title has the exclusive rights to do and to authorize any of the following:

(1)   to reproduce the copyrighted work in copies or phonorecords;

(2)   to prepare derivative works based upon the copyrighted work;

(3)   to distribute copies or phonorecords of the copyrighted work to the public by sale or other transfer of ownership, or by rental, lease, or lending;

(4)   in the case of literary, musical, dramatic, and choreographic works, pantomimes, and motion pictures and other audiovisual works, to perform the copyrighted work publicly; and

(5)   in the case of literary, musical, dramatic, and choreographic works, pantomimes, and pictorial, graphic, or sculptural works, including the individual images of a motion picture or other audiovisual work, to display the copyrighted work publicly.

---

[37]Beam v. Bank of Am., 6 Cal. 3d 12, 490 P.2d 257, 98 Cal. Rptr. 137 (1971); Van Kamp v. Van Kamp, 53 Cal. App. 17, 199 P. 885 (2d Dist. 1921).

[38]See cases cited note 36 supra.

[39]See CAL. CIV. CODE § 5110 (West Supp. 1974).

§ 107. Limitations on Exclusive Rights: Fair Use

Notwithstanding the provisions of section 106, the fair use of a copyrighted work, including such use by reproduction in copies or phonorecords or by any other means specified by that section, for purposes such as criticism, comment, news reporting, teaching (including multiple copies for classroom use), scholarship, or research, is not an infringement of copyright. In determining whether the use made of a work in any particular case is a fair use the factors to be considered shall include—

(1)   the purpose and character of the use, including whether such use is of a commercial nature or is for nonprofit educational purposes;
(2)   the nature of the copyrighted work;
(3)   the amount and substantiality of the portion used in relation to the copyrighted work as a whole; and
(4)   the effect of the use upon the potential market for or value of the copyrighted work.

FROM THE HOUSE REPORT ON THE COPYRIGHT ACT OF 1976*

Section 106. Exclusive Rights in Copyrighted Works

General scope of copyright

The five fundamental rights that the bill gives to copyright owners— the exclusive rights of reproduction, adaptation, publication, performance, and display—are stated generally in section 106. These exclusive rights, which comprise the so-called "bundle of rights" that is a copyright, are cumulative and may overlap in some cases. Each of the five enumerated rights may be subdivided indefinitely and . . . each subdivision of an exclusive right may be owned and enforced separately.

The approach of the bill is to set forth the copyright owner's exclusive rights in broad terms in section 106, and then to provide various limitations, qualifications, or exemptions in the 12 sections that follow. Thus, everything in section 106 is made "subject to sections 107 through 118," and must be read in conjunction with those provisions.

• • •

Section 107. Fair Use

General background of the problem

The judicial doctrine of fair use, one of the most important and well-established limitations on the exclusive right of copyright owners,

*H.R. Rep. No. 94–1478.

would be given express statutory recognition for the first time in section 107. The claim that a defendant's acts constituted a fair use rather than an infringement has been raised as a defense in innumerable copyright actions over the years, and there is ample case law recognizing the existence of the doctrine and applying it. The examples enumerated at page 24 of the Register's 1961 Report, while by no means exhaustive, give some idea of the sort of activities the courts might regard as fair use under the circumstances: "quotation of excerpts in a review or criticism for purposes of illustration or comment; quotation of short passages in a scholarly or technical work, for illustration or clarification of the author's observations; use in a parody of some of the content of the work parodied; summary of an address or article, with brief quotations, in a news report; reproduction by a library of a portion of a work to replace part of a damaged copy; reproduction by a teacher or student of a small part of a work to illustrate a lesson; reproduction of a work in legislative or judicial proceedings or reports; incidental and fortuitous reproduction, in a newsreel or broadcast, of a work located in the scene of an event being reported."

Although the courts have considered and ruled upon the fair use doctrine over and over again, no real definition of the concept has ever emerged. Indeed, since the doctrine is an equitable rule of reason, no generally applicable definition is possible, and each case raising the question must be decided on its own facts. On the other hand, the courts have evolved a set of criteria which, though in no case definitive or determinative, provide some gauge for balancing the equities. These criteria have been stated in various ways, but essentially they can all be reduced to the four standards which have been adopted in section 107.

• • •

General intention behind the provision

The statement of the fair use doctrine in section 107 offers some guidance to users in determining when the principles of the doctrine apply. However, the endless variety of situations and combinations of circumstances that can rise in particular cases precludes the formulation of exact rules in the statute. The bill endorses the purpose and general scope of the judicial doctrine of fair use, but there is no disposition to freeze the doctrine in the statute, especially during a period of rapid technological change. Beyond a very broad statutory explanation of what fair use is and some of the criteria applicable to it, the courts must be free to adapt the doctrine to particular situations on a case-by-case basis. Section 107 is intended to restate the present judicial doctrine of fair use, not to change, narrow, or enlarge it in any way.

• • •

Intention as to classroom reproduction

Although the works and uses to which the doctrine of fair use is applicable are as broad as the copyright law itself, most of the discussion of section 107 has centered around questions of classroom reproduction, particularly photocopying. The arguments on the question are summarized at pp. 30–31 of this Committee's 1967 report (H.R. Rep. No. 83, 90th Cong., 1st Sess.), and have not changed materially in the intervening years.

The Committee also adheres to its earlier conclusion, that "a specific exemption freeing certain reproductions of copyrighted works for educational and scholarly purposes from copyright control is not justified." At the same time the Committee recognizes, as it did in 1967, that there is a "need for greater certainty and protection for teachers." In an effort to meet this need the Committee has not only adopted further amendments to section 107, but has also amended section 504(c) to provide innocent teachers and other non-profit users of copyrighted material with broad insulation against unwarranted liability for infringement.

• • •

At the Judiciary Subcommittee hearings in June 1975, Chairman Kastenmeier and other members urged the parties to meet together independently in an effort to achieve a meeting of the minds as to permissible educational uses of copyrighted material. The response to these suggestions was positive, and a number of meetings of three groups, dealing respectively with classroom reproduction of printed material, music, and audio-visual material, were held beginning in September 1975.

• • •

In a joint letter to Chairman Kastenmeier, dated March 19, 1976, the representatives of the Ad Hoc Committee of Educational Institutions and Organizations on Copyright Law Revision, and of the Authors League of America, Inc., and the Association of American Publishers, Inc., stated:

> You may remember that in our letter of March 8, 1976 we told you that the negotiating teams representing authors and publishers and the Ad Hoc Group had reached tentative agreement on guidelines to insert in the Committee Report covering Educational copying from books and periodicals under Section 107 of H.R. 2223 and S. 22, and that as part of that tentative agreement each side would accept the amendments to Sections 107 and 504 which were adopted by your Subcommittee on March 3, 1976.
>
> We are now happy to tell you that the agreement has been approved by the principals and we enclose a copy herewith. We had originally intended to translate the agreement into language suitable for inclusion in the legislative report dealing with Section 107, but we have since been advised by committee staff that this will not be necessary.

As stated above, the agreement refers only to copying from books and periodicals, and it is not intended to apply to musical or audiovisual works.

The full text of the agreement is as follows:

AGREEMENT ON GUIDELINES FOR CLASSROOM COPYING IN NOT-FOR-PROFIT EDUCATIONAL INSTITUTIONS WITH RESPECT TO BOOKS AND PERIODICALS

The purpose of the following guidelines is to state the minimum and not the maximum standards of educational fair use under Section 107 of H.R. 2223. The parties agree that the conditions determining the extent of permissible copying for educational purposes may change in the future; that certain types of copying permitted under these guidelines may not be permissible in the future; and conversely that in the future other types of copying not permitted under these guidelines may be permissible under revised guidelines.

Moreover, the following statement of guidelines is not intended to limit the types of copying permitted under the standards of fair use under judicial decision and which are stated in Section 107 of the Copyright Revision Bill. There may be instances in which copying which does not fall within the guidelines stated below may nonetheless be permitted under the criteria of fair use.

GUIDELINES

I. *Single Copying for Teachers*

A single copy may be made of any of the following by or for a teacher at his or her individual request for his or her scholarly research or use in teaching or preparation to teach a class:

A. A chapter from a book;

B. An article from a periodical or newspaper;

C. A short story, short essay or short poem, whether or not from a collective work;

D. A chart, graph, diagram, drawing, cartoon or picture from a book, periodical, or newspaper.

II. *Multiple Copies for Classroom Use*

Multiple copies (not to exceed in any event more than one copy per pupil in a course) may be made by or for the teacher giving the course for classroom use or discussion; *provided that:*

A. The copying meets the tests of brevity and spontaneity as defined below; *and*

B. Meets the cumulative effect test as defined below; *and*

C. Each copy includes a notice of copyright.

Definitions

Brevity

(i) Poetry: (a) A complete poem if less than 250 words and if printed on not more than two pages or, (b) from a longer poem, an excerpt of not more than 250 words.

(ii) Prose: (a) Either a complete article, story or essay of less than 2,500 words, or (b) an excerpt from any prose work of not more than 1,000 words or 10% of the work, whichever is less, but in any event a minimum of 500 words.

[Each of the numerical limits stated in "i" and "ii" above may be expanded to permit the completion of an unfinished line of a poem or of an unfinished prose paragraph.]

(iii) Illustration: One chart, graph, diagram, drawing, cartoon or picture per book or per periodical issue.

(iv) "Special" works: Certain works in poetry, prose or in "poetic prose" which often combine language with illustrations and which are intended sometimes for children and at other times for a more general audience fall short of 2,500 words in their entirety. Paragraph "ii" above notwithstanding such "special works" may not be reproduced in their entirety; however, an excerpt comprising not more than two of the published pages of such special work and containing not more than 10% of the words found in the text thereof, may be reproduced.

Spontaneity

(i) The copying is at the instance and inspiration of the individual teacher, and

(ii) The inspiration and decision to use the work and the moment of its use for maximum teaching effectiveness are so close in time that it would be unreasonable to expect a timely reply to a request for permission.

Cumulative Effect

(i) The copying of the material is for only one course in the school in which the copies are made.

(ii) Not more than one short poem, article, story, essay or two excerpts may be copied from the same author, nor more than three from the same collective work or periodical volume during one class term.

(iii) There shall not be more than nine instances of such multiple copying for one course during one class term.

[The limitations stated in "ii" and "iii" above shall not apply to current news periodicals and newspapers and current news sections of other periodicals.]

III. *Prohibitions as to I and II Above*

Notwithstanding any of the above, the following shall be prohibited:

(A) Copying shall not be used to create or to replace or substitute for anthologies, compilations or collective works. Such replacement or substitution may occur whether copies of various works or excerpts therefrom are accumulated or reproduced and used separately.

(B) There shall be no copying of or from works intended to be "consumable" in the course of study or of teaching. These include workbooks, exercises, standardized tests and test booklets and answer sheets and like consumable material.

(C) Copying shall not:
   (a) substitute for the purchase of books, publishers' reprints or periodicals;
   (b) be directed by higher authority;
   (c) be repeated with respect to the same item by the same teacher from term to term.

(D)   No charge shall be made to the student beyond the actual cost of the photocopying.

Agreed March 19, 1976.
Ad Hoc Committee on Copyright Law Revision:
                    By Sheldon Elliott Steinbach.
Author-Publisher Group:
Authors League of America:
                    By Irwin Karp, *Counsel.*
Association of American Publishers, Inc.:
                    By Alexander C. Hoffman,
                    Chairman, Copyright Committee.

Suggestions for Further Reading

A detailed treatment of some of the changes described by Macpherson—and their relation to the development of capitalism—is given in Thomas F. Bergin and Paul G. Haskell, *Preface to Estates in Land and Future Interests* (Brooklyn: Foundation Press, 1966). The reader may also wish to consult Richard Schlatter, *Private Property: The History of an Idea* (New Brunswick, N.J.: Rutgers University Press, 1951); and Morton J. Horwitz, "The Transformation in the Conception of Property in American Law," 40 *University of Chicago Law Review* 248 (1973).

   Many of the supplementary materials relevant to Reich's article, as well as to the articles by Levine and Schaefer, and to the piece on copyright, were noted in "Suggestions for Further Reading" at the end of Part One, Section One (pp. 26–27). Two later pieces by Charles Reich are "Individual Rights and Social Welfare: The Emerging Legal Issues," 74 *Yale Law Journal* 1245 (1965); and "Social Welfare in the Public-Private State," 114 *University of Pennsylvania Law Review* 487 (1966). See also the comment "Unemployment as a Taking without Just Compensation," 43 *Southern California Law Review* 488 (1970).

PART THREE
CRITIQUES

The first man who, having enclosed a piece of ground, bethought himself of saying "This is mine," and found people simple enough to believe him, was the real founder of civil society. From how many crimes, wars, and murders, from how many horrors and misfortunes might not any one have saved mankind, by pulling up the stakes, or filling up the ditch, and crying to his fellows: "Beware of listening to this imposter; you are undone if you once forget that the fruits of the earth belong to us all, and the earth itself to nobody."

> Jean Jacques Rousseau,
> *Discourse on the Origin of Inequality*

Place one hundred men on an island from which there is no escape, and whether you make one of these men the absolute owner of the other ninety-nine, or the absolute owner of the soil of the island, will make no difference either to him or to them.

In the one case, as the other, the one will be the absolute master of the ninety-nine. . . .

> Henry George,
> *Progress and Poverty*

It [is] in vain to repeat: "I built this wall; I gained this spot by my industry." Who gave you your standing, it might be answered, and what right have you to demand payment of us for doing what we never asked you to do? Do you not know that numbers of your fellow creatures are starving, for want of what you have too much of? You ought to have had the express and universal consent of mankind, before appropriating more of the common subsistence than you needed for your own maintenance.

> Jean Jacques Rousseau,
> *Discourse on the Origin of Inequality*

What constitutes the rightful basis of property? . . . Is it not, primarily, the right of a man to himself, to the use of his own powers, to the enjoyment of the fruits of his own exertions? Is it not this individual right . . . which alone justifies individual ownership? As a man belongs to himself, so his labor when put in concrete form belongs to him.

Henry George,
Progress and Poverty

If I were asked to answer the following question: *What is slavery?* and I should answer in one word, *It is murder,* my meaning would be understood at once. No extended argument would be required to show that the power to take from a man his thought, his will, his personality, is a power of life and death; and that to enslave a man is to kill him. Why, then, to this other question: *What is property?* may I not likewise answer, *It is robbery,* without the certainty of being misunderstood; the second proposition being no other than a transformation of the first?

Pierre Proudhon,
What Is Property?

No one can doubt, that the convention for the distinction of property, and for the stability of possession, is of all circumstances the most necessary to the establishment of human society, and that after the agreement for the fixing and observing of this rule, there remains little or nothing to be done towards settling a perfect harmony and concord.

David Hume,
Treatise of Human Nature

OVERVIEW

While the materials of Part Two introduced the reader to some of the main attempts to understand property, the materials of this last part concern questions of justification. We have chosen to organize the selections here along thematic lines reflecting what we take to be some of the central concerns in both classical and contemporary writings. To be sure, there is significant overlap: The issues raised in the earlier sections are reconsidered in these. But one will generally notice revealing shifts in perspective and changes in emphasis.

Section One focuses on the connection between labor and ownership: the "labor theory" of property. Does the fact that someone has made something provide a justifying basis for a claim of ownership? Does it always do this, or are there occasions when labor alone will not suffice to ground a property right? Section Two explores the relevance of patterns of distribution of goods within society. It is common for systems of property to be associated with wide variations in the amounts owned by people: great wealth can exist side by side with extreme poverty. Do these inequalities provide the basis for rejecting or revising our social practices? Section Three contains materials that discuss the relationships between the private interests of property owners and the public interest, between the individual holder of property and the community itself. A recurring question here involves compensation for takings: When the community determines that it cannot allow the private ownership of something—a slave or a plot of land—when must it pay compensation to the owner who has been dispossessed? The fourth and last section looks at property in the context of the modern economy. Considered here are contemporary questions involving governmental regulation of property, employment contracts, modernization, pollution, and corporate responsibility.

The materials here have been assembled with the intention of achieving great diversity in the collection and providing an antidote to the tendency to give quick answers to questions involved in justifying property. We hope to have contributed to the effort to formulate responsible judgments on these most basic of social issues.

SECTION ONE
THE LABOR THEORY
OF PROPERTY

The moral force of the claim "It is mine because I made it" has probably always been recognized. But it is safe to say that this "labor principle" did not acquire its central place in Western theorizing about property until the seventeenth century. That is, the notion of labor as a sufficient condition for title to property—independent of considerations of utility, convention, and divine law—did not emerge in a theoretically powerful form until then. The classic text is Chapter V of John Locke's *Second Treatise of Government* (1690).

Locke apparently had at least two distinct labor theories. One, standardly quoted, starts with the idea that people own their own bodies and, hence, their labor. People thus own whatever things they "mix" their labor with or "add value" to. The second theory proceeds from the observations that labor is painful and is the source of most of what is of value to us. Since people would not work if they could not expect some benefit from it, it would be unjust not to let them have what they want (and deserve?): namely, a property right in the things produced by their labor. Both theories are subject to the restrictions that people are entitled only to as much as they can use, and must leave "enough and as good" for others.

As is the case with many works that break new ground, Locke's essay is not always easy to follow and contains much that is puzzling or illogical.

Most of these defects, however, arise from deep problems within the labor theory itself—problems which remain unsolved to this day. Robert Nozick in his discussion of "Locke's Theory of Acquisition" (from his recent book *Anarchy, State and Utopia*) elegantly summarizes the difficulties with Locke's labor theory of property. Particular attention should be paid to what he calls the Lockean "proviso"—the restriction that one must leave "enough and as good" for others, or at any rate, not leave them worse off than they were. At what point does Locke's labor theory become inapplicable in appropriating scarce resources in a crowded world?

As we shall see in later sections, Locke's arguments have been targets of abuse for nearly three centuries by both friends and foes of private property. But the driving force behind them—the notion that the people who work to produce things have a special claim upon us—is a powerful idea. Libertarians use the idea as a barrier against social control of property: "If I *earned* it, what right do you have to tax it or to tell me what to do with it?" Socialists use the idea to attack capitalism: "If the workers are entitled to the value of the goods they produce, then they are entitled to the *whole* value. Idle capitalists are not entitled to skim off 'surplus value' as profits." Everyone, however, must face the same problem that Locke had: How do you prove that the special claims of laborers amount to property rights? Why doesn't labor just entitle people to our gratitude, and to an equal share in the sum total of what we all produce?

Of Property

JOHN LOCKE

25. Whether we consider natural reason, which tells us that men being once born have a right to their preservation, and consequently to meat and drink and such other things as nature affords for their subsistence; or revelation, which gives us an account of those grants God made of the world to Adam, and to Noah and his sons, 'tis very clear that God, as King David says, Psalm cxv. 16, "has given the earth to the children of men," given it to mankind in common. But this being supposed, it seems to some a very great difficulty how anyone should ever come to have a property in anything. I will not content myself to answer that if it be difficult to make out property upon a supposition that God gave the world to Adam and his posterity in common, it is impossible that any man but one universal monarch should have any property upon a supposition

From *Second Treatise of Government* by John Locke.

that God gave the world to Adam and his heirs in succession, exclusive of all the rest of his posterity. But I shall endeavor to show how men might come to have a property in several parts of that which God gave to mankind in common, and that without any express compact of all the commoners.

26. God, who hath given the world to men in common, hath also given them reason to make use of it to the best advantage of life and convenience. The earth and all that is therein is given to men for the support and comfort of their being. And though all the fruits it naturally produces, and beasts it feeds, belong to mankind in common, as they are produced by the spontaneous hand of nature; and nobody has originally a private dominion exclusive of the rest of mankind in any of them as they are thus in their natural state; yet being given for the use of men, there must of necessity be a means to appropriate them some way or other before they can be of any use or at all beneficial to any particular man. The fruit or venison which nourishes the wild Indian, who knows no enclosure, and is still a tenant in common, must be his, and so his, i.e., a part of him, that another can no longer have any right to it, before it can do any good for the support of his life.

27. Though the earth and all inferior creatures be common to all men, yet every man has a property in his own person; this nobody has any right to but himself. The labor of his body and the work of his hands we may say are properly his. Whatsoever, then, he removes out of the state that nature hath provided and left it in, he hath mixed his labor with, and joined to it something that is his own, and thereby makes it his property. It being by him removed from the common state nature placed it in, it hath by this labor something annexed to it that excludes the common right of other men. For this labor being the unquestionable property of the laborer, no man but he can have a right to what that is once joined to, at least where there is enough, and as good left in common for others.

28. He that is nourished by the acorns he picked up under an oak or the apples he gathered from the trees in the wood, has certainly appropriated them to himself. Nobody can deny but the nourishment is his. I ask, then, When did they begin to be his—when he digested, or when he ate, or when he boiled, or when he brought them home, or when he picked them up? And 'tis plain if the first gathering made them not his, nothing else could. That labor put a distinction between them and common; that added something to them more than nature, the common mother of all, had done, and so they became his private right. And will anyone say he had no right to those acorns or apples he thus appropriated, because he had not the consent of all mankind to make them his? Was it a robbery thus to assume to himself what belonged to all in common? If such a consent as that was necessary, man had starved, notwithstanding the plenty God had given him. We see in commons which remain so by compact that 'tis the taking any part of what is common and removing it out of the state nature leaves it in, which begins the property; without which the common is of no use. And the taking of this or that part does not depend on the express consent of all the commoners. Thus

the grass my horse has bit, the turfs my servant has cut, and the ore I have dug in any place where I have a right to them in common with others, become my property without the assignation or consent of anybody. The labor that was mine removing them out of that common state they were in, hath fixed my property in them.

29. By making an explicit consent of every commoner necessary to anyone's appropriating to himself any part of what is given in common. Children or servants could not cut the meat which their father or master had provided for them in common without assigning to everyone his peculiar part. Though the water running in the fountain be everyone's, yet who can doubt but that in the pitcher is his only who drew it out? His labor hath taken it out of the hands of Nature where it was common, and belonged equally to all her children, and hath thereby appropriated it to himself.

30. Thus this law of reason makes the deer that Indian's who hath killed it; it is allowed to be his goods who hath bestowed his labor upon it, though, before, it was the common right of everyone. And amongst those who are counted the civilized part of mankind, who have made and multiplied positive laws to determine property, this original law of nature for the beginning of property, in what was before common, still takes place, and by virtue thereof, what fish anyone catches in the ocean, that great and still remaining common of mankind; or what ambergris anyone takes up here is by the labor that removes it out of that common state nature left it in, made his property who takes that pains about it. And even amongst us, the hare that anyone is hunting is thought his who pursues her during the chase. For being a beast that is still looked upon as common, and no man's private possession, whoever has employed so much labor about any of that kind as to find and pursue her has thereby removed her from the state of nature wherein she was common, and hath began a property.

31. It will perhaps be objected to this, that if gathering the acorns, or other fruits of the earth, etc., makes a right to them, then anyone may engross as much as he will. To which I answer, Not so. The same law of nature that does by this means give us property, does also bound that property too. "God has given us all things richly" (I Tim. vi. 17), is the voice of reason confirmed by inspiration. But how far has He given it us? To enjoy. As much as anyone can make use of to any advantage of life before it spoils, so much he may by his labor fix a property in; whatever is beyond this, is more than his share, and belongs to others. Nothing was made by God for man to spoil or destroy. And thus considering the plenty of natural provisions there was a long time in the world, and the few spenders, and to how small a part of that provision the industry of one man could extend itself, and engross it to the prejudice of others—especially keeping within the bounds, set by reason, of what might serve for his use—there could be then little room for quarrels or contentions about property so established.

32. But the chief matter of property being now not the fruits of the earth, and the beasts that subsist on it, but the earth itself, as that which

takes in and carries with it all the rest, I think it is plain that property in that, too, is acquired as the former. As much land as a man tills, plants, improves, cultivates, and can use the product of, so much is his property. He by his labor does as it were enclose it from the common. Nor will it invalidate his right to say, everybody else has an equal title to it; and therefore he cannot appropriate, he cannot enclose, without the consent of all his fellow-commoners, all mankind. God, when He gave the world in common to all mankind, commanded man also to labor, and the penury of his condition required it of him. God and his reason commanded him to subdue the earth, i.e., improve it for the benefit of life, and therein lay out something upon it that was his own, his labor. He that, in obedience to this command of God, subdued, tilled, and sowed any part of it, thereby annexed to it something that was his property, which another had no title to, nor could without injury take from him.

33. Nor was this appropriation of any parcel of land, by improving it, any prejudice to any other man, since there was still enough and as good left; and more than the yet unprovided could use. So that in effect there was never the less left for others because of his enclosure for himself. For he that leaves as much as another can make use of, does as good as take nothing at all. Nobody could think himself injured by the drinking of another man, though he took a good draught, who had a whole river of the same water left him to quench his thirst; and the case of land and water, where there is enough of both, is perfectly the same.

34. God gave the world to men in common; but since He gave it them for their benefit, and the greatest conveniences of life they were capable to draw from it, it cannot be supposed He meant it should always remain common and uncultivated. He gave it to the use of the industrious and rational (and labor was to be his title to it), not to the fancy or covetousness of the quarrelsome and contentious. He that had as good left for his improvement as was already taken up, needed not complain, ought not to meddle with what was already improved by another's labor; if he did, it is plain he desired the benefit of another's pains, which he had no right to, and not the ground which God had given him in common with others to labor on, and whereof there was as good left as that already possessed, and more than he knew what to do with, or his industry could reach to.

35. It is true, in land that is common in England, or any other country where there is plenty of people under Government, who have money and commerce, no one can enclose or appropriate any part without the consent of all his fellow-commoners: because this is left common by compact, i.e., by the law of the land, which is not to be violated. And though it be common in respect of some men, it is not so to all mankind; but is the joint property of this country, or this parish. Besides, the remainder, after such enclosure, would not be as good to the rest of the commoners as the whole was, when they could all make use of the whole; whereas in the beginning and first peopling of the great common of the world it was quite otherwise. The law man was under was rather for appropriating. God commanded, and his wants forced him, to labor. That

was his property, which could not be taken from him wherever he had fixed it. And hence subduing or cultivating the earth, and having dominion, we see are joined together. The one gave title to the other. So that God, by commanding to subdue, gave authority so far to appropriate. And the condition of human life, which requires labor and materials to work on, necessarily introduces private possessions.

36. The measure of property nature has well set by the extent of men's labor and the conveniency of life. No man's labor could subdue or appropriate all, nor could his enjoyment consume more than a small part; so that it was impossible for any man, this way, to entrench upon the right of another or acquire to himself a property to the prejudice of his neighbor, who would still have room for as good and as large a possession (after the other had taken out his) as before it was appropriated. Which measure did confine every man's possession to a very moderate proportion, and such as he might appropriate to himself without injury to anybody in the first ages of the world, when men were more in danger to be lost, by wandering from their company, in the then vast wilderness of the earth than to be straitened for want of room to plant in.

The same measure may be allowed still, without prejudice to anybody, full as the world seems. For, supposing a man or family, in the state they were at first, peopling of the world by the children of Adam or Noah, let him plant in some inland vacant places of America. We shall find that the possessions he could make himself, upon the measures we have given, would not be very large, nor, even to this day, prejudice the rest of mankind or give them reason to complain or think themselves injured by this man's encroachment, though the race of men have now spread themselves to all the corners of the world, and do infinitely exceed the small number was at the beginning. Nay, the extent of ground is of so little value without labor that I have heard it affirmed that in Spain itself a man may be permitted to plough, sow, and reap, without being disturbed, upon land he has no other title to, but only his making use of it. But, on the contrary, the inhabitants think themselves beholden to him who, by his industry on neglected, and consequently waste land, has increased the stock of corn, which they wanted. But be this as it will, which I lay no stress on, this I dare boldly affirm, that the same rule of propriety—viz., that every man should have as much as he could make use of, would hold still in the world, without straitening anybody, since there is land enough in the world to suffice double the inhabitants, had not the invention of money, and the tacit agreement of men to put a value on it, introduced (by consent) larger possessions and a right to them; which, how it has done, I shall by and by show more at large.

37. This is certain, that in the beginning, before the desire of having more than man needed had altered the intrinsic value of things, which depends only on their usefulness to the life of man; or had agreed that a little piece of yellow metal which would keep without wasting or decay should be worth a great piece of flesh or a whole heap of corn, though men had a right to appropriate by their labor, each one to himself, as much of the things of nature as he could use, yet this could not be much,

nor to the prejudice of others, where the same plenty was still left to those who would use the same industry.

Before the appropriation of land, he who gathered as much of the wild fruit, killed, caught, or tamed as many of the beasts as he could; he that so employed his pains about any of the spontaneous products of nature as any way to alter them from the state which nature put them in, by placing any of his labor on them, did thereby acquire a propriety in them. But if they perished in his possession without their due use; if the fruits rotted, or the venison putrefied before he could spend it, he offended against the common law of nature, and was liable to be punished; he invaded his neighbor's share, for he had no right further than his use called for any of them and they might serve to afford him conveniences of life.

38. The same measures governed the possessions of land, too. Whatsoever he tilled and reaped, laid up, and made use of before it spoiled, that was his peculiar right; whatsoever he enclosed and could feed and make use of, the cattle and product was also his. But if either the grass of his enclosure rotted on the ground, or the fruit of his planting perished without gathering and laying up, this part of the earth, notwithstanding his enclosure, was still to be looked on as waste, and might be the possession of any other. Thus, at the beginning, Cain might take as much ground as he could till and make it his own land, and yet leave enough for Abel's sheep to feed on; a few acres would serve for both their possessions. But as families increased, and industry enlarged their stocks, their possessions enlarged with the need of them; but yet it was commonly without any fixed property in the ground they made use of, till they incorporated, settled themselves together, and built cities; and then, by consent, they came in time to set out the bounds of their distinct territories, and agree on limits between them and their neighbors, and, by laws within themselves, settled the properties of those of the same society. For we see that in that part of the world which was first inhabited, and therefore like to be best peopled, even as low down as Abraham's time, they wandered with their flocks and their herds, which was their substance, freely up and down—and this Abraham did in a country where he was a stranger; whence it is plain that, at least, a great part of the land lay in common, that the inhabitants valued it not, nor claimed property in any more than they made use of; but when there was not room enough in the same place for their herds to feed together, they, by consent, as Abraham and Lot did (Gen. xiii. 5), separated and enlarged their pasture where it best liked them. And for the same reason, Esau went from his father and his brother, and planted in Mount Seir (Gen. xxxvi. 6).

39. And thus, without supposing any private dominion and property in Adam over all the world, exclusive of all other men, which can no way be proved, nor any one's property be made out from it, but supposing the world, given as it was to the children of men in common, we see how labor could make men distinct titles to several parcels of it for their private uses, wherein there could be no doubt of right, no room for quarrel.

40. Nor is it so strange, as perhaps before consideration it may appear, that the property of labor should be able to overbalance the community of land. For it is labor indeed that puts the difference of value on everything; and let anyone consider what the difference is between an acre of land planted with tobacco or sugar, sown with wheat or barley, and an acre of the same land lying in common without any husbandry upon it, and he will find that the improvement of labor makes the far greater part of the value. I think it will be but a very modest computation to say that of the products of the earth useful to the life of man nine-tenths are the effects of labor; nay, if we will rightly estimate things as they come to our use, and cast up the several expenses about them—what in them is purely owing to nature, and what to labor—we shall find that in most of them ninety-nine hundredths are wholly to be put on the account of labor.

41. There cannot be a clearer demonstration of anything than several nations of the Americans are of this, who are rich in land and poor in all the comforts of life; whom nature, having furnished as liberally as any other people with the materials of plenty—i.e., a fruitful soil, apt to produce in abundance what might serve for food, raiment, and delight; yet, for want of improving it by labor, have not one hundredth part of the conveniences we enjoy, and a king of a large and fruitful territory there feeds, lodges, and is clad worse than a day laborer in England.

42. To make this a little clearer, let us but trace some of the ordinary provisions of life, through their several progresses, before they come to our use, and see how much they receive of their value from human industry. Bread, wine, and cloth are things of daily use and great plenty; yet, notwithstanding, acorns, water, and leaves or skins, must be our bread, drink, and clothing, did not labor furnish us with these more useful commodities. For whatever bread is more worth than acorns, wine than water, and cloth or silk than leaves, skins, or moss, that is wholly owing to labor and industry: the one of these being the food and raiment which unassisted nature furnishes us with; the other, provisions which our industry and pains prepare for us; which how much they exceed the other in value when anyone hath computed, he will then see how much labor makes the far greatest part of the value of things we enjoy in this world. And the ground which produces the materials is scarce to be reckoned in as any, or at most but a very small part of it; so little that even amongst us land that is left wholly to nature, that hath no improvement of pasturage, tillage, or planting, is called, as indeed it is, "waste," and we shall find the benefit of it amount to little more than nothing.

43. An acre of land that bears here twenty bushels of wheat, and another in America which, with the same husbandry, would do the like, are without doubt of the same natural intrinsic value; but yet the benefit mankind receives from the one in a year is worth £5, and from the other possibly not worth a penny, if all the profit an Indian received from it were to be valued and sold here; at least, I may truly say, not one-thousandth. 'Tis labor, then, which puts the greatest part of value upon land, without which it would scarcely be worth anything; 'tis to

that we owe the greatest part of all its useful products, for all that the straw, bran, bread, of that acre of wheat is more worth than the product of an acre of as good land which lies waste, is all the effect of labor. For 'tis not barely the ploughman's pains, the reaper's and thresher's toil, and the baker's sweat, is to be counted into the bread we eat; the labor of those who broke the oxen, who dug and wrought the iron and stones, who felled and framed the timber employed about the plough, mill, oven, or any other utensils, which are a vast number, requisite to this corn, from its sowing, to its being made bread, must all be charged on the account of labor, and received as an effect of that. Nature and the earth furnished only the almost worthless materials as in themselves. 'Twould be a strange catalogue of things that industry provided, and made use of, about every loaf of bread before it came to our use, if we could trace them—iron, wood, leather, bark, timber, stone, bricks, coals, lime, cloth, dyeing drugs, pitch, tar, masts, ropes, and all the materials made use of in the ship that brought any of the commodities made use of by any of the workmen to any part of the work all which it would be almost impossible—at least, too long—to reckon up.

44. From all which it is evident that, though the things of nature are given in common, yet man, by being master of himself and proprietor of his own person and the actions or labor of it, had still in himself the great foundation of property; and that which made up the great part of what he applied to the support or comfort of his being, when invention and arts had improved the conveniences of life, was perfectly his own, and did not belong in common to others.

45. Thus labor, in the beginning, gave a right of property, wherever anyone was pleased to employ it upon what was common, which remained a long while the far greater part, and is yet more than mankind makes use of. Men at first, for the most part, contented themselves with what unassisted nature offered to their necessities; and though afterwards, in some parts of the world (where the increase of people and stock, with the use of money, had made land scarce, and so of some value), the several communities settled the bounds of their distinct territories, and, by laws within themselves, regulated the properties of the private men of their society, and so, by compact and agreement, settled the property which labor and industry began—and the leagues that have been made between several states and kingdoms, either expressly or tacitly disowning all claim and right to the land in the other's possession, have, by common consent, given up their pretenses to their natural common right, which originally they had to those countries; and so have, by positive agreement, settled a property amongst themselves in distinct parts of the world—yet there are still great tracts of ground to be found which, the inhabitants thereof not having joined with the rest of mankind in the consent of the use of their common money, lie waste, and are more than the people who dwell on it do or can make use of, and so still lie in common; though this can scarce happen amongst that part of mankind that have consented to the use of money.

46. The greatest part of things really useful to the life of man, and

such as the necessity of subsisting made the first commoners of the world look after, as it doth the Americans now, are generally things of short duration, such as, if they are not consumed by use, will decay and perish of themselves: gold, silver, and diamonds are things that fancy or agreement have put the value on more than real use and the necessary support of life. Now, of those good things which nature hath provided in common, everyone hath a right, as hath been said, to as much as he could use, and had a property in all he could effect with his labor—all that his industry could extend to, to alter from the state nature had put it in, was his. He that gathered a hundred bushels of acorns or apples had thereby a property in them; they were his goods as soon as gathered. He was only to look that he used them before they spoiled, else he took more than his share, and robbed others; and, indeed, it was a foolish thing, as well as dishonest, to hoard up more than he could make use of. If he gave away a part to anybody else, so that it perished not uselessly in his possession, these he also made use of; and if he also bartered away plums that would have rotted in a week, for nuts that would last good for his eating a whole year, he did no injury; he wasted not the common stock, destroyed no part of the portion of goods that belonged to others, so long as nothing perished uselessly in his hands. Again, if he would give his nuts for a piece of metal, pleased with its color, or exchange his sheep for shells, or wool for a sparkling pebble or a diamond, and keep those by him all his life, he invaded not the right of others; he might heap up as much of these durable things as he pleased, the exceeding of the bounds of his just property not lying in the largeness of his possessions, but the perishing of anything uselessly in it.

47. And thus came in the use of money—some lasting thing that men might keep without spoiling, and that, by mutual consent, men would take in exchange for the truly useful but perishable supports of life.

48. And as different degrees of industry were apt to give men possessions in different proportions, so this invention of money gave them the opportunity to continue and enlarge them; for supposing an island, separate from all possible commerce with the rest of the world, wherein there were but a hundred families—but there were sheep, horses, and cows, with other useful animals, wholesome fruits, and land enough for corn for a hundred thousand times as many, but nothing in the island, either because of its commonness or perishableness, fit to supply the place of money—what reason could anyone have there to enlarge his possessions beyond the use of his family and a plentiful supply to its consumption, either in what their own industry produced, or they could barter for like perishable useful commodities with others? Where there is not something both lasting and scarce, and so valuable to be hoarded up, there men will not be apt to enlarge their possessions of land, were it never so rich, never so free for them to take; for I ask, what would a man value ten thousand or a hundred thousand acres of excellent land, ready cultivated, and well stocked too with cattle, in the middle of the inland parts of America, where he had no hopes of commerce with other parts of the

world, to draw money to him by the sale of the product? It would not be worth the enclosing, and we should see him give up again to the wild common of nature whatever was more than would supply the conveniences of life to be had there for him and his family.

49. Thus in the beginning all the world was America, and more so than is now, for no such thing as money was anywhere known. Find out something that hath the use and value of money amongst his neighbors, you shall see the same man will begin presently to enlarge his possessions.

50. But since gold and silver, being little useful to the life of man in proportion to food, raiment, and carriage, has its value only from the consent of men, whereof labor yet makes, in great part, the measure, it is plain that the consent of men have agreed to a disproportionate and unequal possession of the earth—I mean out of the bounds of society and compact; for in governments the laws regulate it; they having, by consent, found out and agreed in a way how a man may rightfully and without injury possess more than he himself can make use of by receiving gold and silver, which may continue long in a man's possession, without decaying for the overplus, and agreeing those metals should have a value.

51. And thus, I think, it is very easy to conceive without any difficulty how labor could at first begin a title of property in the common things of nature, and how the spending it upon our uses bounded it; so that there could then be no reason of quarrelling about title, nor any doubt about the largeness of possession it gave. Right and conveniency went together; for as a man had a right to all he could employ his labor upon, so he had no temptation to labor for more than he could make use of. This left no room for controversy about the title, nor for encroachment on the right of others; what portion a man carved to himself was easily seen, and it was useless, as well as dishonest, to carve himself too much, or take more than he needed.

Locke's Theory of Acquisition

ROBERT NOZICK

Locke views property rights in an unowned object as originating through someone's mixing his labor with it. This gives rise to many questions. What are the boundaries of what labor is mixed with? If a private

From pp. 174–178 of *Anarchy, State and Utopia* by Robert Nozick. Copyright © 1974 by Basic Books, Inc. Reprinted by permission of the author and the publishers, Basic Books, Inc., and Basil Blackwell. Footnotes renumbered.

astronaut clears a place on Mars, has he mixed his labor with (so that he comes to own) the whole planet, the whole uninhabited universe, or just a particular plot? Which plot does an act bring under ownership? The minimal (possibly disconnected) area such that an act decreases entropy in that area, and not elsewhere? Can virgin land (for the purposes of eco-logical investigation by high-flying airplane) come under ownership by a Lockean process? Building a fence around a territory presumably would make one the owner of only the fence (and the land immediately under-neath it).

Why does mixing one's labor with something make one the owner of it? Perhaps because one owns one's labor, and so one comes to own a previously unowned thing that becomes permeated with what one owns. Ownership seeps over into the rest. But why isn't mixing what I own with what I don't own a way of losing what I own rather than a way of gaining what I don't? If I own a can of tomato juice and spill it in the sea so that its molecules (made radioactive, so I can check this) mingle evenly throughout the sea, do I thereby come to own the sea, or have I foolishly dissipated my tomato juice? Perhaps the idea, instead, is that laboring on something improves it and makes it more valuable; and anyone is entitled to own a thing whose value he has created. (Reinforc-ing this, perhaps, is the view that laboring is unpleasant. If some people made things effortlessly, as the cartoon characters in *The Yellow Subma-rine* trail flowers in their wake, would they have lesser claim to their own products whose making didn't *cost* them anything?) Ignore the fact that laboring on something may make it less valuable (spraying pink enamel paint on a piece of driftwood that you have found). Why should one's entitlement extend to the whole object rather than just to the *added value* one's labor has produced? (Such reference to value might also serve to delimit the extent of ownership; for example, substitute "increases the value of" for "decreases entropy in" in the above entropy criterion.) No workable or coherent value-added property scheme has yet been de-vised, and any such scheme presumably would fall to objections (similar to those) that fell the theory of Henry George.

It will be implausible to view improving an object as giving full ownership to it, if the stock of unowned objects that might be improved is limited. For an object's coming under one person's ownership changes the situation of all others. Whereas previously they were at liberty (in Hoh-feld's sense) to use the object, they now no longer are. This change in the situation of others (by removing their liberty to act on a previously un-owned object) need not worsen their situation. If I appropriate a grain of sand from Coney Island, no one else may now do as they will with *that* grain of sand. But there are plenty of other grains of sand left for them to do the same with. Or if not grains of sand, then other things. Alterna-tively, the things I do with the grain of sand I appropriate might improve the position of others, counterbalancing their loss of the liberty to use that grain. The crucial point is whether appropriation of an unowned object worsens the situation of others.

Locke's proviso that there be "enough and as good left in common for others" (sect. 27) is meant to ensure that the situation of others is not worsened. (If this proviso is met is there any motivation for his further condition of nonwaste?) It is often said that this proviso once held but now no longer does. But there appears to be an argument for the conclusion that if the proviso no longer holds, then it cannot ever have held so as to yield permanent and inheritable property rights. Consider the first person Z for whom there is not enough and as good left to appropriate. The last person Y to appropriate left Z without his previous liberty to act on an object, and so worsened Z's situation. So Y's appropriation is not allowed under Locke's proviso. Therefore the next to last person X to appropriate left Y in a worse position, for X's act ended permissible appropriation. Therefore X's appropriation wasn't permissible. But then the appropriator two from last, W, ended permissible appropriation and so, since it worsened X's position, W's appropriation wasn't permissible. And so on back to the first person A to appropriate a permanent property right.

This argument, however, proceeds too quickly. Someone may be made worse off by another's appropriation in two ways: first, by losing the opportunity to improve his situation by a particular appropriation or any one; and second, by no longer being able to use freely (without appropriation) what he previously could. A *stringent* requirement that another not be made worse off by an appropriation would exclude the first way if nothing else counterbalances the diminution in opportunity, as well as the second. A *weaker* requirement would exclude the second way, though not the first. With the weaker requirement, we cannot zip back so quickly from Z to A, as in the above argument; for though person Z can no longer *appropriate*, there may remain some for him to *use* as before. In this case Y's appropriation would not violate the weaker Lockean condition. (With less remaining that people are at liberty to use, users might face more inconvenience, crowding, and so on; in that way the situation of others might be worsened, unless appropriation stopped far short of such a point.) It is arguable that no one legitimately can complain if the weaker provision is satisfied. However, since this is less clear than in the case of the more stringent proviso, Locke may have intended this stringent proviso by "enough and as good" remaining, and perhaps he meant the nonwaste condition to delay the end point from which the argument zips back.

Is the situation of persons who are unable to appropriate (there being no more accessible and useful unowned objects) worsened by a system allowing appropriation and permanent property? Here enter the various familiar social considerations favoring private property: it increases the social product by putting means of production in the hands of those who can use them most efficiently (profitably); experimentation is encouraged, because with separate persons controlling resources, there is no one person or small group whom someone with a new idea must convince to try it out; private property enables people to decide on the pattern and types of risks they wish to bear, leading to specialized types of risk bearing; private property protects future persons by leading some to hold back resources from current consumption for future markets; it provides alternate sources of employment for unpopular persons who don't have to convince any one person or small group to hire them, and so on. These considerations enter a Lockean theory to support the claim that appropriation of private property satisfies the intent behind the "enough and as good left over" proviso, *not* as a utilitarian justification of property. They enter to rebut the claim that because the proviso is violated no natural right to private property can arise by a Lockean process. The difficulty in working such an argument to show that the proviso is satisfied is in fixing the appropriate baseline for comparison. Lockean appropriation makes people no worse off than they would be *how?*[1] This question of fixing the baseline needs more detailed investigation than we are able to give it here. It would be desirable to have an estimate of the general economic importance of original appropriation in order to see how much leeway there is for differing theories of appropriation and of the location of the baseline. Perhaps this importance can be measured by the percentage of all income that is based upon untransformed raw materials and given resources (rather than upon human actions), mainly rental income representing the unimproved value of land, and the price of raw material *in situ,* and by the percentage of current wealth which represents such income in the past.[2]

We should note that it is not only persons favoring *private* property who need a theory of how property rights ligitimately originate. Those believing in collective property, for example those believing that a group of persons living in an area jointly own the territory, or its mineral resources, also must provide a theory of how such property rights arise; they must show why the persons living there have rights to determine what is done with the land and resources there that persons living elsewhere don't have (with regard to the same land and resources).

Suggestions for Further Reading

A detailed evaluation of the cogency of the labor theory is given in Lawrence C. Becker, *Property Rights: Philosophic Foundations* (London and Boston: Routledge & Kegan Paul, 1977), chap. 4. An extensive account of the historical context of Locke's theory, together with an argument that it

---

[1]Compare this with Robert Paul Wolff's "A Refutation of Rawls' Theorem on Justice," *Journal of Philosophy,* March 31, 1966, sect. 2. Wolff's criticism does not apply to Rawls' conception under which the baseline is fixed by the difference principle.

[2]I have not seen a precise estimate. David Friedman, *The Machinery of Freedom* (N.Y.: Harper & Row, 1973), pp. xiv, xv, discusses this issue and suggests 5 percent of U.S. national income as an upper limit for the first two factors mentioned. However he does not attempt to estimate the percentage of current wealth which is based upon such income in the past. (The vague notion of "based upon" merely indicates a topic needing investigation.)

has been badly misunderstood by writers who ignore its Natural Law origins, may be found in James Tully, *A Discourse on Property: John Locke and His Adversaries* (Cambridge, Eng.: Cambridge University Press, 1980). On the point that the labor theory may well provide the foundation for socialism rather than "possessive individualism," see Hastings Rashdall, "The Philosophical Theory of Property," in J. V. Bartlett, ed., *Property: Its Duties and Rights*, 2d ed. (London: Macmillan, 1915). A helpful discussion of Locke's ideas of property and its place in his political theory is to be found in C. B. Macpherson's *The Political Theory of Possessive Individualism* (London: Oxford University Press, 1962). Note also the discussions by Bentham, Honoré, Rousseau, Mill, George, Cohen, Ellerman, and Schumacher in Sections Two, Three, and Four below.

SECTION TWO
SCARCITY AND
DISTRIBUTION

The three discussions of this section consider, in various ways, the relationships between laws governing property and the distribution of goods within society. Each of the authors is aware that a system of property will affect distribution and that distributions may or may not exhibit equality. How are the relationships between property and distribution to be understood?

David Hume (1711–1776), in his classic discussion reprinted here, invites us to imagine what would happen to our ideas about property if certain very general features of the human condition were different from what they are. If the things we desired to own as property were so abundant that we would not suffer the least inconvenience if we lost everything that was "ours," if the human condition were not, in other words, marked by moderate scarcity of goods, then our laws concerning property would be very different from what they are. And if universal love were the rule in our attitudes toward one another, if each of us felt no more concern for his or her own interests than for those of others, then there would be little point in drawing distinctions between "mine" and "yours." Our ideas about virtue, equity, and justice are thus dependent upon the conditions in which we find ourselves. Hume's emphases here upon moderate scarcity and moderate self-interest are crucial. While we are "partial to ourselves," we are "capable of learning the advantage resulting from a more equitable conduct." In Hume's view, property and justice are finally to be valued in terms of their public "usefulness" under the conditions that appear to obtain for most of us, most of the time.

Jeremy Bentham (1748–1832), one of the founders of modern utilitarianism, finds in the idea of property "nothing but a basis of expectation." While Bentham advocated radical social reforms in a great many areas, when it came to property he saw great risk in any sudden movement toward equality and away from "fixed and durable possession" guaranteed by law. Bentham argued that the legal protection of possession was utterly necessary for security and that security was the foundation for subsistence, abundance, happiness, and life itself. Thus, "[w]hen security and equality are in conflict, it will not do to hesitate a moment. Equality must yield." Even those with no property to protect are better off under laws which protect property.

A. M. Honoré, whom we have considered earlier in Part Two, does not share Bentham's assessment of the tension between property (security) and equality. His criticisms here of Robert Nozick's views are incidental and, of course, cannot be evaluated properly without reading Nozick's *Anarchy, State and Utopia.* What concerns us is his argument that a system of just entitlements to property can be conducive to social equality. Drawing upon the work of economic anthropologists, Honoré tries to show that certain non-Western systems of property law can be both morally defensible (even in terms of the labor theory) *and* inherently redistributive. The critical issue for Honoré is thus not whether to choose property or equality but, rather, how much redistribution to build into our very notion of property.

Of Justice

DAVID HUME

That Justice is useful to society, and consequently that *part* of its merit, at least, must arise from that consideration, it would be a superfluous undertaking to prove. That public utility is the *sole* origin of Justice, and that reflections on the beneficial consequences of this virtue are the *sole* foundation of its merit, this proposition, being more curious and important, will better deserve our examination and inquiry.

Let us suppose that nature has bestowed on the human race such profuse *abundance* of all *external* conveniences that, without any uncer-

From *Inquiry Concerning the Principles of Morals* by David Hume.

tainty in the event, without any care or industry on our part, every individual finds himself fully provided with whatever his most voracious appetites can want or luxurious imagination wish or desire. His natural beauty, we shall suppose, surpasses all acquired ornaments: the perpetual clemency of the seasons renders useless all clothes or covering; the raw herbage affords him the most delicious fare; the clear fountain the richest beverage. No laborious occupation required: no tillage, no navigation. Music, poetry, and contemplation form his sole business; conversation, mirth, and friendship, his sole amusement.

It seems evident that in such a happy state every other social virtue would flourish and receive tenfold increase; but the cautious, jealous virtue of justice would never once have been dreamed of. For what purpose make a partition of goods where everyone has already more than enough? Why give rise to property where there cannot possibly be any injury? Why call this object *mine* when, upon the seizing of it by another, I need but stretch out my hand to possess myself of what is equally valuable? Justice, in that case, being totally *useless*, would be an idle ceremonial and could never possibly have place in the catalogue of virtues.

We see, even in the present necessitous condition of mankind, that, wherever any benefit is bestowed by nature in an unlimited abundance, we leave it always in common among the whole human race and make no subdivisions of right and property. Water and air, though the most necessary of all objects, are not challenged as the property of individuals; nor can any man commit injustice by the most lavish use and enjoyment of these blessings. In fertile, extensive countries, with few inhabitants, land is regarded on the same footing. And no topic is so much insisted on, by those who defend the liberty of the seas, as the unexhausted use of them in navigation. Were the advantages procured by navigation as inexhaustible, these reasoners had never had any adversaries to refute, nor had any claims ever been advanced of a separate, exclusive dominion over the ocean.

It may happen in some countries, at some periods, that there be established a property in water, none in land,[1] if the latter be in greater abundance than can be used by the inhabitants, and the former be found with difficulty and in very small quantities.

Again: suppose that, though the necessities of the human race continue the same as at present, yet the mind is so enlarged and so replete with friendship and generosity that every man has the utmost tenderness for every man, and feels no more concern for his own interest than for that of his fellows: It seems evident that the *use* of Justice would, in this case, be suspended by such an extensive benevolence, nor would the divisions and barriers of property and obligation have ever been thought of. Why should I bind another, by a deed or promise, to do me any good office when I know that he is already prompted by the strongest inclination to seek my happiness and would of himself perform the desired service, except the hurt he thereby receives be greater than the benefit

---

[1]Genesis, Chaps. 13 and 21.

accruing to me; in which case he knows that, from my innate humanity and friendship, I should be the first to oppose myself to his imprudent generosity? Why raise landmarks between my neighbor's field and mine when my heart has made no division between our interests, but shares all his joys and sorrows with the same force and vivacity as if originally my own? Every man, upon this supposition, being a second self to another, would trust all his interests to the discretion of every man without jealousy, without partition, without distinction. And the whole human race would form only one family where all would lie in common and be used freely, without regard to property; but cautiously too, with an entire regard to the necessities of each individual, as if our own interests were most intimately concerned.

In the present disposition of the human heart, it would perhaps be difficult to find complete instances of such enlarged affections; but still we may observe that the case of families approaches toward it; and the stronger the mutual benevolence is among the individuals, the nearer it approaches, till all distinction of property be, in a great measure, lost and confounded among them. Between married persons, the cement of friendship is by the laws supposed so strong as to abolish all division of possessions, and has often, in reality, the force ascribed to it. And it is observable that, during the ardor of new enthusiasms, when every principle is inflamed into extravagance, the community of goods has frequently been attempted; and nothing but experience of its inconveniences, from the returning or disguised selfishness of men, could make the imprudent fanatics adopt anew the ideas of justice and of separate property. So true is it that this virtue derives its existence entirely from its necessary *use* to the intercourse and social state of mankind.

To make this truth more evident, let us reverse the foregoing suppositions and, carrying everything to the opposite extreme, consider what would be the effect of these new situations. Suppose a society to fall into such want of all common necessaries that the utmost frugality and industry cannot preserve the greater number from perishing and the whole from extreme misery: it will readily, I believe, be admitted that the strict laws of justice are suspended in such a pressing emergency and give place to the stronger motives of necessity and self-preservation. Is it any crime, after a shipwreck, to seize whatever means or instrument of safety one can lay hold of, without regard to former limitations of property? Or if a city besieged were perishing with hunger, can we imagine that men will see any means of preservation before them and lose their lives from a scrupulous regard to what, in other situations, would be the rules of equity and justice? The *use* and *tendency* of that virtue is to procure happiness and security, by preserving order in society. But where the society is ready to perish from extreme necessity, no greater evil can be dreaded from violence and injustice, and every man may now provide for himself by all the means which prudence can dictate or humanity permit. The public, even in less urgent necessities, opens granaries without the consent of proprietors, as justly supposing that the authority of magistracy may, consistent with equity, extend so far. But were any number of men to

assemble without the tie of laws or civil jurisdiction, would an equal partition of bread in a famine, though effected by power and even violence, be
regarded as criminal or injurious?

Suppose, likewise, that it should be a virtuous man's fate to fall into
the society of ruffians, remote from the protection of laws and government, what conduct must he embrace in that melancholy situation? He
sees such a desperate rapaciousness prevail, such a disregard to equity,
such contempt of order, such stupid blindness to future consequences, as
must immediately have the most tragical conclusion and must terminate
in destruction to the greater number and in a total dissolution of society
to the rest. He, meanwhile, can have no other expedient than to arm
himself, to whomever the sword he seizes, or the buckler, may belong; to
make provision of all means of defense and security. And his particular
regard to justice being no longer of *use* to his own safety or that of others,
he must consult the dictates of self-preservation alone, without concern
for those who no longer merit his care and attention.

When any man, even in political society, renders himself by his
crimes obnoxious to the public, he is punished by the laws in his goods
and person; that is, the ordinary rules of justice are, with regard to him,
suspended for a moment, and it becomes equitable to inflict on him, for
the *benefit* of society, what otherwise he could not suffer without wrong or
injury.

The rage and violence of public war, what is it but a suspension of
justice among the warring parties who perceive that this virtue is now no
longer of any *use* or advantage to them? The laws of war, which then
succeed to those of equity and justice, are rules calculated for the *advantage* and *utility* of that particular state in which men are now placed. And
were a civilized nation engaged with barbarians who observed no rules
even of war, the former must also suspend their observance of them
where they no longer serve to any purpose, and must render every
action or rencounter as bloody and pernicious as possible to the first
aggressors.

Thus the rules of equity or justice depend entirely on the particular
state and condition in which men are placed, and owe their origin and
existence to that *utility* which results to the public from their strict and
regular observance. Reverse, in any considerable circumstance, the condition of men: produce extreme abundance or extreme necessity, implant
in the human breast perfect moderation and humanity or perfect rapaciousness and malice; by rendering justice totally *useless,* you thereby totally destroy its essence and suspend its obligation upon mankind.

The common situation of society is a medium amidst all these extremes. We are naturally partial to ourselves and to our friends, but are
capable of learning the advantage resulting from a more equitable conduct. Few enjoyments are given us from the open and liberal hand of
nature; but by art, labor, and industry we can extract them in great
abundance. Hence the ideas of property become necessary in all civil
society; hence justice derives its usefulness to the public; and hence alone
arises its merit and moral obligation.

• • •

If we examine the *particular* laws by which justice is directed and property determined, we shall still be presented with the same conclusions. The good of mankind is the only object of all these laws and regulations. Not only is it requisite for the peace and interest of society that men's possessions should be separated, but the rules which we follow in making the separation are such as can best be contrived to serve further the interests of society.

From Principles of the Civil Code

JEREMY BENTHAM

CHAPTER VII: OF SECURITY

We come now to the principle object of law,—the care of security. That inestimable good, the distinctive index of civilization, is entirely the work of law. Without law there is no security; and, consequently, no abundance, and not even a certainty of subsistence; and the only equality which can exist in such a state of things is an equality of misery.

To form a just idea of the benefits of law, it is only necessary to consider the condition of savages. They strive incessantly against famine; which sometimes cuts off entire tribes. Rivalry for subsistence produces among them the most cruel wars; and, like beasts of prey, men pursue men, as a means of sustenance. The fear of this terrible calamity silences the softer sentiments of nature; pity unites with insensibility in putting to death the old men who can hunt no longer.

Let us now examine what passes at those terrible epochs when civilized society returns almost to the savage state; that is, during war, when the laws on which security depends are in part suspended. Every instant of its duration is fertile in calamities; at every step which it prints upon the earth, at every movement which it makes, the existing mass of riches, the fund of abundance and of subsistence, decreases and disappears. The cottage is ravaged as well as the palace; and how often the rage, the caprice even of a moment, delivers up to destruction the slow produce of the labours of an age!

Law alone has done that which all the natural sentiments united have not the power to do. Law alone is able to create a fixed and durable possession which merits the name of property. Law alone can accustom men to bow their heads under the yoke of foresight, hard at first to bear, but afterwards light and agreeable. Nothing but law can encourage men to labours superfluous for the present, and which can be enjoyed only in the future. Economy has as many enemies as there are dissipators—men who wish to enjoy without giving themselves the trouble of producing. Labour is too painful for idleness; it is too slow for impatience. Fraud and injustice secretly conspire to appropriate its fruits. Insolence and audacity think to ravish them by open force. Thus security is assailed on every side—ever threatened, never tranquil, it exists in the midst of alarms. The legislator needs a vigilance always sustained, a power always in action, to defend it against this crowd of indefatigable enemies.

Law does not say to man, *Labour, and I will reward you;* but it says: *Labour, and I will assure to you the enjoyment of the fruits of your labor—that natural and sufficient recompense which without me you cannot preserve; I will insure it by arresting the hand which may seek to ravish it from you.* If industry creates, it is law which preserves; if at the first moment we owe all to labour, at the second moment, and at every other, we are indebted for everything to law.

To form a precise idea of the extent to which ought to be given to the principle of security, we must consider that man is not like the animals, limited to the present, whether as respects suffering or enjoyment; but that he is susceptible of pains and pleasures by anticipation; and that it is not enough to secure him from actual loss, but it is necessary also to guarantee him, as far as possible, against future loss. It is necessary to prolong the idea of his security through all the perspective which his imagination is capable of measuring.

This presentiment, which has so marked an influence upon the fate of man, is called *expectation*. It is hence that we have the power of forming a general plan of conduct; it is hence that the successive instants which compose the duration of life are not like isolated and independent points, but become continuous parts of a whole. *Expectation* is a chain which unites our present existence to our future existence, and which passes beyond us to the generation which is to follow. The sensibility of man extends through all the links of this chain.

The principle of security extends to the maintenance of all these expectations; it requires that events, so far as they depend upon laws, should conform to the expectations which law itself has created.

Every attack upon this sentiment produces a distinct and special evil, which may be called a *pain of disappointment.*

It is a proof of great confusion in the ideas of lawyers, that they have never given any particular attention to a sentiment which exercises so powerful an influence upon human life. The word *expectation* is scarcely found in their vocabulary. Scarce a single argument founded upon that principle appears in their writings. They have followed it, without doubt, in many respects; but they have followed it by instinct rather than by reason. If they had known its extreme importance they would not have failed to *name* it and to mark it, instead of leaving it unnoticed in the crowd.

CHAPTER VIII: OF PROPERTY

The better to understand the advantages of law, let us endeavour to form a clear idea of *property*. We shall see that there is no such thing as natural property, and that it is entirely the work of law.

Property is nothing but a basis of expectation; the expectation of deriving certain advantages from a thing which we are said to possess, in consequence of the relation in which we stand towards it.

There is no image, no painting, no visible trait, which can express the relation that constitutes property. It is not material, it is metaphysical; it is a mere conception of the mind.

To have a thing in our hands, to keep it, to make it, to sell it, to work it up into something else, to use it—none of these physical circumstances, nor all united, convey the idea of property. A piece of stuff which is actually in the Indies may belong to me, while the dress I wear may not. The aliment which is incorporated into my very body may belong to another, to whom I am bound to account for it.

The idea of property consists in an established expectation; in the persuasion of being able to draw such or such an advantage from the thing possessed, according to the nature of the case. Now this expectation, this persuasion, can only be the work of law. I cannot count upon the enjoyment of that which I regard as mine, except through the promise of the law which guarantees it to me. It is law alone which permits me to forget my natural weakness. It is only through the protection of law that I am able to inclose a field, and to give myself up to its cultivation with the sure though distant hope of harvest.

But it may be asked, What is it that serves as a basis to law, upon which to begin operations, when it adopts objects which, under the name of property, it promises to protect? Have not men, in the primitive state, a *natural* expectation of enjoying certain things—an expectation drawn from sources anterior to law?

Yes. There have been from the beginning, and there always will be, circumstances in which a man may secure himself, by his own means, in the enjoyment of certain things. But the catalogue of these cases is very limited. The savage who has killed a deer may hope to keep it for himself, so long as his cave is undiscovered; so long as he watches to defend it, and is stronger than his rivals; but that is all. How miserable and precarious is such a possession! If we suppose the least agreement among savages to respect the acquisitions of each other, we see the introduction of a principle to which no name can be given but that of law. A feeble and momentary expectation may result from time to time from circumstances purely physical; but a strong and permanent expectation can result only from law. That which, in the natural state, was an almost invisible thread, in the social state becomes a cable.

Property and law are born together, and die together. Before laws were made there was no property; take away laws, and property ceases.

As regards property, security consists in receiving no check, no shock, no derangement to the expectation founded on the laws, of enjoying such and such a portion of good. The legislator owes the greatest respect to this expectation which he has himself produced. When he does not contradict it, he does what is essential to the happiness of society; when he disturbs it, he always produces a proportionate sum of evil.

CHAPTER IX: ANSWER TO AN OBJECTION

But perhaps the laws of property are good for those who have property, and oppressive to those who have none. The poor man, perhaps, is more miserable than he would be without laws.

The laws, in creating property, have created riches only in relation to poverty. Poverty is not the work of the laws; it is the primitive condition of the human race. The man who subsists only from day to day is precisely the man of nature—the savage. The poor man, in civilized society, obtains nothing, I admit, except by painful labour; but, in the natural state, can he obtain anything except by the sweat of his brow? Has not the chase its fatigues, fishing its dangers, and war its uncertainties? And if man seems to love this adventurous life; if he has an instinct warm for this kind of perils; if the savage enjoys with delight an idleness so dearly bought;—must we thence conclude that he is happier than our cultivators? No. Their labour is more uniform, but their reward is more sure; the woman's lot is far more agreeable; childhood and old age have more resources; the species multiplies in a proportion a thousand times greater,—and that alone suffices to show on which side is the superiority of happiness. Thus the laws, in creating riches, are the benefactors of those who remain in the poverty of nature. All participate more or less in the pleasures, the advantages, and the resources of civilized society. The industry and the labour of the poor place them among the candidates of fortune. And have they not the pleasures of acquisition? Does not hope mix with their labours? Is the security which the law gives of no importance to them? Those who look down from above upon the inferior ranks see all objects smaller; but towards the base of the pyramid it is the summit which in turn is lost. Comparisons are never dreamed of; the wish of what seems impossible does not torment. So that, in fact, all things considered, the protection of the laws may contribute as much to the happiness of the cottage as to the security of the palace.

It is astonishing that a writer so judicious as Beccaria has interposed, in a work dictated by the soundest philosophy, a doubt subversive of social order. *The right of property*, he says, *is a terrible right, which perhaps is not necessary.* Tyrannical and sanguinary laws have been founded upon that right; it has been frightfully abused; but the right itself presents only ideas of pleasure, abundance, and security. It is that right which has vanquished the natural aversion to labour; which has given to man the empire of the earth; which has brought to an end the migratory life of nations; which has produced the love of country and a regard for posterity. Men universally desire to enjoy speedily—to enjoy without labour. It is that desire which is terrible; since it arms all who have not against all who have. The law which restrains that desire is the noblest triumph of humanity over itself.

CHAPTER X: ANALYSIS OF THE EVILS WHICH RESULT FROM ATTACKS UPON PROPERTY

We have already seen that subsistence depends upon the laws which assure to the labourer the produce of his labour. But it is desirable more exactly to analyze the evils which result from violations of property. They may be reduced to four heads.

1st. *Evil of Non-Possession.*—If the acquisition of a portion of wealth is a good, it follows that the non-possession of it is an evil, though only a negative evil. Thus, although men in the condition of primitive poverty may not have specially felt the want of a good which they knew not, yet it is clear that they have lost all the happiness which might have resulted from its possession, and of which we have the enjoyment. The loss of a portion of good, though we knew nothing of it, is still a loss. Are you doing me no harm when, by false representations, you deter my friend from conferring upon me a favour which I did not expect? In what consists the harm? In the negative evil which results from not possessing that which, but for your falsehoods, I should have had.

2nd. *Pain of Losing.*—Everything which I possess, or to which I have a title, I consider in my own mind as destined always to belong to me. I make it the basis of my expectations, and of the hopes of those dependent upon me; and I form my plan of life accordingly. Every part of my property may have, in my estimation, besides its intrinsic value, a value of affection—as an inheritance from my ancestors, as the reward of my own labour, or as the future dependence of my children. Everything about it represents to my eye that part of myself which I have put into it—those cares, that industry, that economy which denied itself present pleasures to make provision for the future. Thus our property becomes a part of our being, and cannot be torn from us without rending us to the quick.

3rd. *Fear of Losing.*—To regret for what we have lost is joined inquietude as to what we possess, and even as to what we may acquire. For the greater part of the objects which compose subsistence and abundance being perishable matters, future acquisitions are a necessary supplement to present possessions. When insecurity reaches a certain point, the fear of losing prevents us from enjoying what we possess already. The care of preserving condemns us to a thousand sad and painful precautions, which yet are always liable to fail of their end. Treasures are hidden or conveyed away. Enjoyment becomes sombre, furtive, and solitary. It fears to show itself, lest cupidity should be informed of a chance to plunder.

4th. *Deadening of Industry.*—When I despair of making myself sure of the produce of my labour, I only seek to exist from day to day. I am unwilling to give myself cares which will only be profitable to my enemies. Besides, the will to labour is not enough; means are wanting. While waiting to reap, in the meantime I must live. A single loss may deprive me of the capacity of action, without having quenched the spirit of industry, or without having paralyzed my will. Thus the three first evils affect the passive faculties of the individual, while the fourth extends to his active faculties, and more or less benumbs them.

It appears from this analysis that the two first evils do not go beyond the individual injured; while the two latter spread through society, and occupy an indefinite space. An attack upon the property of an individual excites alarm among other proprietors. This sentiment spreads from neighbour to neighbour, till at last the contagion possesses the entire body of the state. . . .

CHAPTER XI: OPPOSITION BETWEEN SECURITY AND EQUALITY

In consulting the grand principle of security, what ought the legislator to decree respecting the mass of property already existing?

He ought to maintain the distribution as it is actually established. It is this which, under the name of *justice,* is regarded as his first duty. This is a general and simple rule, which applies itself to all states; and which adapts itself to all places, even those of the most opposite character. There is nothing more different than the state of property in America, in England, in Hungary, and in Russia. Generally, in the first of these countries, the cultivator is a proprietor; in the second, a tenant; in the third, attached to the glebe; in the fourth, a slave. However, the supreme principle of security commands the preservation of all these distributions, though their nature is so different, and though they do not produce the same sum of happiness. How make another distribution without taking away from each that which he has? And how despoil any without attacking the security of all? When your new repartition is disarranged—that is to say, the day after its establishment—how avoid making a second? Why not correct it in the same way? And in the meantime, what becomes of security? Where is happiness? Where is industry?

When security and equality are in conflict, it will not do to hesitate a moment. Equality must yield. The first is the foundation of life; subsistence, abundance, happiness, everything depends upon it. Equality produces only a certain portion of good. Besides, whatever we may do, it will never be perfect; it may exist a day; but the revolutions of the morrow will overturn it. The establishment of perfect equality is a chimera; all we can do is to diminish inequality.

If violent causes, such as a revolution of government, a division, or a conquest, should bring about an overturn of property, it would be a great calamity; but it would be transitory; it would diminish; it would repair itself in time. Industry is a vigorous plant which resists many amputations, and through which a nutritious sap begins to circulate with the first rays of returning summer. But if property should be overturned with the direct intention of establishing an equality of possessions, the evil would be irreparable. No more security, no more industry, no more abundance! Society would return to the savage state whence it emerged. . . .

CHAPTER XII: MEANS OF UNITING
SECURITY AND EQUALITY

Is it necessary that between these two rivals, *Security* and *Equality,* there should be an opposition, an eternal war? To a certain point they are incompatible; but with a little patience and address they may, in a great measure, be reconciled.

The only mediator between these contrary interests is time. Do you wish to follow the counsels of equality without contravening those of security?—await the natural epoch which puts an end to hopes and fears, the epoch of death.

When property by the death of the proprietor ceases to have an owner, the law can interfere in its distribution, either by limiting in certain respects the testamentary power, in order to prevent too great an accumulation of wealth in the hands of an individual; or by regulating the succession in favour of equality in cases where the deceased has left no consort, nor relation in the direct line, and has made no will. The question then relates to new acquirers who have formed no expectations; and equality may do what is best for all without disappointing any. At present I only indicate the principle: the development of it may be seen in the second book.

When the question is to correct a kind of civil inequality, such as slavery, it is necessary to pay the same attention to the right of property; to submit it to a slow operation, and to advance towards the subordinate object without sacrificing the principal object. Men who are rendered free by these gradations, will be much more capable of being so than if you had taught them to tread justice under foot, for the sake of introducing a new social order. . . .

Property, Title and Redistribution

A. M. HONORÉ

This discussion paper is concerned with the relationship between the institution of private property and the notion of economic equality. Is it inconsistent, or morally obtuse to recognize the value of the institution

From pp. 107–115 of Carl Wellman (ed.), *Equality and Freedom: Past, Present and Future,* Beiheft Neue Folge nr. 10, *Archiv für Rechts- und Sozialphilosophie* (Wiesbaden: Franz Steiner Verlag, 1977). © 1977 by *Archiv für Rechts- und Sozialphilosophie.* Reprinted by permission of the author and publisher.

and at the same time to argue that each member of a society is entitled
to an equal or approximately equal standard of living? I shall be particularly concerned with the argument of *R. Nozick,* in *Anarchy, State and
Utopia*[1] to the effect that under a system of 'just entitlements' such as he
specifies there is no room to admit that the state has the right or duty to
redistribute benefits so as to secure an equal or more equal spread,
because 'the particular rights over things fill the space of rights, leaving
no room for general rights to be in a certain material condition'[2].
Though *Nozick's* 'just entitlements'[3] are not confined to titles to property
I shall so confine myself. Rights of a more personal character could in
theory be the subjects of redistribution and indeed *Nozick* discusses the
case for transplanting organs from A to B in order to correct physical
maldistribution of parts of the body[4]. Fascinating as such speculations
may be, the physical and technical difficulties involved in such a programme would be stupendous and the moral objections to the invasion
of people's bodies for whatever purpose are much stronger than they
are when what is proposed is to tax or, in some cases, to expropriate.
Nor can one concede the argument that the redistribution of part of
what A has earned to B goes beyond the invasion of property rights and
amounts to a system of forced labour[5] by which A is compelled to work
part of his day for B, so that redistribution of property is really an
invasion of the status and freedom of the person taxed or expropriated.
This is no more compelling than the Marxist argument that a wage-
earner whose surplus product is appropriated by the employer is a sort
of wageslave. The objection to this is not that the income-earner freely
works under a system in which he knows that part of what he produces
will be appropriated by his employer or transferred to other people by
means of taxes. He may have no choice, if he is to earn a living, but to
accept a system which he dislikes. The argument is open to attack rather
because it rests on the morally questionable view that a person is entitled
to keep exclusively and indefinitely for himself whatever he makes or
produces. This would be true of a man working in complete isolation;
no serious argument has been advanced to show that it is true of a social
being.

   Nozick's argument depends on accepting this questionable view.
Against those who favour a principle of social justice by which things are
to be distributed according to need, desert, the principle of equal claims
or the like, he argues that the just allocation is the historically justifiable

[1]Oxford 1974.
[2]Nozick p. 238.
[3]Nozick pp. 150–182.
[4]Nozick p. 206.
[5]Nozick pp. 169 f, arguing that redistributive arrangements give B a sort of Property
right in A. This mistake stems from the Lockean argument that we own ourselves and *hence*
what we make etc. If human beings are free they cannot own themselves; their relationship
to themselves and their bodies is more like one of "sovereignty" which cannot be alienated or
foregone, though it can be restricted by (lawful) contract or treaty.

one. This can be ascertained, in relation to any given item of property, by asking whether the holder acquired it by a just title or derived his title justly from another who so held it, either originally or by derivation from such a just acquirer. Consequently just distribution depends on just acquisition and transfer, and redistribution is confined to those instances in which the original acquisition or the subsequent transmission of the property was unjust.

All therefore turns on what count as just principles of acquisition and transfer of title. According to *Nozick*—

1. a person who acquires a holding in accordance with the principle of justice in acquisition is entitled to that holding
2. a person who acquires a holding in accordance with the principle of justice in transfer from some one else entitled to the holding is entitled to the holding
3. no one is entitled to a holding except by (repeated) applications of 1 and 2.

The complete principle of distributive justice would say simply that a distribution is just if everyone is entitled to the holdings they possess under the distribution.

What is presupposed by this set of rules for tracing title is apparently only that the principles of acquisition and transfer should be morally respectable. For acquisition something like *Locke's* theory of property is understood[6]. Transfers in a free society will be consensual. But that is only the appearance. What *Nozick* additionally presupposes, without seeking to justify, is that the interest acquired and transmitted is the ownership of property as conceived in western society on the model of Roman law[7]. He is assuming, first, that the acquirer obtains an exclusive right to the thing acquired, that he is entitled, having cleared the land, made the tool etc. to deny access and use to everyone else. Secondly he is supposing that the right acquired is of indefinite duration. The man who has made the clearing can remain there for his lifetime. He is not obliged to move on after so many years, and leave the fruits of his labour to another, nor does he lose his right by leaving. Thirdly the right is supposed to be transmissible inter vivos and on death, so that it can be sold, given, inherited, mortgaged and the like again without limit of time. Under such a system of property law, of course, the initial acquisition is decisive. Once A has cleared the land his neighbours, friends, associates and, if it comes to that, his family are obliged to look on while he enjoys and transmits his 'entitlement' to whomsoever he chooses, irrespective of the fact that in a wider context they, along with him, form part of a single group[8] which is dedicated, among other objects, to the preservation of all. This system of property law, whatever its economic merits, is not self-evidently just. If the interest acquired

[6]Nozick pp. 174 ff.

[7]For an analysis see Honoré, "Ownership", in Guest, *Oxford Essays in Jurisprudence* (London 1961).

[8]For an analysis see Honoré ARSP 61 (1975) 161.

(western type ownership) is greater than can be morally justified, then however just the methods by which A acquires the thing in question and transfers it to X, the distribution of property under which the thing is allocated to X is not thereby saved from criticism. Indeed, quite the contrary. If the interest awarded to owners under the system is greater than can reasonably be justified on moral, as opposed to economic grounds, any distribution of property will be inherently unjust. Hence the intervention of the state will be needed if justice is to be done.

There is no doubt that the *Nozick* rules about just acquisition, transfer and distribution reproduce in outline western systems of property law based on the liberal conception of ownership. According to these notions, ownership is a permanent, exclusive and transmissible interest in property. But this type of property system is neither the only conceivable system, nor the easiest to justify from a moral point of view, nor does it predominate in those societies which are closest to a 'state of nature'.

In so far as the *Nozick* principles are meant to reproduce western property law they are incomplete in that they omit provision for lapse of title and for compulsory acquisition. Lapse of title is not perhaps of great moral importance, but it is worth noting that legal rules about limitation of actions and prescription embody the idea that an owner who neglects his property may be deprived of it. The acquirer (squatter or the like) obtains it by a sort of private expropriation. More important is expropriation by the state or public authority. It is not at all clear why the parts of western property law favourable to the private owner should be reproduced in the system of entitlements to the exclusion of those which favour the claims of the community. The latter, after all, balance the former. The individualistic bias of property law is corrected by the admission of state claims to tax and expropriate.

Aside from the omission of rules about lapse and compulsory acquisition one may note that *Nozick's* principles rest on the assumption that whether a justification exists for acquiring or transferring property can be decided in abstraction from the historical and social context. A just acquisition in 1066 or 1620 remains a just root of title in 1975. If this were really so one would have to say either that the acquisition of slaves is seen in retrospect always to have been unjust and that the state would have been justified in intervening in a slave-owning society to correct the injustice, or that the descendants of slave-owners are entitled to own the descendants of freed slaves. So with colonies, *mutatis mutandis*. Are we to say that as a result of the post-war movement to free colonies we now see that the acquisition of colonies, apparently valid at the time in international law and morality, was always wrong and that the international society would have been justified, had it been so minded, in intervening even in the nineteenth century to free the existing colonies and prevent further acquisitions. If so, how can we be sure that there are not equally unjustified forms of property ownership in present-day society which in fact justify state intervention in a redistributive sense? And how can we be sure in any future society that these objectionable forms of acquisition are not present? In which case, outside Utopia, the thesis advanced by *Nozick* has no application. But if the acquisition of slaves and colonies was initially just, surely some provision should be made in his system for the redistribution of entitlements when the moral basis on which they originally rested has become eviscerated. These instances would count morally as cases of lapse of title owing to changing views of right and wrong. Legally they would furnish examples of just expropriation. There would have to be a further exception in *Nozick's* system to cater for changing conditions of fact. Suppose, apart from any question of the justification for colonies, that in the nineteenth century Metropolitania occupied a deserted tract which it proceeded to colonize, building roads and irrigating the land. As a result a numerous indigenous population crowded in from the neighbouring areas. These people now claim to be free and to decide their own destinies. Whether or not colonization is in general thought a permissible form of 'entitlement' the changed situation must surely change one's moral evaluation of Metropolitania's title to the formerly deserted tract. So with the Mayflowerite who bagged a large stretch of unoccupied land in 1620. If the situation is now that irrespective of title the tracts in question are occupied by people who have nowhere else to live, surely the moral basis of the title of the Mayflowerite's successors must at least be open to debate. Once there was more than enough to go round, now there is not. And is the case very different if the thousands without property instead of occupying the colonies or tracts in question crowd the periphery and make claims on the unused resources inside: All this is intended to make the simple point that it is obtuse to suppose that the justification for acquiring or transmitting property could be settled once and for all at the date of acquisition or transfer. Legally it may be so, subject to the rules of lapse and expropriation. This is because of the need to frame rules of law in such a way as to ensure certainty of title. They are meant however to be applied in a context in which social and moral criticism may be directed against their operation and in which their defects may be corrected by legislation or similar means. Apart from positive law, can it seriously be maintained that the rules about what constitutes a just acquisition or transfer both express unchanging verities and, in their application to the facts of a given acquisition or transfer, are exempt from reassessment in the light of changed circumstances?

Systems of property law which diverge from the orthodox western type based on liberal conceptions of ownership are conceivable, morally defensible and have actually obtained in certain societies. To begin with the conceivable, let us take an imaginary case. Suppose that, in a 'state of nature' a group of people live near a river and subsist on fish, which they catch by hand, and berries. There is great difficulty in catching fish by hand. Berries are however fairly plentiful. There are bits of metal lying around and I discover how to make one of them into a fishhook. With this invention I quadruple my catch of fish. My neighbours cannot discover the knack and I decline to tell them. They press me to lend them the fishhook or to give them lessons in acquiring the technique. I have however acquired western notions of property law and Lockean ideas about entitlement, I point out that I have a just title to the fishhook, since according to *Nozick's* version of *Locke* they are no worse off as a result of my invention. I am therefore entitled to the exclusive, permanent and transmissible use of the fishhook. My neighbours may try their hands at finding out how to make one, of course, but if they fail they may look forward to eating berries and from time to time a bit of fish while I and those persons whom I choose to invite to a meal propose to enjoy ourselves with daily delicacies. If they object that this is unfair I shall point out (though the relevance is not obvious) that they are not actually starving. Nor am I monopolizing materials. There are other pieces of metal lying around. They are no worse off than they were before or than they would have been without my find [in fact they *are* worse off, relatively to me]. As to the parrot cry that they protect me and my family from marauders, wild animals and the like, so that I ought to share my good fortune with them, I reply that they have not grasped what is implied by a system of just entitlements. Are they saying that I am not entitled to the fishhook?

One of my brighter neighbours might well answer me as follows. 'I do not deny that you have a right to the fishhook. As you say you made it and you invented the system of using it to catch fish. But it does not follow that, as you assert, your right to it is exclusive, permanent and transmissible. Your views seem to be coloured by reading books about sophisticated societies. In those societies men are dedicated to increasing production, come what may, and in order to achieve that they accept institutions which to us seem very unfair. We are simple people used to sharing our fortunes and misfortunes. We recognize that you have a right to the fishhook but not that the right has the unlimited content which you assign to it. You ought to allow each of us to use it in turn. Naturally as the maker and inventor you are entitled to a greater share in the use than the rest of us individually, and if you like to call that share 'ownership' we shall not object. But please stop looking up the definition of 'ownership' in foreign books. These notions will only disrupt our way of life'.

The point my neighbor is making is that a system of private property can be inherently distributive. In the system envisaged there is an 'owner' in the sense of a person whose right to the use of the thing is greater than that of others, who has a residual claim if others do not want to use the thing, and in whom powers of management will be vested. He will be responsible for lending the fishhook out, it will be returned to him each evening, he will keep it in repair. But these powers of use, management and reversion fall short of western conception of ownership. In such a system the redistributive power of the state will be unnecessary unless the members of the group fail to keep the rules. For the rules themselves ensure an even distribution of property, subject to the recognition of desert and choice—a recognition which is not allowed to subvert the principle of sharing.

Is the projected system of property law obviously unjust? How does it compare with western notions of ownership? From the point of view of justice, though perhaps not of economic efficiency, it seems to compare rather favourably. It is designed to give effect to the interdependence of the members of the group and to recognize overtly that they cannot survive in isolation. It rejects the notion that I do no harm to a member of my group if as a result of my effort I am better off, and he is no worse off than he would otherwise be. That notion, which is common to the outlook of *Nozick* and *Rawls,* however much they otherwise differ, rests on the assumption that a person who is *comparatively* worse off is not worse off. But he is, and the precise wrong he suffers is that of being treated as an unequal by the more fortunate member or members of the group.

The fruits of an invention which raises production have therefore, in the projected system, to be shared, either by a system of compulsory loan or, in a weaker version, by a system of surplus sharing, under which what an owner 'has in excess of his needs or is not using must be made available to other members of his group'[9].

The sort of system envisaged is unlikely to survive the division of labour, viz. specialisation. The members of the group other than the inventor are likely to feel that he can fish better than they and that they would do well to get him to fish for them. But then they must pay him. At first perhaps the payment is a fraction of the catch. Later the inventor is bemused by the idea that he is entitled to the whole product of his invention. So he argues that his neighbours owe him the whole of his catch and, if they want any of it, must pay in some other way, as by repairing his hut. As he has possession on his side his views may prevail. We slide insensibly, therefore, from a participatory to an exclusive system of property law, and it is difficult to keep alive, in a society of economic specialisation, the notion that each participates in a common enterprise. The remedy for this is not, or is only to a minor extent, a return to rotatory labour. It is rather that the community as a whole, the state, must act as the surrogate of the participatory principles. The inventor of the fishhook will have to be taxed. In that way the economic advantages of specialisation can be combined with a just, or juster distribution of the benefits derived from it. The tax will be used to give the other members of the group benefits corresponding to their former rights to use the fishhook.

There is no point in attempting to work out in detail what a participatory system of property law would be like. The idea is easy to grasp. If such a system is morally sound, then it follows that in a western-type system the intervention of the state, so far from being, as *Nozick* thinks,[10] ruled out except in peripheral instances, (initially unjust acquisitions, subsequently unjust transfers) is essential in order to achieve justice in distribution. Whether one says that this is because in a western-type system all the holdings are unjust (because they are holdings of an unjust sort of property interest) or that they were initially just but that their permanent retention cannot be justified, is debatable: the former seems more appealing. In any event either *Nozick's* conclusion is empty because the premises

---

[9]Herskowitz, below n. 12, p. 372.

[10]Nozick, pp. 174 ff. However one interprets Locke's requirement that the acquirer must leave enough and as good in common for others (Second Treatise sec. 27) the intention behind it is not satisfied unless entitlements are adjusted from time to time according to what *then* remains for others.

are never fulfilled, or if the premises are fulfilled, they do not lead to the conclusion to which they seem to lead.

If it is accepted that the sort of property system described is conceivable and morally defensible that is sufficient to rebut the argument which denies a redistributive function to the state. It is not irrelevant, however, to draw attention to the fact that among the variety of property arrangements found in simple societies there are some which approximate to the distributive arrangement outlined. Among other things this will serve to rebut any argument that I am relying on a gimmicky obligatory principle of transfer[11]. A convenient outline of the variety of such property systems is to be found in *M. J. Herskowitz'* work[12]. They are of course multifold: apart from arrangements which resemble the western institution of ownership there are to be found types of group (e.g. family or clan) ownership, public ownership, rotating individual use (e.g. of fishing grounds) and also the sort of arrangement here envisaged, namely what may be called private ownership subject to compulsory loan or sharing. Thus among the Bushmen[13] 'all kinds of food are private property' and 'one who takes without the permission of the owner is liable to punishment for theft' but 'one who shoots a buck or discovers a terrain where vegetable food is to be gathered is nevertheless expected to share with those who have nothing', so that 'all available food, though from the point of view of customary law privately owned, is actually distributed among the members of a given group'. The dividing is done by the owner and the skin, sinews etc. belong to him to deal with as he pleases. Among the Indians of the Pacific North-West[14] a man is said to have 'owned' an economically important tract and this 'ownership' was expressed by his 'giving permission', to his fellows to exploit the locality each season but 'no instance was ever heard of an "owner" refusing to give the necessary permission. Such a thing is inconceivable'. The individual 'ownership' is a sort of stewardship or ownership in trust carrying with it management and the right to use but not excluding the right of others to a similar use. Among certain tribes of Hottentots[15] a person who dug a waterhole or opened a spring made this his property and all who wished to use it had to have his permission, but he was under an obligation to see that no stranger or stranger's stock was denied access to it. Among the Tswana[16] where the chief allocates (and in that sense 'owns') the land he will allot cattle-posts to individuals, but not exclusively. The allocee, whose position is closest to that of the private owner, 'must share with a number of other people the pastures of the place where his cattle-post is situated, although

[11]Nozick p. 157.

[12]M. J. Herskowitz, *Economic Anthropology* (New York 1952), part IV. Property.

[13]Herskowitz pp. 321–2, citing L. Shapera, *The Khosian Peoples of South Africa, Bushmen and Hottentots* (London 1930) p. 148.

[14]Herskowitz pp. 332–3, citing P. Drucker "Rank, Wealth and Kinship in Northwest Coast Society", *Amer. Anth.* 41 (1939) p. 59.

[15]Herskowitz pp. 343–4, citing Schapera, above n. 13, at pp. 286–291.

[16]Herskowitz p. 344, citing L. Schapera and A. J. H. Goodwin "Work and Wealth" in *The Bantu-Speaking Tribes of South Africa* (ed. L. Schapera) pp. 156–7.

no one else may bring his cattle there without permission'. Yet occupation does give a certain prior right. 'If a man builds a hut and so indicates that it is not merely for temporary use, he established a form of lien over the place, and can return to it at any time'.

There are also examples of what I have termed surplus sharing, which give effect to the principle that what a person has in excess of his needs, or is not using must be made available to other members of the group. Among the Eskimos the principle that 'personal possession is conditioned by actual use of the property' comes into play. A fox-trap lying idle may be taken by anyone who will use it. In Greenland a man already owning a tent or large boat does not inherit another, since it is assumed that one person can never use more than one possession of this type. 'Though what a person uses is generally acknowledged to be his alone any excess must be at the disposal of those who need it and can make good use of it'[17].

These examples show that there is nothing unnatural about distributive property arrangements in a simple society. The mechanism, or one of the possible mechanisms by which such arrangements are secured, is that of what it seems preferable to call private ownership subject to a trust or a duty to permit sharing. The 'ownership' is not of course ownership of the classical western type, but neither is it 'primitive communism'. Its essential feature is that the titles to acquisition are much the same as in modern societies—finding, invention, occupation, making and the like—and the types of transfer—sale, gift, inheritance—are not necessarily dissimilar, but the type of interest acquired and transmitted is different. The principle of sharing is written into the delineation of interests of property.

There is no special reason to think that our moral consciousness is superior to that of simple societies. So if compulsory sharing commends itself to some of them it should not be dismissed out of hand for societies in which the division of labour has made those simple arrangements out of date: but in these, given the weakened social cohesion which the division of labour introduces, the central authority (the state) is needed to see that sharing takes place.

Suggestions for Further Reading

The reader may wish to compare Hume's views in the *Inquiry,* printed here, with the section on property in his earlier *Treatise of Human Nature,* ed. L. A. Selby-Bigge (Oxford: Clarendon Press, 1960), Book III, Part II, §II.

---

[17]Herskowitz pp. 373–4, citing K. Birket-Smith, *The Eskimos* (London 1936) pp. 148–151.

For a better appreciation of Bentham's general approach to moral questions, see the article by D. H. Monro, "Bentham," in Paul Edwards, ed., *The Encyclopedia of Philosophy*, (New York: Collier-Macmillan, 1967). David Lyons, *In the Interest of the Governed* (Oxford: Oxford University Press, 1973) offers an unusual interpretation of Bentham.

A relevant book of readings on distributive justice is John Arthur and William H. Shaw, eds., *Justice and Economic Distribution* (Englewood Cliffs, N.J.: Prentice-Hall, 1978), which also contains significant portions of John Rawls's *A Theory of Justice* (Cambridge, Mass.: Belknap Press of Harvard University Press, 1971) and Robert Nozick's *Anarchy, State and Utopia* (New York: Basic Books, 1974). For an overview of the problems of distributive (but not *re*distributive) justice, see Nicholas Rescher, *Distributive Justice* (Indianapolis: Bobbs-Merrill, 1966). Some helpful discussions are to be found in Virginia Held's anthology *Property, Profits, and Economic Justice* (Belmont, Calif.: Wadsworth, 1980).

SECTION THREE
THE COMMUNITY AND
THE PUBLIC INTEREST

Sometimes the justification of moral or legal rules is rested on the notion of an agreement: "If we all have agreed to a certain arrangement, then that arrangement is fair and binding." A moment's reflection, however, can raise problems with this sort of account. How do we know that the agreement is fair? Can't people be manipulated into believing that they want things that aren't good for them? Can't they be intimidated into agreeing to things they don't want? Don't people sometimes make bad bargains out of ignorance? Further, what happens when someone does not agree? Majority rule, since it does not imply unanimity, raises questions of fairness. And how are new arrivals to be treated? Must a society reach a new consensus every time it admits an immigrant or every time a child comes of age?

Such difficulties drove most social contract theorists to the notion of *hypothetical* agreement. Here the idea is that an arrangement is justifiable *if* people who thought about it (rationally? fairmindedly? thoroughly?) *would* agree to it. For the most part hypothetical contract theory does not make a distinctive contribution to property theory. This is largely because these theorists must find a basis for saying that people would agree to whatever property arrangement they propose. This basis typically turns out to be either some version of natural rights theory or some version of utility theory.

172

Jean Jacques Rousseau (1712–1778) may be the exception. Though he appears to ground the property rights necessary for survival in a natural right of some sort, his contention is that the social contract involves the total transfer (alienation) of all individual rights to the community. This has consequences for property theory which are not directly reducible to natural rights or utility theory. Specifically, it provides a rationale for public, rather than private, ownership of most property.

In the selections here from *The Social Contract*, Rousseau distinguishes between possessions—what one holds on to in the state of nature, if one can—and property—legitimate entitlement to things in civil society. Rousseau's view is that a property right is not held *against* the government but rather is held *through* the government. Note especially what Rousseau has to say about land ownership: specifically about the right of first occupancy and the relevance of labor. The question of land ownership will be a central one in this section.

The utilitarian tradition in social philosophy has long been the major alternative to the contractarian tradition. Though John Stuart Mill was Jeremy Bentham's successor in arguing, along utilitarian lines, that social institutions should be assessed by the degree to which they could be expected to contribute to public happiness, his views on property represented a significant departure from those of his predecessor. In the selections here from Mill's *Principles of Political Economy*, first published in 1848, he defends an extensive system of private property. (He is concerned, however, to show that communism cannot be dismissed out of hand on utilitarian grounds.) Mill draws an important distinction between reasons for adopting *some system* of property where none existed before and reasons for adopting reforms within a stable system. He clearly thinks that the former types of reason (the need to establish social order out of chaos) cannot be used to object to sweeping changes in an existing regime of property. The principal reforms that Mill advocates involve the rights to own land and inherit property. But note that, in Mill's view, when the community decides that it can no longer entrust land—a common inheritance—to an unfit landlord, it must pay compensation.

Henry George (1839–1897), an American economist and author of the highly influential book *Progress and Poverty*, excerpted here, turns the Lockean labor theory of property acquisition against the ownership of land. Since labor is the only means of acquiring just title to property, and since labor cannot produce land, no one can acquire land by labor. Since he believes that monopolization of land is the cause of poverty and that poverty is the major cause of social instability, expediency as well as justice argue for the abolition of property in land. While Mill recommended compensation of expropriated landlords, George scorns this suggestion. If the land rightly belongs to the people and not to the landlords, why should the people have to pay the landlords for it?

Morris Raphael Cohen, in the selections here from his 1927 article, "Property and Sovereignty," reviews some of the principal approaches to the justification of property rights. While he is careful to try to extract the kernels of truth in each of these, it is clear that for Cohen none of these justifications can be sustained when the needs of the community are compromised. "The issue before thoughtful people is therefore not the maintenance or abolition of private property, but the determination of the precise lines along which private enterprise must be given free scope and where it must be restricted in the interests of the common good." In taking up the question of compensating expropriated owners, Cohen holds that, while payment is "generally advisable in order not to disturb the general feeling of security, no absolute principle of justice requires it." He compares the claims of these dispossessed owners to those heard from industry when a protective tariff is lifted. Notice especially Cohen's characterization of the tenement landlord as a "public official."

From The Social Contract

JEAN JACQUES ROUSSEAU

CHAPTER VIII: THE CIVIL STATE

The passage from the state of nature to the civil state produces a very remarkable change in man, by substituting justice for instinct in his conduct, and giving his actions the morality they had formerly lacked. Then only, when the voice of duty takes the place of physical impulses and right of appetite, does man, who so far had considered only himself, find that he is forced to act on different principles, and to consult his reason before listening to his inclinations. Although, in this state, he deprives himself of some advantages which he got from nature, he gains in return others so great, his faculties are so stimulated and developed, his ideas so extended, his feelings so ennobled, and his whole soul so uplifted, that, did not the abuses of this new condition often degrade him below that which he left, he would be bound to bless continually the happy moment which took him from it for ever, and, instead of a stupid and unimaginative animal, made him an intelligent being and a man.

Let us draw up the whole account in terms easily commensurable. What man loses by the social contract is his natural liberty and an unlimited right to everything he tries to get and succeeds in getting; what he gains is civil liberty and the proprietorship of all he possesses. If we are to

From Jean Jacques Rousseau's *The Social Contract and Discourses*, translated by G. D. H. Cole, Everyman's Library Series, London: J. M. Dent & Sons, Ltd. Reprinted by permission of the publishers.

avoid mistake in weighing one against the other, we must clearly distinguish natural liberty, which is bounded only by the strength of the individual, from civil liberty, which is limited by the general will; and possession, which is merely the effect of force or the right of the first occupier,
from property, which can be founded only on a positive title.

We might, over and above all this, add, to what man acquires in the
civil state, moral liberty, which alone makes him truly master of himself;
for the mere impulse of appetite is slavery, while obedience to a law which
we prescribe to ourselves is liberty. But I have already said too much on
this head, and the philosophical meaning of the word liberty does not
now concern us.

CHAPTER IX: REAL PROPERTY

Each member of the community gives himself to it, at the moment of its
foundation, just as he is, with all the resources at his command, including
the goods he possesses. This act does not make possession, in changing
hands, change its nature, and become property in the hands of the Sovereign; but, as the forces of the city are incomparably greater than those of
an individual, public possession is also, in fact, stronger and more irrevo-
cable, without being any more legitimate, at any rate from the point of
view of foreigners. For the State, in relation to its members, is master of
all their goods by the social contract, which, within the State, is the basis of
all rights; but, in relation to other powers, it is so only by the right of the
first occupier, which it holds from its members.

The right of the first occupier, though more real than the right of
the strongest, becomes a real right only when the right of property has
already been established. Every man has naturally a right to everything
he needs; but the positive act which makes him proprietor of one thing
excludes him from everything else. Having his share, he ought to keep
to it, and can have no further right against the community. This is why
the right of the first occupier, which in the state of nature is so weak,
claims the respect of every man in civil society. In this right we are
respecting not so much what belongs to another as what does not belong
to ourselves.

In general, to establish the right of the first occupier over a plot of
ground, the following conditions are necessary: first, the land must not
yet be inhabited; secondly, a man must occupy only the amount he needs
for his subsistence; and, in the third place, possession must be taken, not
by an empty ceremony, but by labour and cultivation, the only sign of
proprietorship that should be respected by others, in default of a legal
title.

In granting the right of first occupancy to necessity and labour, are
we not really stretching it as far as it can go? Is it possible to leave such a
right unlimited? Is it to be enough to set foot on a plot of common
ground, in order to be able to call yourself at once the master of it? Is it to

be enough that a man has the strength to expel others for a moment, in order to establish his right to prevent them from ever returning? How can a man or a people seize an immense territory and keep it from the rest of the world except by a punishable usurpation, since all others are being robbed, by such an act, of the place of habitation and the means of subsistence which nature gave them in common? When Nuñez Balboa, standing on the seashore, took possession of the South Seas and the whole of South America in the name of the crown of Castille, was that enough to dispossess all their actual inhabitants, and to shut out from them all the princes of the world? On such a showing, these ceremonies are idly multiplied, and the Catholic King need only take possession all at once, from his apartment, of the whole universe, merely making a subsequent reservation about what was already in the possession of other princes.

We can imagine how the lands of individuals, where they were contiguous and came to be united, became the public territory, and how the right of Sovereignty, extending from the subjects over the lands they held, became at once real and personal. The possessors were thus made more dependent, and the forces at their command used to guarantee their fidelity. The advantage of this does not seem to have been felt by ancient monarchs, who called themselves King of the Persians, Scythians, or Macedonians, and seemed to regard themselves more as rulers of men than as masters of a country. Those of the present day more cleverly call themselves Kings of France, Spain, England, etc.: thus holding the land, they are quite confident of holding the inhabitants.

The peculiar fact about this alienation is that, in taking over the goods of individuals, the community, so far from despoiling them, only assures them legitimate possession, and changes usurpation into a true right and enjoyment into proprietorship. Thus the possessors, being regarded as depositaries of the public good, and having their rights respected by all the members of the State and maintained against foreign aggression by all its forces, have, by a cession which benefits both the public and still more themselves, acquired, so to speak, all that they gave up. This paradox may easily be explained by the distinction between the rights which the Sovereign and the proprietor have over the same estate, as we shall see later on.

It may also happen that men begin to unite one with another before they possess anything, and that, subsequently occupying a tract of country which is enough for all, they enjoy it in common, or share it out among themselves, either equally or according to a scale fixed by the Sovereign. However the acquisition be made, the right which each individual has to his own estate is always subordinate to the right which the community has over all: without this, there would be neither stability in the social tie, nor real force in the exercise of Sovereignty.

I shall end this chapter and this book by remarking on a fact on which the whole social system should rest: i.e. that, instead of destroying natural inequality, the fundamental compact substitutes, for such physical inequality as nature may have set up between men, an equality that is moral and legitimate, and that men, who may be unequal in strength or intelligence, become every one equal by convention and legal right.[1]

From Principles of Political Economy

JOHN STUART MILL

Private property, as an institution, did not owe its origin to any of those considerations of utility, which plead for the maintenance of it when established. Enough is known of rude ages, both from history and from analogous states of society in our own time, to show, that tribunals (which always precede laws) were originally established, not to determine rights, but to repress violence and terminate quarrels. With this object chiefly in view, they naturally enough gave legal effect to first occupancy, by treating as the aggressor the person who first commenced violence, by turning, or attempting to turn, another out of possession. The preservation of the peace, which was the original object of civil government, was thus attained; while by confirming, to those who already possessed it, even what was not the fruit of personal exertion, a guarantee was incidentally given to them and others that they would be protected in what was so. . . .

• • •

The assailants of the principle of individual property may be divided into two classes: those whose scheme implies absolute equality in the distribution of the physical means of life and enjoyment, and those who admit inequality, but grounded on some principle, or supposed principle, of justice or general expediency, and not, like so many of the existing social inequalities, dependent on accident alone.

• • •

Whatever may be the merits or defects of these various schemes, they cannot be truly said to be impracticable. No reasonable person can

[1]Under bad governments, this equality is only apparent and illusory; it serves only to keep the pauper in his poverty and the rich man in the position he has usurped. In fact, laws are always of use to those who possess and harmful to those who have nothing: from which it follows that the social state is advantageous to men only when all have something and none too much.

doubt that a village community, composed of a few thousand inhabitants cultivating in joint ownership the same extent of land which at present feeds the number of people, and producing by combined labour and the most improved processes the manufactured articles which they required, could raise an amount of productions sufficient to maintain them in comfort; and would find the means of obtaining, and if need be, exacting, the quantity of labour necessary for this purpose, from every member of the association who was capable of work.

The objection ordinarily made to a system of community of property and equal distribution of the produce, that each person would be incessantly occupied in evading his fair share of the work, points, undoubtedly, to a real difficulty. But those who urge this objection, forget to how great an extent the same difficulty exists under the system on which nine-tenths of the business of society is now conducted. The objection supposes, that honest and efficient labour is only to be had from those who are themselves individually to reap the benefit of their own exertions. But how small a part of all the labour performed in England, from the lowest paid to the highest, is done by persons working for their own benefit. From the Irish reaper or hodman to the chief justice or the minister of state, nearly all the work of society is remunerated by day wages or fixed salaries. A factory operative has less personal interest in his work than a member of a Communist association, since he is not, like him, working for a partnership of which he is himself a member. It will no doubt be said, that though the labourers themselves have not, in most cases, a personal interest in their work, they are watched and superintended, and their labour directed, and the mental part of the labour performed, by persons who have. Even this, however, is far from being universally the fact. In all public, and many of the largest and most successful private undertakings, not only the labours of detail but the control and superintendence are entrusted to salaried officers. And though the "master's eye," when the master is vigilant and intelligent, is of proverbial value, it must be remembered that in a Socialist farm or manufactory, each labourer would be under the eye not of one master, but of the whole community. In the extreme case of obstinate perseverance in not performing the due share of work, the community would have the same resources which society now has for compelling conformity to the necessary conditions of the association. Dismissal, the only remedy at present, is no remedy when any other labourer who may be engaged does no better than his predecessor: the power of dismissal only enables an employer to obtain from his workmen the customary amount of labour, but that customary labour may be of any degree of inefficiency. Even the labourer who loses his employment by idleness or negligence, has nothing worse to suffer, in the most unfavourable case, than the discipline of a workhouse, and if the desire to avoid this be a sufficient motive in the one system, it would be sufficient in the other. . . .

. . . [Further,] mankind are capable of a far greater amount of public spirit than the present age is accustomed to suppose possible. History bears witness to the success with which large bodies of human beings may be trained to feel the public interest their own. And no soil could be more favourable to the growth of such a feeling, than a Communist association, since all the ambition, and the bodily and mental activity, which are now exerted in the pursuit of separate and self-regarding interests, would require another sphere of employment, and would naturally find it in the pursuit of the general benefit of the community. The same cause, so often assigned in explanation of the devotion of the Catholic priest or monk to the interest of his order—that he has no interest apart from it—would, under Communism, attach the citizen to the community. And independently of the public motive, every member of the association would be amenable to the most universal, and one of the strongest, of personal motives, that of public opinion. The force of this motive in deterring from any act or omission positively reproved by the community, no one is likely to deny; but the power also of emulation, in exciting to the most strenuous exertions for the sake of the approbation and admiration of others, is borne witness to by experience in every situation in which human beings publicly compete with one another, even if it be in things frivolous, or from which the public derive no benefit. A contest, who can do most for the common good, is not the kind of competition which Socialists repudiate. To what extent, therefore, the energy of labour would be diminished by Communism, or whether in the long run it would be diminished at all, must be considered for the present an undecided question. . . .

If . . . the choice were to be made between Communism with all its chances, and the present state of society with all its sufferings and injustices; if the institution of private property necessarily carried with it as a consequence, that the produce of labour should be apportioned as we now see it, almost in an inverse ratio to the labour—the largest portions to those who have never worked at all, the next largest to those whose work is almost nominal, and so in a descending scale, the remuneration dwindles as the work grows harder and more disagreeable, until the most-fatiguing and exhausting bodily labour cannot count with certainty on being able to earn even the necessaries of life; if this, or Communism, were the alternative, all the difficulties, great or small, of Communism, would be but as dust in the balance. But to make the comparison applicable, we must compare Communism at its best, with the régime of individual property, not as it is, but as it might be made. The principle of private property has never yet had a fair trial in any country; and less so, perhaps, in this country than in some others. The social arrangements of modern Europe commenced from a distribution of property which was the result, not of just partition, or acquisition by industry, but of conquest and violence: and notwithstanding what industry has been doing for many centuries to modify the work of force, the system still retains many and large traces of its origin. The laws of property have never yet conformed to the principles on which the justification of private property rests. They have made property of things which never ought to be property, and absolute property where only a qualified property ought to exist. They have not held the balance fairly between human beings, but have heaped impediments upon some, to give advantage to others; they have purposely fostered inequalities, and prevented all from starting fair in the race. . . .

. . .

It is next to be considered, what is included in the idea of private property, and by what considerations the application of the principle should be bounded.

The institution of property, when limited to its essential elements, consists in the recognition, in each person, of a right to the exclusive disposal of what he or she have produced by their own exertions, or received either by gift or by fair agreement, without force or fraud, from those who produced it. The foundation of the whole is, the right of producers to what they themselves have produced. It may be objected, therefore, to the institution as it now exists, that it recognises rights of property in individuals over things which they have not produced. For example (it may be said) the operatives in a manufactory create, by their labour and skill, the whole produce; yet, instead of its belonging to them, the law gives them only their stipulated hire, and transfers the produce to some one who has merely supplied the funds, without perhaps contributing anything to the work itself, even in the form of superintendence. The answer to this is, that the labour of manufacture is only one of the conditions which must combine for the production of the commodity. The labour cannot be carried on without materials and machinery, nor without a stock of necessaries provided in advance, to maintain the labourers during the production. All these things are the fruits of previous labour. If the labourers were possessed of them, they would not need to divide the produce with any one; but while they have them not, an equivalent must be given to those who have, both for the antecedent labour, and for the abstinence by which the produce of that labour, instead of being expended on indulgences, has been reserved for this use. The capital may not have been, and in most cases was not, created by the labour and abstinence of the present possessor; but it was created by the labour and abstinence of some former person, who may indeed have been wrongfully dispossessed of it, but who, in the present age of the world, much more probably transferred his claims to the present capitalist by gift or voluntary contract: and the abstinence at least must have been continued by each successive owner, down to the present. If it be said, as it may with truth, that those who have inherited the savings of others have an advantage which they have in no way deserved, over the industrious whose predecessors have not left them anything; I not only admit, but strenuously contend, that this unearned advantage should be curtailed, as much as is consistent with justice to those who thought fit to dispose of their savings by giving them to their descendants. But while it is true that the labourers are at a disadvantage compared with those whose predecessors have saved, it is also true that the labourers are far better off than if those predecessors had not saved. They share in the advantage, though not to an equal extent with the inheritors. The terms of co-operation between present labour and the fruits of past labour and saving, are a subject for adjustment between the two parties. Each is necessary to the other. The capitalist can do nothing without labourers, nor the labourers without capital. If the labourers compete for employment, the capitalists on their part compete for labour, to the full extent of the circulating capital of the country. Competition is often spoken of as if it were necessarily a cause of misery and degradation to the labouring class; as if high wages were not precisely as much a product of competition as low wages. The remuneration of labour is as much the result of the law of competition in the United States, as it is in Ireland, and much more completely so than in England.

The right of property includes, then, the freedom of acquiring by contract. The right of each to what he has produced, implies a right to what has been produced by others, if obtained by their free consent; since the producers must either have given it from good will, or exchanged it for what they esteemed an equivalent, and to prevent them from doing so would be to infringe their right of property in the product of their own industry.

Before proceeding to consider the things which the principle of individual property does not include, we must specify one more thing which it does include: and this is that a title, after a certain period, should be given by prescription. According to the fundamental idea of property, indeed, nothing ought to be treated as such, which has been acquired by force or fraud, or appropriated in ignorance of a prior title vested in some other person; but it is necessary to the security of rightful possessors, that they should not be molested by charges of wrongful acquisition, when by the lapse of time witnesses must have perished or been lost sight of, and the real character of the transaction can no longer be cleared up. Possession which has not been legally questioned within a moderate number of years, ought to be, as by the laws of all nations it is, a complete title. Even when the acquisition was wrongful, the dispossession, after a generation has elapsed, of the probably *bonâ fide* possessors, by the revival of a claim which had been long dormant, would generally be a greater injustice, and almost always a greater private and public mischief, than leaving the original wrong without atonement. It may seem hard that a claim, originally just, should be defeated by mere lapse of time; but there is a time after which, (even looking at the individual case, and without regard to the general effect on the security of possessors,) the balance of hardship turns the other way. With the injustices of men, as with the convulsions and disasters of nature, the longer they remain unrepaired, the greater become the obstacles to repairing them, arising from the after-growths which would have to be torn up or broken through. In no human transactions, not even in the simplest and clearest, does it follow that a thing is fit to be done now, because it was fit to be done sixty years ago. It is scarcely needful to remark, that these reasons for not disturbing acts of injustice of old date, cannot apply to unjust systems or institutions; since a bad law or usage is not one bad act, in the remote past, but a perpetual repetition of bad acts, as long as the law or usage lasts.

Such, then, being the essentials of private property, it is now to be considered, to what extent the forms in which the institution has existed in different states of society, or still exists, are necessary consequences of its principle, or are recommended by the reasons on which it is grounded.

Nothing is implied in property but the right of each to his (or her) own faculties, to what he can produce by them, and to whatever he can get for them in a fair market: together with his right to give this to any other person if he chooses, and the right of that other to receive and enjoy it.

It follows, therefore, that although the right of bequest, or gift after death, forms part of the idea of private property, the right of inheritance, as distinguished from bequest, does not. That the property of persons who have made no disposition of it during their lifetime, should pass first to their children, and failing them, to the nearest relations, may be a proper arrangement or not, but is no consequence of the principle of private property. Although there belong to the decision of such questions many considerations besides those of political economy, it is not foreign to the plan of this work to suggest, for the judgment of thinkers, the view of them which most recommends itself to the writer's mind. . . .

Whether the power of bequest should itself be subject to limitation is an ulterior question of great importance. Unlike inheritance *ab intestato,* bequest is one of the attributes of property: the ownership of a thing cannot be looked upon as complete without the power of bestowing it, at death or during life, at the owner's pleasure: and all the reasons, which recommend that private property should exist, recommend *pro tanto* this extension of it. But property is only a means to an end, not itself the end. Like all other proprietary rights, and even in a greater degree than most, the power of bequest may be so exercised as to conflict with the permanent interests of the human race. It does so, when, not content with bequeathing an estate to A, the testator prescribes that on A's death it shall pass to his eldest son, and to that son's son, and so on for ever. No doubt, persons have occasionally exerted themselves more strenuously to acquire a fortune from the hope of founding a family in perpetuity; but the mischiefs to society of such perpetuities outweigh the value of this incentive to exertion, and the incentives in the case of those who have the opportunity of making large fortunes are strong enough without it. A similar abuse of the power of bequest is committed when a person who does the meritorious act of leaving property for public uses, attempts to prescribe the details of its application in perpetuity; when in founding a place of education (for instance) he dictates, for ever, what doctrines shall be taught. It being impossible that any one should know what doctrines will be fit to be taught after he has been dead for centuries, the law ought not to give effect to such dispositions of property, unless subject to the perpetual revision (after a certain interval has elapsed) of a fitting authority. . . .

The next point to be considered is, whether the reasons on which the institution of property rests, are applicable to all things in which a right of exclusive ownership is at present recognized; and if not, on what other grounds the recognition is defensible.

The essential principle of property being to assure to all persons what they have produced by their labour and accumulated by their abstinence, this principle cannot apply to what is not the produce of labour, the raw material of the earth. If the land derived its productive power wholly from nature, and not at all from industry, or if there were any means of discriminating what is derived from each source, it not only would not be necessary, but it would be the height of injustice, to let the gift of nature be engrossed by individuals. The use of the land in agriculture must indeed, for the time being, be of necessity exclusive; the same person who has ploughed and sown must be permitted to reap: but the land might be occupied for one season only, as among the ancient Germans; or might be periodically redivided as population increased: or the State might be the universal landlord, and the cultivators tenants under it, either on lease or at will.

But though land is not the produce of industry, most of its valuable qualities are so. Labour is not only requisite for using, but almost equally so for fashioning, the instrument. Considerable labour is often required at the commencement, to clear the land for cultivation. In many cases, even when cleared, its productiveness is wholly the effect of labour and art. . . .

•   •   •

. . . Cultivation also requires buildings and fences, which are wholly the produce of labour. The fruits of this industry cannot be reaped in a short period. The labour and outlay are immediate, the benefit is spread over many years, perhaps over all future time. A holder will not incur this labour and outlay when strangers and not himself will be benefited by it. If he undertakes such improvements, he must have a sufficient period before him in which to profit by them; and he is in no way so sure of having always a sufficient period as when his tenure is perpetual. . . .

•   •   •

These are the reasons which form the justification in an economical point of view, of property in land. It is seen, that they are only valid, in so far as the proprietor of land is its improver. Whenever, in any country, the proprietor, generally speaking, ceases to be the improver, political economy has nothing to say in defence of landed property, as there established. In no sound theory of private property was it ever contemplated that the proprietor of land should be merely a sinecurist quartered on it. . . .

•   •   •

When the "sacredness of property" is talked of, it should always be remembered, that any such sacredness does not belong in the same degree to landed property. No man made the land. It is the original inheritance of the whole species. Its appropriation is wholly a question of general expediency. When private property in land is not expedient, it is unjust. It is no hardship to any one, to be excluded from what others have produced: they were not bound to produce it for his use, and he loses nothing by not sharing in what otherwise would not have existed at all. But is some hardship to be born into the world and to find all nature's gifts previously engrossed, and no place left for the new-comer. To reconcile people to this, after they have once admitted into their minds the idea that any moral rights belong to them as human beings, it will always be necessary to convince them that the exclusive appropriation is good for mankind on the whole, themselves included. But this is what no sane human being could be persuaded of, if the relation between the landowner and the cultivator were the same everywhere as it has been in Ireland.

Landed property is felt, even by those most tenacious of its rights, to be a different thing from other property; and where the bulk of the community have been disinherited of their share of it, and it has become the exclusive attribute of a small minority, men have generally tried to reconcile it, at least in theory, to their sense of justice, by endeavouring to attach duties to it, and erecting it into a sort of magistracy, either moral or legal. But if the state is at liberty to treat the possessors of land as public functionaries, it is only going one step further to say, that it is at liberty to discard them. The claim of the landowners to the land is altogether subordinate to the general policy of the state. The principle of property gives them no right to the land, but only a right to compensation for whatever portion of their interest in the land it may be the policy of the state to deprive them of. To that, their claim is indefeasible. It is due to landowners, and to owners of any property whatever, recognized as such by the state, that they should not be dispossessed of it without receiving its pecuniary value, or an annual income equal to what they derived from it. This is due on the general principles on which property rests. If the land was bought with the produce of the labour and abstinence of themselves or their ancestors, compensation is due to them on that ground; even if otherwise, it is still due on the ground of prescription. Nor can it ever be necessary for accomplishing an object by which the community altogether will gain, that a particular portion of the community should be immolated. When the property is of a kind to which peculiar affections attach themselves, the compensation ought to exceed a bare pecuniary equivalent. But, subject to this proviso, the state is at liberty to deal with landed property as the general interests of the community may require, even to the extent, if it so happen, of doing with the whole, what is done with a part whenever a bill is passed for a railroad or a new street. The community has too much at stake in the proper cultivation of the land, and in the conditions annexed to the occupancy of it, to leave these things to the discretion of a class of persons called landlords, when they have shown themselves unfit for the trust. . . .

. . . To me it seems almost an axiom that property in land should be interpreted strictly, and that the balance in all cases of doubt should incline against the proprietor. The reverse is the case with property in moveables, and in all things the product of labour: over these, the owner's power both of use and of exclusion should be absolute, except where positive evil to others would result from it; but in the case of land, no exclusive right should be permitted in any individual, which cannot be shown to be productive of positive good. To be allowed any exclusive right at all, over a portion of the common inheritance, while there are others who have no portion, is already a privilege. No quantity of moveable goods which a person can acquire by his labour, prevents others from acquiring the like by the same means; but from the very nature of the case, whoever owns land, keeps others out of the enjoyment of it. The privilege, or monopoly, is only defensible as a necessary evil; it becomes an injustice when carried to any point to which the compensating good does not follow it.

For instance, the exclusive right to the land for purposes of cultivation does not imply an exclusive right to it for purposes of access; and no such right ought to be recognized, except to the extent necessary to protect the produce against damage, and the owner's privacy against invasion. The pretension of two Dukes to shut up a part of the Highlands, and exclude the rest of mankind from many square miles of mountain scenery to prevent disturbance to wild animals, is an abuse; it exceeds the legitimate bounds of the right of landed property. When land is not intended to be cultivated, no good reason can in general be given for its being private property at all; and if any one is permitted to call it his, he ought to know that he holds it by sufferance of the community, and on an implied condition that his ownership, since it cannot possibly do them any good, at least shall not deprive them of any, which they could have derived from the land if it had been unappropriated. Even in the case of cultivated land, a man whom, though only one among millions, the law permits to hold thousands of acres as his single share, is not entitled to think that all this is given to him to use and abuse, and deal with as if it concerned nobody but himself. The rents or profits which he can obtain from it are at his sole disposal; but with regard to the land, in everything which he does with it, and in everything which he abstains from doing, he is morally bound, and should whenever the case admits be legally compelled, to make his interest and pleasure consistent with the public good. The species at large still retains, of its original claim to the soil of the planet which it inhabits, as much as is compatible with the purposes for which it has parted with the remainder.

Besides property in the produce of labour, and property in land, there are other things which are or have been subjects of property, in which no proprietary rights ought to exist at all. But as the civilized world has in general made up its mind on most of these, there is no necessity for dwelling on them in this place. At the head of them, is property in human beings. It is almost superfluous to observe, that this institution can have no place in any society even pretending to be founded on justice, or on fellowship between human creatures. But, iniquitous as it is, yet when the state has expressly legalized it, and human beings, for generations, have been bought, sold, and inherited under sanction of law, it is another wrong, in abolishing the property, not to make full compensation. . . . Other examples of property which ought not to have been created, are properties in public trusts; such as judicial offices under the old French régime, and the heritable jurisdictions which, in countries not wholly emerged from feudality, pass with the land. Our own country affords, as cases in point, that of a commission in the army, and of an advowson, or right of nomination to an ecclesiastical benefice. A property is also sometimes created in a right of taxing the public; in a monopoly, for instance, or other exclusive privilege. These abuses prevail most in semibarbarous countries; but are not without example in the most civilized. In France there are several important trades and professions, including notaries, attorneys, brokers, appraisers, printers, even bakers, and (until lately) butchers, of which the numbers are limited by law. The *brevet* or privilege of one of the permitted number consequently brings a high price in the market. In these cases, compensation probably could not with justice be refused, on the abolition of the privilege. There are other cases in which this would be more doubtful. The question would turn upon what, in the peculiar circumstances, was sufficient to constitute prescription; and whether the legal recognition which the abuse had obtained, was sufficient to constitute it an institution, or amounted only to an occasional license. It would be absurd to claim compensation for losses caused by changes in a tariff, a thing confessedly variable from year to year; or for monopolies like those granted to individuals by Queen Elizabeth, favours of a despotic authority, which the power that gave was competent at any time to recall.

So much on the institution of property, a subject of which, for the purposes of political economy, it was indispensable to treat, but on which we could not usefully confine ourselves to economical considerations. We have now to inquire on what principles and with what results the distribution of the produce of land and labour is effected, under the relations which this institution creates among the different members of the community.

From Progress and Poverty

HENRY GEORGE

[The] strange and unnatural spectacle of large numbers of willing men who cannot find employment is enough to suggest the true cause [of poverty] to whosoever can think consecutively. For, though custom has dulled us to it, it *is* a strange and unnatural thing that men who wish to labor, in order to satisfy their wants, cannot find the opportunity—as, since labor is that which produces wealth, the man who seeks to exchange labor for food, clothing, or any other form of wealth, is like one who proposes to give bullion for coin, or wheat for flour. We talk about the supply of labor and the demand for labor, but, evidently, these are only relative terms. The supply of labor is everywhere the same—two hands always come into the world with one mouth, twenty-one boys to every twenty girls; and the demand for labor must always exist as long as men want things which labor alone can procure. We talk about the "want of work," but, evidently, it is not work that is short while want continues; evidently, the supply of labor cannot be too great, nor the demand for labor too small, when people suffer for the lack of things that labor produces. The real trouble must be that supply is somehow prevented from satisfying demand, that somewhere there is an obstacle which prevents labor from producing the things that laborers want. . . .

Now, what is necessary to enable labor to produce these things, is land. When we speak of labor creating wealth, we speak metaphorically. Man creates nothing. The whole human race, were they to labor forever, could not create the tiniest mote that floats in a sunbeam—could not make this rolling sphere one atom heavier or one atom lighter. In producing wealth, labor, with the aid of natural forces, but works up, into the forms desired, pre-existing matter, and, to produce wealth, must, therefore, have access to this matter and to these forces—that is to say, to land. The land is the source of all wealth. It is the mine from which must be drawn the ore that labor fashions. It is the substance to which labor gives the form. And, hence, when labor cannot satisfy its wants, may we not with certainty infer that it can be from no other cause than that labor is denied access to land? . . .

Now, why is it that . . . unemployed labor cannot employ itself upon the land? Not that the land is all in use. Though all the symptoms that in older countries are taken as showing a redundancy of population are beginning to manifest themselves in San Francisco, it is idle to talk of redundancy of population in a State that with greater natural resources than France has not yet a million of people. Within a few miles of San Francisco is unused land enough to give employment to every man who wants it. I do not mean to say that every unemployed man could turn farmer or build himself a house, if he had the land; but that enough could and would do so to give employment to the rest. What is it, then, that prevents labor from employing itself on this land? Simply, that it has been monopolized. . . .

There is but one way to remove an evil—and that is, to remove its cause. Poverty deepens as wealth increases, and wages are forced down while productive power grows, because land, which is the source of all wealth and the field of all labor, is monopolized. To extirpate poverty, to make wages what justice commands they should be, the full earnings of the laborer, we must therefore substitute for the individual ownership of land a common ownership. Nothing else will go to the cause of the evil—in nothing else is there the slightest hope.

This, then, is the remedy for the unjust and unequal distribution of wealth apparent in modern civilization, and for all the evils which flow from it:

We must make land common property.

• • •

When it is proposed to abolish private property in land the first question that will arise is that of justice. . . .

What constitutes the rightful basis of property? What is it that enables a man justly to say of a thing, "It is mine!" From what springs the sentiment which acknowledges his exclusive right as against all the world? Is it not, primarily, the right of a man to himself, to the use of his own powers, to the enjoyment of the fruits of his own exertions? Is it not this individual right, which springs from and is testified to by the natural facts of individual organization—the fact that each particular pair of hands obey a particular brain and are related to a particular stomach; the fact that each man is a definite, coherent, independent whole—which alone justifies individual ownership? As a man belongs to himself, so his labor when put in concrete form belongs to him.

And for this reason, that which a man makes or produces is his own, as against all the world—to enjoy or to destroy, to use, to exchange, or to give. No one else can rightfully claim it, and his exclusive right to it involves no wrong to any one else. Thus there is to everything produced by human exertion a clear and indisputable title to exclusive possession and enjoyment, which is perfectly consistent with justice, as it descends from the original producer, in whom it vested by natural law. The pen with which I am writing is justly mine. No other human being can rightfully lay claim to it, for in me is the title of the producers who made it. It has become mine, because transferred to me by the stationer, to whom it was transferred by the importer, who obtained the exclusive right to it by transfer from the manufacturer, in whom, by the same process of purchase, vested the rights of those who dug the material from the ground and shaped it into a pen. Thus, my exclusive right of ownership in the pen springs from the natural right of the individual to the use of his own faculties.

Now, this is not only the original source from which all ideas of exclusive ownership arise—as is evident from the natural tendency of the mind to revert to it when the idea of exclusive ownership is questioned, and the manner in which social relations develop—but it is necessarily the only source. There can be to the ownership of anything no rightful title which is not derived from the title of the producer and does not rest upon the natural right of the man to himself. There can be no other rightful title, because (1st) there is no other natural right from which any other title can be derived, and (2d) because the recognition of any other title is inconsistent with and destructive of this.

For (1st) what other right exists from which the right to the exclusive possession of anything can be derived, save the right of a man to himself?

With what other power is man by nature clothed, save the power of exerting his own faculties? How can he in any other way act upon or affect material things or other men? Paralyze the motor nerves, and your man has no more external influence or power than a log or stone. From what else, then, can the right of possessing and controlling things be derived? If it spring not from man himself, from what can it spring? Nature acknowledges no ownership or control in man save as the result of exertion. In no other way can her treasures be drawn forth, her powers directed, or her forces utilized or controlled. She makes no discriminations among men, but is to all absolutely impartial. She knows no distinction between master and slave, king and subject, saint and sinner. All men to her stand upon an equal footing and have equal rights. She recognizes no claim but that of labor, and recognizes that without respect to the claimant. . . . Hence, as nature gives only to labor, the exertion of labor in production is the only title to exclusive possession.

(2d) This right of ownership that springs from labor excludes the possibility of any other right of ownership. If a man be rightfully entitled to the produce of his labor, then no one can be rightfully entitled to the ownership of anything which is not the produce of his labor, or the labor of some one else from whom the right has passed to him. If production give to the producer the right to exclusive possession and enjoyment, there can rightfully be no exclusive possession and enjoyment of anything not the production of labor, and the recognition of private property in land is a wrong. For the right to the produce of labor cannot be enjoyed without the right to the free use of the opportunities offered by nature, and to admit the right of property in these is to deny the right of property in the produce of labor. When nonproducers can claim as rent a portion of the wealth created by producers, the right of the producers to the fruits of their labor is to that extent denied.

There is no escape from this position. To affirm that a man can rightfully claim exclusive ownership in his own labor when embodied in material things, is to deny that any one can rightfully claim exclusive ownership in land. To affirm the rightfulness of property in land, is to affirm a claim which has no warrant in nature, as against a claim founded in the organization of man and the laws of the material universe. . . .

Whatever may be said for the institution of private property in land, it is therefore plain that it cannot be defended on the score of justice.

The equal right of all men to the use of land is as clear as their equal right to breathe the air—it is a right proclaimed by the fact of their existence. For we cannot suppose that some men have a right to be in this world and others no right. . . .

The right to exclusive ownership of anything of human production is clear. No matter how many the hands through which it has passed, there was, at the beginning of the line, human labor—some one who, having procured or produced it by his exertions, had to it a clear title as against all the rest of mankind, and which could justly pass from one to another by sale or gift. But at the end of what string of conveyances or grants can be shown or supposed a like title to any part of the material universe? To improvements, such an original title can be shown; but it is a title only to the improvements, and not to the land itself. If I clear a forest, drain a swamp, or fill a morass, all I can justly claim is the value given by these exertions. They give me no right to the land itself, no claim other than to my equal share with every other member of the community in the value which is added to it by the growth of the community.

But it will be said: There are improvements which in time become indistinguishable from the land itself! Very well; then the title to the improvements becomes blended with the title to the land; the individual right is lost in the common right. It is the greater that swallows up the less, not the less that swallows up the greater. Nature does not proceed from man, but man from nature, and it is into the bosom of nature that he and all his works must return again.

Yet, it will be said: As every man has a right to the use and enjoyment of nature, the man who is using land must be permitted the exclusive right to its use in order that he may get the full benefit of his labor. But there is no difficulty in determining where the individual right ends and the common right begins. A delicate and exact test is supplied by value and with its aid there is no difficulty, no matter how dense population may become, in determining and securing the exact rights of each, the equal rights of all. . . .

As for the deduction of a complete and exclusive individual right to land from priority of occupation, that is, if possible, the most absurd ground on which landownership can be defended. Priority of occupation give exclusive and perpetual title to the surface of a globe on which, in the order of nature, countless generations succeed each other! Had the men of the last generation any better right to the use of this world than we of this? or the men of a hundred years ago? or of a thousand years ago? Had the mound builders, or the cave dwellers, the contemporaries of the mastodon and the three-toed horse, or the generations still further back, who, in dim æons that we can think of only as geologic periods, followed each other on the earth we now tenant for our little day?

Has the first comer at a banquet the right to turn back all the chairs and claim that none of the other guests shall partake of the food provided, except as they make terms with him? Does the first man who presents a ticket at the door of a theater, and passes in, acquire by his priority the right to shut the doors and have the performance go on for him alone? Does the first passenger who enters a railroad car obtain the right to scatter his baggage over all the seats and compel the passengers who come in after him to stand up?

The cases are perfectly analogous. We arrive and we depart, guests at a banquet continually spread, spectators and participants in an entertainment where there is room for all who come; passengers from station to station, on an orb that whirls through space—our rights to take and possess cannot be exclusive; they must be bounded everywhere by the equal rights of others. Just as the passenger in a railroad car may spread himself and his baggage over as many seats as he pleases, until other passengers come in, so may a settler take and use as much land as he chooses, until it is needed by others—a fact which is shown by the land acquiring a value—when his right must be curtailed by the equal rights of the others, and no priority of appropriation can give a right which will bar these equal rights of others. If this were not the case, then by priority of appropriation one man could acquire and could transmit to whom he pleased, not merely the exclusive right to 160 acres, or to 640 acres, but to a whole township, a whole state, a whole continent.

And to this manifest absurdity does the recognition of individual right to land come when carried to its ultimate—that any one human being, could he concentrate in himself the individual rights to the land of any country, could expel therefrom all the rest of its inhabitants; and could he thus concentrate the individual rights to the whole surface of the globe, he alone of all the teeming population of the earth would have the right to live. . . .

The examination through which we have passed has proved conclusively that private property in land cannot be justified on the ground of utility—that, on the contrary, it is the great cause to which are to be traced the poverty, misery, and degradation, the social disease and the political weakness which are showing themselves so menacingly amid advancing civilization. Expediency, therefore, joins justice in demanding that we abolish it.

When expediency thus joins justice in demanding that we abolish an institution that has no broader base or stronger ground than a mere municipal regulation, what reason can there be for hesitation?

The consideration that seems to cause hesitation, even on the part of those who see clearly that land by right is common property, is the idea that having permitted land to be treated as private property for so long, we should in abolishing it be doing a wrong to those who have been suffered to base their calculations upon its permanence; that having permitted land to be held as rightful property, we should by the resumption of common rights be doing injustice to those who have purchased it with what was unquestionably their rightful property. Thus, it is held that if we abolish private property in land, justice requires that we should fully compensate those who now possess it, as the British Government, in abolishing the purchase and sale of military commissions, felt itself bound to compensate those who held commissions which they had purchased in the belief that they could sell them again, or as in abolishing slavery in the British West Indies $100,000,000 was paid the slaveholders. . . .

It is this idea that suggests the proposition, which finds advocates in Great Britain, that the government shall purchase at its market price the individual proprietorship of the land of the country, and it was this idea which led John Stuart Mill, although clearly perceiving the essential injustice of private property in land, to advocate, not a full resumption of the land, but only a resumption of accruing advantages in the future. His plan was that a fair and even liberal estimate should be made of the market value of all the land in the kingdom, and that future additions to that value, not due to the improvements of the proprietor, should be taken by the state.

To say nothing of the practical difficulties which such cumbrous plans involve, in the extension of the functions of government which they would require and the corruption they would beget, their inherent and essential defect lies in the impossibility of bridging over by any compromise the radical difference between wrong and right. Just in proportion as the interests of the landholders are conserved, just in that proportion must general interests and general rights be disregarded, and if landholders are to lose nothing of their special privileges, the people at large can gain nothing. To buy up individual property rights would merely be to give the landholders in another form a claim of the same kind and amount that their possession of land now gives them; it would be to raise for them by taxation the same proportion of the earnings of labor and capital that they are now enabled to appropriate in rent. Their unjust advantage would be preserved and the unjust disadvantage of the non-landholders would be continued. . . .

Such inefficient and impracticable schemes may do to talk about, where any proposition more efficacious would not at present be entertained, and their discussion is a hopeful sign, as it shows the entrance of the thin end of the wedge of truth. Justice in men's mouths is cringingly humble when she first begins a protest against a time-honored wrong, and we of the English-speaking nations still wear the collar of the Saxon thrall, and have been educated to look upon the "vested rights" of landowners with all the superstitious reverence that ancient Egyptians looked upon the crocodile. But when the times are ripe for them, ideas grow, even though insignificant in their first appearance. One day, the Third Estate covered their heads when the king put on his hat. A little while thereafter, and the head of a son of St. Louis rolled from the scaffold. The antislavery movement in the United States commenced with talk of compensating owners, but when four millions of slaves were emancipated, the owners got no compensation, nor did they clamor for any. And by the time the people of any such country as England or the United States are sufficiently aroused to the injustice and disadvantages of individual ownership of land to induce them to attempt its nationalization, they will be sufficiently aroused to nationalize it in a much more direct and easy way than by purchase. They will not trouble themselves about compensating the proprietors of land.

Nor is it right that there should be any concern about the proprietors of land. That such a man as John Stuart Mill should have attached so much importance to the compensation of landowners as to have urged the confiscation merely of the future increase in rent, is explainable only by his acquiescence in the current doctrines that wages are drawn from capital and that population constantly tends to press upon subsistence. These blinded him as to the full effects of the private appropriation of land. He saw that "the claim of the landholder is altogether subordinate to the general policy of the state." and that "when private property in land is not expedient, it is unjust,"[1] but, entangled in the toils of the

---

[1]"Principles of Political Economy," Book I, Chap. 2, Sec. 6.

Malthusian doctrine, he attributed, as he expressly states in a paragraph I have previously quoted, the want and suffering that he saw around him to "the niggardliness of nature, not to the injustice of man," and thus to him the nationalization of land seemed comparatively a little thing, that could accomplish nothing toward the eradication of pauperism and the abolition of want—ends that could be reached only as men learned to repress a natural instinct. Great as he was and pure as he was—warm heart and noble mind—he yet never saw the true harmony of economic laws, nor realized how from this one great fundamental wrong flow want and misery, and vice and shame. Else he could never have written this sentence: "This land of Ireland, the land of every country, belongs to the people of the country. The individuals called landowners have no right in morality and justice to anything but the rent, or compensation for its salable value."

In the name of the Prophet—figs! If the land of any country belong to the people of that country, what right, in morality and justice, have the individuals called landowners to the rent? If the land belong to the people, why in the name of morality and justice should the people pay its salable value for their own?

Herbert Spencer says:[2] "Had we to deal with the parties who originally robbed the human race of its heritage, we might make short work of the matter." Why not make short work of the matter anyhow? For this robbery is not like the robbery of a horse or a sum of money, that ceases with the act. It is a fresh and continuous robbery, that goes on every day and every hour. It is not from the produce of the past that rent is drawn; it is from the produce of the present. It is a toll levied upon labor constantly and continuously. Every blow of the hammer, every stroke of the pick, every thrust of the shuttle, every throb of the steam engine, pays it tribute. It levies upon the earnings of the men who, deep under ground, risk their lives, and of those who over white surges hang to reeling masts; it claims the just reward of the capitalist and the fruits of the inventor's patient effort; it takes little children from play and from school, and compels them to work before their bones are hard or their muscles are firm; it robs the shivering of warmth; the hungry, of food; the sick, of medicine; the anxious, of peace. It debases, and embrutes, and embitters. It crowds families of eight and ten into a single squalid room; it herds like

---

[2]"Social Statics," page 142. [It may be well to say in the new reprint of this book (1897) that this and all other references to Herbert Spencer's "Social Statics" are from the edition of that book published by D. Appleton & Co., New York, with his consent, from 1864 to 1892. At that time "Social Statics" was repudiated, and a new edition under the name of "Social Statics, abridged and revised," has taken its place. From this, all that the first "Social Statics" had said in denial of property in land has been eliminated, and it of course contains nothing here referred to. Mr. Spencer has also been driven by the persistent heckling of the English single tax men, who insisted on asking him the questions suggested in the first "Social Statics," to bring out a small volume, entitled "Mr. Herbert Spencer on the Land Question," in which are reprinted in parallel columns Chap. IX of "Social Statics" with what he considers valid answers to himself as given in "Justice," 1891. This has also been reprinted by D. Appleton & Co., and constitutes, I think, the very funniest answer to himself ever made by a man who claimed to be a philosopher.]

swine agricultural gangs of boys and girls; it fills the gin palace and groggery with those who have no comfort in their homes; it makes lads who might be useful men candidates for prisons and penitentiaries; it fills brothels with girls who might have known the pure joy of motherhood; it sends greed and all evil passions prowling through society as a hard winter drives the wolves to the abodes of men; it darkens faith in the human soul, and across the reflection of a just and merciful Creator draws the veil of a hard, and blind, and cruel fate!

It is not merely a robbery in the past; it is a robbery in the present—a robbery that deprives of their birthright the infants that are now coming into the world! Why should we hesitate about making short work of such a system? Because I was robbed yesterday, and the day before, and the day before that, is it any reason that I should suffer myself to be robbed today and tomorrow? any reason that I should conclude that the robber has acquired a vested right to rob me? . . .

Try the case of the landholders by the maxims of the common law by which the rights of man and man are determined. The common law we are told is the perfection of reason, and certainly the landowners cannot complain of its decision, for it has been built up by and for landowners. Now what does the law allow to the innocent possessor when the land for which he paid his money is adjudged rightfully to belong to another? Nothing at all. That he purchased in good faith gives him no right or claim whatever. The law does not concern itself with the "intricate question of compensation" to the innocent purchaser. . . . And not only this, it takes from him all the improvements that he has in good faith made upon the land. You may have paid a high price for land, making every exertion to see that the title is good; you may have held it in undisturbed possession for years without thought or hint of an adverse claimant; made it fruitful by your toil or erected upon it a costly building of greater value than the land itself, or a modest home in which you hope, surrounded by the fig trees you have planted and the vines you have dressed, to pass your declining days; yet if Quirk, Gammon & Snap can mouse out a technical flaw in your parchments or hunt up some forgotten heir who never dreamed of his rights, not merely the land, but all your improvements, may be taken away from you. And not merely that. According to the common law, when you have surrendered the land and given up your improvements, you may be called upon to account for the profits you derived from the land during the time you had it.

Now if we apply to this case of The People vs. The Landowners the same maxims of justice that have been formulated by landowners into law, and are applied every day in English and American courts to disputes between man and man, we shall not only not think of giving the landholders any compensation for the land, but shall take all the improvements and whatever else they may have as well.

But I do not propose, and I do not suppose that any one else will propose, to go so far. It is sufficient if the people resume the ownership of the land. Let the landowners retain their improvements and personal property in secure possession.

And in this measure of justice would be no oppression, no injury to any class. The great cause of the present unequal distribution of wealth, with the suffering, degradation, and waste that it entails, would be swept away. Even landholders would share in the general gain. The gain of even the large landholders would be a real one. The gain of the small landholders would be enormous. For in welcoming Justice, men welcome the handmaid of Love. Peace and Plenty follow in her train, bringing their good gifts, not to some, but to all.

Property and Sovereignty

MORRIS RAPHAEL COHEN

II. THE JUSTIFICATION OF PROPERTY

1. The Occupation Theory

The oldest and up to recently the most influential defense of private property was based on the assumed right of the original discoverer and occupant to dispose of that which thus became his. This view dominated the thought of Roman jurists and of modern philosophers—from Grotius to Kant—so much so that the right of the laborer to the produce of his work was sometimes defended on the ground that the laborer "occupied" the material which he fashioned into the finished product.

It is rather easy to find fatal flaws in this view. Few accumulations of great wealth were ever simply found. Rather were they acquired by the labor of many, by conquest, by business manipulation, and by other means. It is obvious that today at any rate few economic goods can be acquired by discovery and first occupancy.[1] Even in the few cases when they are, as in fishing and trapping, we are apt rather to think of the labor involved as the proper basis of the property acquired. Indeed, there seems nothing ethically self-evident in the motto that "findings is keepings." There seems nothing wrong in a law that a treasure trove shall belong to the king or the state rather than to the finder. Shall the finder of a river be entitled to all the water in it?

From 13 *Cornell Law Quarterly* 8 (1927). © copyright 1927 by Cornell University. Reprinted by permission of Cornell University, Fred B. Rothman & Company, and Harry N. Rosenfield. Footnotes renumbered.

[1]In granting patents, copyrights, etc., the principle of reward for useful work or to encourage productivity seems so much more relevant that the principle of discovery and first occupancy seems to have little force.

Moreover, even if we were to grant that the original finder or occupier should have possession as against anyone else, it by no means follows that he may use it arbitrarily or that his rule shall prevail indefinitely after his death. The right of others to acquire the property from him by bargain, by inheritance, or by testamentary disposition, is not determined by the principle of occupation.

Despite all these objections, however, there is a kernel of positive value in this principle. Protecting the discoverer or first occupant, is really part of the more general principle that possession as such should be protected. There is real human economy in doing so until somebody shows a better claim than the possessor. It makes for certainty and security of transaction as well as for public peace—provided the law is ready to set aside possession acquired in ways that are inimical to public order. Various principles of justice may determine the distribution of goods and the retribution to be made for acts of injustice. But the law must not ignore the principle of inertia in human affairs. Continued possession creates expectations in the possessor and in others and only a very poor morality would ignore the hardship of frustrating these expectations and rendering human relations insecure, even to correct some old flaws in the original acquisition. Suppose some remote ancestor of yours did acquire your property by fraud, robbery or conquest, *e.g.* in the days of William of Normandy. Would it be just to take it away from you and your dependents who have held it in good faith? Reflection on the general insecurity that would result from such procedure leads us to see that as habit is the basis of individual life, continued practice must be the basis of social procedure. Any form of property which exists has therefore a claim to continue until it can be shown that the effort to change it is worth while. Continual changes in property laws would certainly discourage enterprise.

Nevertheless, it would be as absurd to argue that the distribution of property must never be modified by law as it would be to argue that the distribution of political power must never be changed. No less a philosopher than Aristotle argued against changing even bad laws, lest the habit of obedience be thereby impaired. There is something to be said for this, but only so long as we are in the realm of merely mechanical obedience. When we introduce the notion of free or rational obedience, Aristotle's argument loses its force in the political realm; and similar considerations apply to any property system that can claim the respect of rational beings.

2. The Labor Theory

That everyone is entitled to the full produce of his labor is assumed as self-evident by both socialists and conservatives who believe that capital is the result of the savings of labor. However, as economic goods are never the result of any one man's unaided labor, our maxim is altogether inapplicable. How shall we determine what part of the value of a table should belong to the carpenter, to the lumberman, to the transport worker, to the policeman who guarded the peace while the work was being done, and to the indefinitely large numbers of others whose cooperation was necessary? Moreover, even if we could tell what any one individual has produced—let us imagine a Robinson Crusoe growing up all alone on an island and in no way indebted to any community—it would still be highly questionable whether he has a right to keep the full produce of his labor when some shipwrecked mariner needs his surplus food to keep from starving.

In actual society no one ever thinks it unjust that a wealthy old bachelor should have part of his presumably just earnings taken away in the form of a tax for the benefit of other people's children, or that one immune to certain diseases, should be taxed to support hospitals, etc. We do not think there is any injustice involved in such cases because social interdependence is so intimate that no man can justly say: "This wealth is entirely and absolutely mine as the result of my own unaided effort."

The degree of social solidarity varies, of course; and it is easy to conceive of a sparsely settled community, such as Missouri at the beginning of the 19th century, where a family of hunters or isolated cultivators of the soil might regard everything which it acquired as the product of its own labor. Generally, however, human beings start with a stock of tools or information acquired from others and they are more or less dependent upon some government for protection against foreign aggression, etc.

Yet despite these and other criticisms, the labor theory contains too much substantial truth to be brushed aside. The essential truth is that labor has to be encouraged and that property must be distributed in such a way as to encourage ever greater efforts at productivity.

As not all things produced are ultimately good, as even good things may be produced at an unjustified expense in human life and worth, it is obvious that other principles besides that of labor or productivity are needed for an adequate basis or justification of any system of property law. We can only say dialectically that all other things being equal, property should be distributed with due regard to the productive needs of the community. We must, however, recognize that a good deal of property accrues to those who are not productive,[2] and a good deal of productivity does not and perhaps should not receive its reward in property. Nor should we leave this theme without recalling the Hebrew-Christian view—and for that matter, the specifically religious view—that the first claim on property is by the man who needs it rather than the man who has created it. Indeed, the only way of justifying the principle of distribution of property according to labor is to show that it serves the larger social need.

The occupation theory has shown us the necessity for security of possession and the labor theory the need for encouraging enterprise. These two needs are mutually dependent. Anything which discourages enterprise makes our possessions less valuable, and it is obvious that it is not worth while engaging in economic enterprise if there is no prospect of securely possessing the fruit of it. Yet there is also a conflict between these two needs. The owners of land, wishing to secure the continued posses-

---

[2]Economists often claim that the unearned increment is the greatest source of wealth. See Bull. of Am. Econ. Ass'n (4th ser., No. 2) 542 ff.

sion by the family, oppose laws which make it subject to free financial transactions or make it possible that land should be taken away from one's heirs by a judgment creditor for personal debts. In an agricultural economy security of possession demands that the owner of a horse should be able to reclaim it no matter into whose hands it has fallen. But in order that markets should be possible, it becomes necessary that the innocent purchaser should have a good title. This conflict between static and dynamic security has been treated most suggestively by Demogue and I need only refer you to his masterly book. *"Les Notions fondementales du Droit privé."*

3. Property and Personality

Hegel, Ahrens, Lorimer, and other idealists have tried to deduce the right of property from the individual's right to act as a free personality. To be free one must have a sphere of self-assertion in the external world. One's private property provides such an opportunity.

Waiving all traditional difficulties in applying the metaphysical idea of freedom to empirical legal acts, we may still object that the notion of personality is too vague to enable us to deduce definite legal consequences by means of it. How, for example, can the principle of personality help us to decide to what extent there shall be private rather than public property in railroads, mines, gas-works, and other public necessities?

Not the extremest communist would deny that in the interest of privacy certain personal belongings such as are typified by the toothbrush, must be under the dominion of the individual owner, to the absolute exclusion of everyone else. This, however, will not carry us far if we recall that the major effect of property in land, in the machinery of production, in capital goods, etc., is to enable the owner to exclude others from *their necessities,* and thus to compel them to serve him. Ahrens, one of the chief expounders of the personality theory, argues "It is undoubtedly contrary to the right of personality to have persons dependent on others on account of material goods."[3] But if this is so, the primary effect of property on a large scale is to limit freedom, since the one thing that private property law does not do is to guarantee a minimum of subsistence or the necessary tools of freedom to everyone. So far as a regime of private property fails to do the latter it rather compels people to part with their freedom.

It may well be argued in reply that just as restraining traffic rules in the end give us greater freedom of motion, so, by giving control over things to individual property owners, greater economic freedom is in the end assured to all. This is a strong argument, as can be seen by comparing the different degrees of economic freedom that prevail in lawless and in law abiding communities. It is, however, an argument for legal order rather than any particular form of government or private property. It argues for a regime where every one has a definite sphere of rights and

[3] II Cours de Droit Naturel (6th ed.) 108.

duties, but it does not tell us where these lines should be drawn. The principle of freedom of personality certainly cannot justify a legal order wherein a few can, by virtue of their legal monopoly over necessities, compel others to work under degrading and brutalizing conditions. A government which limits the right of large land-holders limits the rights of property and yet may promote real freedom. Property owners, like other individuals, are members of a community and must subordinate their ambition to the larger whole of which they are a part. They may find their compensation in spiritually identifying their good with that of the larger life.

4. The Economic Theory

The economic justification of private property is that by means of it a maximum of productivity is promoted. The classical economic argument may be put thus: The successful business man, the one who makes the greatest profit, is the one who has the greatest power to foresee effective demand. If he has not that power his enterprise fails. He is therefore, in fact, the best director of economic activities.

There can be little doubt that if we take the whole history of agriculture and industry, or compare the economic output in countries like Russia with that in the United States, there is a strong *prima facie* case for the contention that more intensive cultivation of the soil and greater productiveness of industry prevail under individual ownership. Many *a priori* psychologic and economic reasons can also be brought to explain why this must be so, why the individual cultivator will take greater care not to exhaust the soil, etc. All this, however, is so familiar that we may take it for granted and look at the other side of the case, at the considerations which show that there is a difference between socially desirable productivity and the desire for individual profits.

In the first place let us note that of many things the supply is not increased by making them private property. This is obviously true of land in cities and of other monopoly or limited goods. Private ownership of land does not increase the amount of rainfall, and irrigation works to make the land more fruitful have been carried through by government more than by private initiative. Nor was the productivity of French or Irish lands reduced when the property of their landlords in rent charges and other incidents of seigniorage was reduced or even abolished. In our own days, we frequently see tobacco, cotton or wheat farmers in distress because they have succeeded in raising too plentiful crops; and manufacturers who are well-informed know when greater profit is to be made by a decreased output. Patents for processes which would cheapen the product are often bought up by manufacturers and never used. Durable goods which are more economic to the consumer are very frequently crowded out of the market by shoddier goods which are more profitable to produce because of the larger turnover. Advertising campaigns often persuade people to buy the less economical goods and to pay the cost of the uneconomic advice.

In the second place, there are inherent sources of waste in a regime of private enterprise and free competition. If the biologic analogy of the struggle for existence were taken seriously, we should see that the natural survival of the economically fittest is attended, as in the biologic field, with frightful wastefulness. The elimination of the unsuccessful competitor may be a gain to the survivor but all business failures are losses to the community.

Finally, a regime of private ownership in industry is too apt to sacrifice social interests to immediate monetary profits. This shows itself in speeding up industry to such a pitch that men are exhausted in a relatively few years whereas a slower expenditure of their energy would prolong their useful years. It shows itself in the way in which private ownership enterprise has wasted a good deal of the natural resources of the United States to obtain immediate profits. Even when the directors of a modern industrial enterprise see the uneconomic consequences of immediate profits, the demand of shareholders of immediate dividends,[4] and the ease with which men can desert a business and leave it to others to stand the coming losses, all tend to encourage ultimately wasteful and uneconomic activity. Possibly the best illustration of this is child labor, which by lowering wages increases immediate profits, but in the end is really wasteful of the most precious wealth of the country, its future manhood and womanhood.

Surveying our arguments thus far: We have seen the roots of property in custom and in the need for economic productivity, in individual needs of privacy and in the need for social utility. But we have also noted that property, being only one among other human interests, cannot be pursued absolutely without detriment to human life. Hence we can no longer maintain Montesquieu's view that private property is sacrosanct and that the general government must in no way interfere with or retrench its domain. The issue before thoughtful people is therefore not the maintenance or abolition of private property, but the determination of the precise lines along which private enterprise must be given free scope and where it must be restricted in the interests of the common good.

III. LIMITATIONS OF PROPERTY RIGHTS

The traditional theory of rights, and the one that still prevails in this country, was molded by the struggle in the 17th and 18th centuries against restrictions on individual enterprise. These restrictions in the interest of special privilege were fortified by the divine (and therefore absolute) rights of kings. As is natural in all revolts, absolute claims on one side were met with absolute denials on the other. Hence the theory of the natural rights of the individual took not only an absolute but a negative

---

[4]Thus the leading brewers doubtless foresaw the coming of prohibition and could have saved millions in losses by separating their interests from that of the saloon. But the large temporary loss involved in such an operation was something that stockholders could never have agreed to.

form; men have *in*alienable rights, the state must never interfere with private property, etc. The state, however, must interfere in order that individual rights should become effective and not degenerate into public nuisances. To permit anyone to do absolutely what he likes with his property in creating noise, smells, or danger of fire, would be to make property in general valueless. To be really effective, therefore, the right of property must be supported by restrictions or positive duties on the part of owners, enforced by the state as much as the right to exclude others which is the essence of property. Unfortunately, however, whether because of the general decline of juristic philosophy after Hegel or because law has become more interested in defending property against attacks by socialists, the doctrine of natural rights has remained in the negative state and has never developed into a doctrine of the positive contents of rights.[5] . . .

As a believer in natural rights, I believe that the state can, and unfortunately often does enact unjust laws. But I think it is a sheer fallacy based on verbal illusion to think that the rights of the community against an individual owner are no better than the rights of a neighbor. Indeed, no one has in fact had the courage of this confusion to argue that the state has no right to deprive an individual of property to which he is so attached that he refuses any money for it. Though no neighbor has such a right the public interest often justly demands that a proprietor shall part with his ancestral home to which he may be attached by all the roots of his being.

When taking away a man's property, is the state always bound to pay a direct compensation? I submit that while this is generally advisable in order not to disturb the general feeing of security, no absolute principle of justice requires it. I have alluded before to the fact that there is no injustice in taxing an old bachelor to educate the children of others, or to tax one immune to typhoid for the construction of sewers or other sanitary measures. We may go farther and say that the whole business of the state depends upon its rightful power to take away the property of some (in the form of taxation) and use it to support others, such as the needy, those invalided in the service of the state in war or peace, and those who are not yet able to produce but in whom the hope of humanity is embodied. Doubtless, taxation and confiscation may be actuated by malice and may impose needless and cruel hardship on some individuals or classes. But this is not to deny that taxation and confiscation are within the just powers of the state. A number of examples may make this clearer.

(a) Slavery. When slavery is abolished by law, the owners have their property taken away. Is the state ethically bound to pay them the full market value of their slaves? It is doubtless a grievous shock to a community to have a large number of slave owners whose wealth often makes

---

[5]Thus our courts are reluctant to admit that rules against unfair competition may be in the interest of the general public and not merely for those whose immediate property interests are directly affected. Levy v. Walker, 10 Ch. D. 436 (1878); American Washboard Co. v. Saginaw Mfg. Co., 103 Fed. 281, 285 (C.C.A. 6th, 1900); Dickenson v. N.R.Co., 76 W.Va. 148, 151, 85 S.E. 71(1915).

them leaders of culture, suddenly deprived of their income. It may also be conceded that it is not always desirable for the slave himself to be suddenly taken away from his master and cut adrift on the sea of freedom. But when one reads of the horrible ways in which some of those slaves were violently torn from their homes in Africa and shamelessly deprived of their human rights, one is inclined to agree with Emerson that compensation should first be paid to the slaves. This compensation need not be in the form of a direct bounty to them. It may be more effectively paid in the form of rehabilitation and education for freedom; and such a charge may take precedence over the claims of the former owners. After all, the latter claims are no greater than those of a protected industry when the tariff is removed. If the state should decide that certain import duties, e. g. those on scientific instruments, or hospital supplies, are unjustified and proceed to abolish them, many manufacturers may suffer. Are they entitled to compensation by the state?

It is undoubtedly for the general good to obviate as much as possible the effect of economic shock to a large number of people. The routine of life prospers on security. But when that security contains a large element of injustice the shock of an economic operation by law may be necessary and ethically justified.

This will enable us to deal with other types of confiscation.

(b) Financial loss through the abolition of public office. It is only in very recent times that we have got into the habit of ignoring the fact that public office is and always has been regarded as a source of revenue like any other occupation. When, therefore, certain public offices are abolished for the sake of good government, a number of people are deprived of their expected income. In the older law and often in popular judgment of today this does not seem fair. But reflection shows that the state is not obligated to pay anyone when it finds that particular services of his are unnecessary. At best, it should help him to find a new occupation.

Part of the prerogative of the English or Scotch landlord was the right to nominate the priest for the parish on his land. To abolish this right of advowson is undoubtedly a confiscation of a definite property right. But while I cannot agree with my friend Mr. Laski[6] that the courts were wrong to refuse to disobey the law which subordinated the religious scruples of a church to the property rights of an individual, I do not see that there could have been any sound ethical objection to the legislature changing the law without compensating the landlord.

(c) In our own day, we have seen the confiscation of many millions of dollars of property through prohibition. Were the distillers and brewers entitled to compensation for their losses? We have seen that property on a large scale is power and the loss of it, while evil to those who are accustomed to exercise it, may not be an evil to the community. In point of fact, the shock to the distillers and brewers was not as serious as to others, e. g. saloon keepers and bartenders who did not lose any legal property since they were only employees, but who found it difficult late in life to enter new employments.

---

[6]LASKI, STUDIES IN SOVEREIGNTY, ch. on the Great Disruption.

History is full of examples of valuable property privileges abolished without any compensation, *e. g.* the immunity of nobles from taxation, their rights to hunt over other people's lands, etc. It would be absurd to claim that such legislation was unjust.

These and other examples of justifiable confiscation without compensation are inconsistent with the absolute theory of private property. An adequate theory of private property, however, should enable us to draw the line between justifiable and unjustifiable cases of confiscation. Such a theory I cannot undertake to elaborate on this occasion, though the doctrine of security of possession and avoidance of unnecessary shock seem to me suggestive. I wish however to urge that if the large property owner is viewed, as he ought to be, as a wielder of power over the lives of his fellow citizens, the law should not hesitate to develop a doctrine as to his positive duties in the public interest. The owner of a tenement house in a modern city is in fact a public official and has all sorts of positive duties. He must keep the halls lighted, he must see that the roof does not leak, that there are fire-escape facilities, he must remove tenants guilty of certain public immoralities, etc., and he is compensated by the fees of his tenants which the law is beginning to regulate. Similar is the case of a factory owner. He must install all sorts of safety appliances, hygienic conveniences, see that the workmen are provided with a certain amount of light, air, etc.

In general, there is no reason for the law insisting that people should make the most economic use of their property. They have a motive in doing so themselves and the cost of the enforcing machinery may be a mischievous waste. Yet there may be times, such as occurred during the late war, when the state may insist that man shall cultivate the soil intensively and be otherwise engaged in socially productive work.

With considerations such as these in mind, it becomes clear that there is no unjustifiable taking away of property when railroads are prohibited from posting notice that they will discharge their employees if the latter join trade unions, and that there is no property taken away without due or just process of law when an industry is compelled to pay its laborers a minimum of subsistence instead of having it done by private or public charity or else systematically starving its workers.

Suggestions for Further Reading

Other social contract theorists differ sharply from Rousseau. Locke, in his *Second Treatise of Government,* holds, as we have seen earlier, a labor theory of property rather than a contractarian one. Thomas Hobbes, in the *Leviathan,* the Second Part, Chapter 21, insists on significant civil liberties for citizens, liberties that are incompatible with Rousseau's idea of total alienation of individual rights. And the major recent work in this tradition—John Rawls's *A Theory of Justice* (Cambridge, Mass.: Belknap Press of Harvard University Press, 1971)—has very little to say about property. What Rawls does say is that the choice between various mixes of public and private ownership in a society is a political judgment that will "turn on which variation will work out best in practice" (p. 274).

For a general introduction to utilitarian theory, the reader can consult David Lyons's *The Forms and Limits of Utilitarianism* (Oxford: Clarendon Press, 1965); Rolf Sartorius's *Individual Conduct and Social Norms* (Encino, Calif.: Dickenson, 1975); and R. B. Brandt's *Theory of the Good and the Right* (Oxford: Clarendon Press, 1979). Other relevant work by Mill includes his *Utilitarianism* and *On Liberty*.

Joseph L. Sax, "Takings, Private Property and Public Rights," 81 *Yale Law Journal* 149 (1971), offers a useful discussion of when the state must pay compensation. Portions of the article are reprinted in Bruce A. Ackerman, ed., *Economic Foundations of Property Law* (Boston: Little, Brown, 1975). Robert Nozick's position on redistribution is very much less permissive about uncompensated takings. See his *Anarchy, State and Utopia* (New York: Basic Books, 1974), 150–153 and 167–173. Lawrence C. Becker also proposes a less permissive account in "Economic Justice: Three Problems," *Ethics* 89 (1979): 385–393.

The justifications referred to in Cohen's article are analyzed in detail in Lawrence C. Becker's *Property Rights: Philosophic Foundations* (London: Routledge & Kegan Paul, 1977). Becker also considers the notion of "property worthiness" and a potential argument from ethological and sociobiological findings.

Primary source material on the "property of personality" view may be found in Immanuel Kant, *The Metaphysics of Morals*, Part I, *The Metaphysical Elements of Justice*, trans. John Ladd (Indianapolis: Bobbs-Merrill, 1965), 44–56; and G. W. F. Hegel, *Philosophy of Right*, trans. T. M. Knox (Oxford: Clarendon Press, 1942), 37–41. The view is criticized in T. H. Green, *Principles of Political Obligation* [reissue of the 1882 edition] (Ann Arbor: University of Michigan Press, 1967), chap. N.

SECTION FOUR
THE ECONOMY AND
THE CORPORATION

Many recent discussions of property have focused upon the place of the concept in the modern economy, characterized as it is by large-scale corporations, mechanized labor, pollution, depletion of natural resources, and governmental regulation. We begin with a parable by Henry G. Manne, intended to show that, whatever the evils of unrestricted ownership rights and a free market, the cure by governmental regulation may well be worse than the disease. While many would readily grant the modest point that regulation can impose high social costs, it may be questioned how far—and to which cases in particular—the parable can be extended.

The opposite idea, that private property can impose high social costs, is central to the argument of W. Michael Hoffman and James V. Fisher in their article "Corporate Responsibility: Property and Liability." The traditional idea of private property would appear to make owners liable for all damages if what they own (or what they have abandoned) does injury to others. The authors maintain that the modern notion of limited liability for corporations would appear to provide a basis for viewing these organizations as common property. "Why should it be considered right to put a limit on liability . . . but not to have some sort of similar limit on the use or benefits?"

David Ellerman, an economist at the University of Massachusetts at Boston, argues that our ordinary ideas about responsibility (in the sense of "Who did it?") lead one to the conclusion that those whose labor produces property should be recognized as legally owning it and legally liable for the obligations created by production. This appears to be the classical labor theory of property. But when Jones goes to work for the ABC Corporation, we think of the widgets he makes as belonging to ABC and not to Jones. From Ellerman's perspective, the contract between ABC and Jones is an invalid contract. Capitalist production is thus a legalized form of theft. While Ellerman's arguments are presented in the context of a sharp criticism of capitalism, they are, as he is concerned to point out, equally applicable to state socialism. What Ellerman favors is what has been called "workers' self-management."

E. F. Schumacher, in this excerpt form his influential book *Small Is Beautiful*, argues for a sweeping revision in the way Western economists have tended to think about work. While in the West we are inclined to think of labor as the *source* of wealth (a "cost" and not a "benefit"), Schumacher, drawing upon the Buddhist idea of "Right Livelihood," argues that, in effect, labor can be counted as wealth itself. In addition to bringing forth the goods required for a "becoming existence," it can permit us to develop our faculties and overcome our "ego-centredness by joining with other people in a common task." Schumacher traces out some of the implications of this view: for mechanization, unemployment, the assessment of economic systems, the use of natural resources, and modernization. Though his concern is more broadly with materialism, he provides us with an appropriate reminder of what has been observed elsewhere: that there is more to the good life than the joys of ownership and more to the moral life than the rights and duties of property.

The Parable of the Parking Lots

H. MANNE

In a city not far away there was a large football stadium. It was used from time to time for various events, but the principal use was for football games played Saturday afternoons by the local college team. The games were tremendously popular, and people drove hundreds of miles to watch them. Parking was done in the usual way. People who arrived early were able to park free on the streets, and latecomers had to pay to park in regular and improvised lots.

Reprinted with permission of the author from: *The Public Interest*, No. 23 (Spring 1971), pp. 10–15. © 1971 by National Affairs, Inc.

There were, at distances ranging from five to twelve blocks from the stadium, approximately twenty-five commercial parking lots, all of which received some business from Saturday afternoon football games. The lots closer to the stadium naturally received more football business than those further away, and some of the very close lots actually raised their price on Saturday afternoons. But they did not raise the price much, and most did not change prices at all. The reason was not hard to find.

For something else happened on football afternoons. A lot of people who during the week were students, lawyers, school teachers, plumbers, factory workers, and even stockbrokers went into the parking lot business. It was not a difficult thing to do. Typically a young boy would put up a crude, homemade sign saying, "Parking $3." He would direct a couple of cars into his parents' driveway, tell the driver to take the key, and collect the three dollars. If the driveway was larger or there was yard space to park in, an older brother, an uncle, or the head of the household would direct the operation, sometimes asking drivers to leave their keys so that shifts could be made if necessary.

Some part-time parking lot operators who lived very close to the stadium charged as much as $5 to park in their driveways. But as the residences-turned-parking-lots were located further from the stadium (and incidentally closer to the commercial parking lots), the price charged at game time declined. In fact, houses at some distance from the stadium charged less than the adjacent commercial lots. The whole system seemed to work fairly smoothly, and though traffic just after a big game was terrible, there were no significant delays parking cars or retrieving parked cars.

But one day the owner of a chain of parking lots called a meeting of all the commercial parking lot owners in the general vicinity of the stadium. They formed an organization known as the Association of Professional Parking Lot Employers, or APPLE. And they were very concerned about the Saturday parking business. One man who owned four parking lots pointed out that honest parking lot owners had heavy capital investments in their businesses, that they paid taxes, and that they employed individuals who supported families. There was no reason, he alleged, why these lots should not handle all the cars coming into the area for special events like football games. "It is unethical," he said, "to engage in cutthroat competition with irresponsible fender benders. After all, parking cars is a profession, not a business." This last remark drew loud applause.

Thus emboldened he continued, stating that commercial parking lot owners recognize their responsibility to serve the public's needs. Ethical car parkers, he said, understand their obligations not to dent fenders, to employ only trustworthy car parkers, to pay decent wages, and generally to care for their customers' automobiles as they would the corpus of a trust. His statement was hailed by others attending the meeting as being very statesmanlike.

Others at the meeting related various tales of horror about nonprofessional car parkers. One homeowner, it was said, actually allowed his fifteen-year-old son to move other peoples' cars around. Another said that he had seen an $8,000 Cadillac parked on a dirt lawn where it would have become mired in mud had it rained that day. Still another pointed out that a great deal of the problem came on the side of the stadium with the lower-priced houses, where there were more driveways per block than on the wealthier side of the stadium. He pointed out that these poor people would rarely be able to afford to pay for damage to other peoples' automobiles or to pay insurance premiums to cover such losses. He felt that a professional group such as APPLE had a duty to protect the public from their folly in using those parking spaces.

Finally another speaker reminded the audience that these "marginal, fly-by-night" parking lot operators generally parked a string of cars in their driveways so that a driver had to wait until all cars behind his had been removed before he could get his out. This, he pointed out, was quite unlike the situation in commercial lots where, during a normal business day, people had to be assured of ready access to their automobiles at any time. The commercial parking lots either had to hire more attendants to shift cars around, or they had to park them so that any car was always accessible, even though this meant that fewer cars could park than the total space would actually hold. "Clearly," he said, "driveway parking constitutes unfair competition."

Emotions ran high at this meeting, and every member of APPLE pledged $1 per parking space for something mysteriously called a "slush fund." It was never made clear exactly whose slush would be bought with these funds, but several months later a resolution was adopted by the city council requiring licensing for anyone in the parking lot business.

The preamble to the new ordinance read like the speeches at the earlier meeting. It said that this measure was designed to protect the public against unscrupulous, unprofessional, and undercapitalized parking lot operators. It required, inter alia, that anyone parking cars for a fee must have a minimum capital devoted to the parking lot business of $25,000, liability insurance in an amount not less than $500,000, bonding for each car parker, and a special driving test for these parkers (which incidentally would be designed and administered by APPLE). The ordinance also required, again in the public's interest, that every lot charge a single posted price for parking and that any change in the posted price be approved in advance by the city council. Incidentally, most members were able to raise their fees by about 20 percent before the first posting.

Then a funny thing happened to drivers on their way to the stadium for the next big game. They discovered city police in unusually large numbers informing them that it was illegal to pay a non-licensed parking lot operator for the right to park a car. These policemen also reminded parents that if their children were found in violation of this ordinance, it could result in a misdemeanor charge being brought against the parents and possible juvenile court proceedings for the children. There were no driveway parking lots that day.

Back at the commercial parking lots, another funny thing occurred. Proceeding from the entrance of each of these parking lots within twelve blocks of the stadium were long lines of cars waiting to park. The line got larger as the lot was closer to the stadium. Many drivers had to wait so long or walk so far that they missed the entire first quarter of the big game.

At the end of the game it was even worse. The confusion was massive. The lot attendants could not cope with the jam-up, and some cars were actually not retrieved until the next day. It was even rumored about town that some automobiles had been lost forever and that considerable liabilities might result for some operators. Industry spokesmen denied this, however.

Naturally there was a lot of grumbling, but there was no agreement on what had caused the difficulty. At first, everyone said there were merely some "bugs" in the new system that would have to be ironed out. But the only bug ironed out was a Volkswagen which was flattened by a careless lot attendant in a Cadillac Eldorado.

The situation did not improve at subsequent games. The members of APPLE did not hire additional employees to park cars, and operators near the stadium were not careful to follow their previous practice of parking cars in such a way as to have them immediately accessible. Employees seemed to become more surly, and the number of dented-fender claims mounted rapidly.

Little by little, too, cars began appearing in residential driveways again. For instance, one enterprising youth regularly went into the car wash business on football afternoons, promising that his wash job would take at least two hours. He charged $5, and got it—even on rainy days—in fact, especially on rainy days. Another homeowner offered to take cars on consignment for three hours to sell them at prices fixed by the owner. He charged $4 for this "service," but his subterfuge was quickly squelched by the authorities. The parking situation remained "critical."

Political pressures on the city council began to mount to "do something" about the inordinate delays in parking and retrieving cars on football afternoons. The city council sent a stern note of warning to APPLE, and APPLE appointed a special study group recruited from the local university's computer science department to look into the matter. This group reported that the managerial and administrative machinery in the parking lot business was archaic. What was needed, the study group said, was less goose quills and stand-up desks and more computers and conveyor belts. It was also suggested that all members of APPLE be hooked into one computer so that cars could readily be shifted to the most accessible spaces.

Spokesmen for the industry took up the cry of administrative modernization. Subtle warnings appeared in the local papers suggesting that if the industry did not get its own house in order, heavy-handed regulation could be anticipated. The city council asked for reports on failures to deliver cars and decreed that this would include any failure to put a driver in his car within five minutes of demand without a new dent.

Some of the professional operators actually installed computer equipment to handle their ticketing and parking logistics problems. And some added second stories to their parking lots. Others bought up additional space, thereby raising the value of vacant lots in the area. But many simply added a few additional car parkers and hoped that the problem would go away without a substantial investment of capital.

The commercial operators also began arguing that they needed higher parking fees because of their higher operating costs. Everyone agreed that costs for operating a parking lot were certainly higher than before the licensing ordinance. So the city council granted a request for an across-the-board 10 percent hike in fees. The local newspaper editorially hoped that this would ease the problem without still higher fees being necessary. In a way, it did. A lot of people stopped driving. They began using city buses, or they chartered private buses for the game. Some stayed home and watched the game on TV. A new study group on fees was appointed.

Just about then several other blows fell on the parking lot business. Bus transportation to the area near the stadium was improved with a federal subsidy to the municipal bus company. And several new suburban shopping centers caused a loss of automobile traffic in the older areas of town. But most dramatic of all, the local university, under severe pressure from its students and faculty, dropped intercollegiate football altogether and converted the stadium into a park for underprivileged children.

The impact of these events on the commercial parking lots was swift. Income declined drastically. The companies that had borrowed money to finance the expansion everyone wanted earlier were hardest hit. Two declared bankruptcy, and many had to be absorbed by financially stronger companies. Layoffs among car parkers were enormous, and APPLE actually petitioned the city council to guarantee the premiums on their liability insurance policies so that people would not be afraid to park commercially. This idea was suggested to APPLE by recent Congressional legislation creating an insurance program for stock brokers.

A spokesman for APPLE made the following public statement: "New organizations or arrangements may be necessary to straighten out this problem. There has been a failure in both the structure of the industry and the regulatory scheme. New and better regulation is clearly demanded. A sound parking lot business is necessary for a healthy urban economy." The statement was hailed by the industry as being very statesmanlike, though everyone speculated about what he really meant.

Others in the industry demanded that the city bus service be curtailed during the emergency. The city council granted every rate increase the lots requested. There were no requests for rate decreases, but the weaker lots began offering prizes and other subtle or covert rebates to private bus companies who would park with them. In fact, this problem became so serious and uncontrollable that one owner of a large chain proclaimed that old-fashioned price competition for this business would be desirable. This again was hailed as statesmanlike, but everyone assumed that he really meant something else. No one proposed repeal of the licensing ordinance.

One other thing happened. Under pressure from APPLE, the city council decreed that henceforth no parking would be allowed on any streets in the downtown area of town. The local merchants were extremely unhappy with this, however, and the council rescinded the ordinance at the next meeting, citing a computer error as the basis for the earlier restriction.

The ultimate resolution of the "new" parking problem is not in sight. The parking lot industry in this town not very far from here is now said to be a depressed business, even a sick one. Everyone looks to the city council for a solution, but things will probably limp along as they are for quite a while, picking up with an occasional professional football game and dropping low with bad weather.

$$* \quad * \quad *$$

MORAL: If you risk your lot under an apple tree, you may get hit in the head.

Corporate Responsibility
Property and Liability

W. MICHAEL HOFFMAN AND JAMES V. FISHER

I

Daniel Bell suggested in the early seventies that the question of social responsibility would be the crux of a debate that would serve as a turning point for the corporation in modern society.[1] This thought has been echoed recently by George Lodge in his book *The New American Ideology*. Bell and Lodge are the most recent in a line of social theorists who portray our society—and particularly the world of business—as in the midst of one of the great transformations of Western civilization. Old ideas that once legitimized our institutions are eroding in the face of changing operational realities. And one of the most important of these ideas being challenged is that of private property.[2] For example Lodge says:

[1] Daniel Bell, *The Coming of Post-Industrial Society: A Venture in Social Forecasting* (New York: Basic Books, 1973), p. 291.

[2] The classic analysis which generated much of the contemporary discussion is A. A. Berle, Jr., and G. G. Means, *The Modern Corporation and Private Property* (New York: The Macmillan Company, 1932). See also A. A. Berle, Jr., *Power Without Property* (London: Sidgwick and Jackson, 1959).

A curious thing has happened to private property—it has stopped being very important. After all, *what difference* does it really make today *whether a person owns or just enjoys property?* . . . The value of property as a legitimizing idea and basis of authority has eroded as well. It is obvious that our large public corporations are not private property at all. . . . It was to (the) notion of *community need,* for example, that ITT appealed in 1971 when it sought to prevent the Justice Department from divesting it of Hartford Fire Insurance. . . . Note that here, *as so often happens, it was the company that argued the ideologically radical case.*[3] [Emphasis added]

At the heart of the entire debate is the question of the nature of the corporation. Is the corporation primarily an instrument of owners or is it an autonomous enterprise which can freely decide where its economic and moral responsibilities lie? This question arose with the advent of the megacorporation and its *de facto* separation of ownership and control. Stockholding owners today have little or no direct control over what they "own," control being for all practical purposes totally in the specially trained hands of management. With this operational shift of power to management, corporate objectives have enlarged to include at least a recognition of social obligations other than providing the greatest possible financial gain or advantage for their stockholders. But herein lie questions not only as to what these corporate social obligations are and how they are to be acted upon, but more importantly, as to what conceptually justifies and legitimizes the corporation itself now that private property theory is said to have eroded. Answers to the former clearly are dependent on answers to the latter.

Through a variety of rather slippery normative moves, corporate revisionists like Galbraith seem to argue that the great corporation must now simply be regarded as no longer a private but really a public institution. This would, presumably, provide a basis for corporate social responsibility that goes significantly beyond Friedman's "one and only one" social responsibility of business—to increase its profits.[4] Such a "corporate revolution" would appear to mean that the corporation is moving away (whether consciously or unconsciously) from legitimizing itself as *private property* to legitimizing itself as more like *common property.* In fact, perhaps the modern corporation should be seen as an exemplification of the philosophical unsoundness of private property, a strange development, to be sure, since the theory of private property has ostensibly been the essential pillar of capitalism itself.

It is important to note that the analysis which we have just sketched has focused almost exclusively on the issue of *control.* Traditionally, three

---

[3] George C. Lodge, *The New American Ideology* (New York: Alfred A. Knopf, Inc., 1975), pp. 17–19. Also see his article "Business Ethics and Ideology" delivered at Bentley College's "First National Conference on Business Ethics," published in the Conference *Proceedings,* edited by W. Michael Hoffman, Center for Business Ethics, 1977.

[4] Milton Friedman, *Capitalism and Freedom* (Chicago: University of Chicago Press, 1962), p. 133.

elements have characterized property: the right to control, to benefit from, and to alienate (to sell or dispose of) something. An analysis of property which focuses exclusively on *control*, however, is seriously deficient, and a somewhat different picture of the question of corporate social responsibility begins to emerge when one focuses on the property rights of benefit and alienation. Clearly there are dangers to a society in the midst of radical change if it proceeds to discard basic legitimizing ideas of such social import as that of private property before it carefully considers the logic of that move.

It is an interesting fact to ponder that no fully adequate explication of a theory of justification of property acquisition has yet been achieved in modern Western social philosophy. By fully adequate is meant (a) a theory which goes beyond the "justification" that possession *is* ownership, i.e., that having an enforceable claim to something is to be understood as having the power to enforce that claim, and (b) a theory which is reasonably congruent with social realities.[5] The lack of a fully adequate theory of property, however, does not preclude examination of the notion of property itself.

In this paper our primary interest is with the internal logic of the notion of property. The logic of *private property*, it will be argued, indicates a class of things which cannot become (or at least remain) private property, and thus the concept of private property suggests an inevitable transition from (some kinds of) private property to common property. Moreover, the theory of the "managerial revolution" will be seen to result in a gerrymandered definition of private property rather than in an innocent discarding of the idea. The social analysts who have focused on corporate control have made an important empirical observation, but, in reference to the issue of the relation of the corporation, private property, and social responsibility, they have generated serious conceptual confusion. Nor have the philosophers helped very much.

II

The property rights of control, benefit, and alienation always imply the right to exclude. Since we intend to focus on the right to benefit, the following is proposed as a working definition of *private property* in order to clarify and highlight the logic of the notion of property.[6]

(1a)   *Something* (x) *is the private property of someone* (S) *if and only if S has the right to exclude all others from the use or benefit of* x.

[5] A more detailed discussion of this issue is contained in J. V. Fisher, "Hegel and Private Property (or, the Case of T$_n$ the Tiger)" (unpublished manuscript), from which portions of this paper were adapted. See also Lawrence Becker, *Property Rights: Philosophic Foundations* (London: Routledge and Kegan Paul, 1978).

[6] These definitions are adapted from C. B. Macpherson, "A Political Theory of Property," in *Democratic Theory: Essays in Retrieval* (Oxford: Clarendon Press, 1973), p. 128.

The right to alienate will be considered directly, though no attempt will be made in this paper to develop a satisfactory definition integrating the errant element of control.

Common property, on the other hand, must be defined in such a way as to include the individual rights of those who share ownership as well as the collective right of the owners to exclude all others.

(2a)   *Something* (x) *is the common property of two or more people* (S_1, S_2, *etc.*) *if and only if* S_1, S_2, *etc. together have the right to exclude all others from the use or benefit of* x, *and* S_1, S_2, *etc. each has the right* not *to be excluded from the use or benefit of* x.

These definitions which emphasize the right to exclude or the right not to be excluded are, it will be argued, incomplete. There is, in fact, a *double-edged* exclusion which will become obvious when we consider the right to alienate or dispose of something.

To elaborate further the concept of common property, let us consider what it means for something to be common property. Suppose an apple tree is the common property of S_1, S_2, etc., and suppose further that it is autumn and the apple tree in question is now full of ripe apples. If S_1 were to pick one of those ripe apples and eat it, and assuming no prior agreement to refrain from eating any apples (say, for example, to save them all for pressing cider), then it would make little sense for S_2 to say to S_1: "You had no right to eat that apple since it was common property and you have now excluded the rest of us from the use or benefit of it." Here being common property would appear to mean (again in the absence of some specific agreement) that while S_1 had indeed excluded S_2 from the use or benefit of that apple, nevertheless S_2 had not been excluded from the use or benefit of the apple tree—at least as long as there is another ripe apple for S_2. The problem becomes somewhat more complicated if that autumn the apple tree in question were to have borne only one edible apple (each gets one bite?), but clearly any individual commoner's right not to be excluded cannot be taken to mean an *absolute* preclusion of any other individual commoner's actual use of the common property. What this suggests is that any notion of common property is incomplete without some (implicit or explicit) procedure for "fair-taking/using."

III

It was Hegel who pointed out, though no one seems to have followed up on the point, that *owning* something is an action. To put the same point somewhat differently, a necessary condition for S's owning x is S's intention to own x. As Hegel put it, ". . . a person puts his (or her) will into a thing—this is just the concept of property. . . ."[7] Clearly I may possess, use, or benefit from something *without* intending or claiming to own it. I

[7] Hegel, *Philosophy of Right*, trans. T. M. Knox (Oxford University Press, 1952), §51A.

cannot *own* something accidentally (though possible modifications of this will be noted in a moment). Without S's intention to own *x*, S's possession of *x* is no more ownership than S's arm moving would be S's action without S's intending that S's arm move. It follows, then, that S's property is S's in precisely the same way and for the same reason that S's action is S's. Since this is true for any theory of property, the (perhaps surprising) consequences apply for any and all theories of property.

In modern Western society it has commonly been assumed that the term "property" automatically (or even necessarily) meant *private* property. It should be clear, however, that if we can talk about common or joint action, we can also talk about common property. We need no such notion as that of some (fictitious) corporate intention (the intention of the whole as if there were such a thing as a group mind). In other words, there is a clear parallel between "S_1 and S_2 together do something (joint action)" and "S_1 and S_2 together own something (common property)." What should be said is *not* that property necessarily takes the form of private property, but that property is a right which necessarily takes the form of an *individual right*. And this is true whether it is a *right to exclude*, on the one hand, or on the other, a *right not to be excluded*, i.e., whether it is a private property or a common property right.

We can talk about at least three modes in which an individual makes a claim (at least a *de facto* claim) to *own* something: (1) taking possession; (2) use; and (3) alienating or *disowning* it. We will elaborate (1) briefly and then move to (3), since it is of greatest interest for the argument being developed in this paper.

Under the first category, taking possession, at least three elements can be distinguished: directly grasping something physically—what is referred to in legal contracts as "taking possession"; shaping, forming, or developing something; and taking possession by simply marking something as one's own. Note the function of the concept of intention in all three of these activities. Not only is it a necessary element in ownership, its scope extends beyond the immediate relation to the thing itself. Thus the claim to ownership extends to not only such things as unknown parts (mineral deposits, etc.) and organic results (eggs, the offspring, etc.), but also connections made by chance subsequent to the original acquisition (alluvial deposits, jetsam, etc.). This is even more explicit when I take possession by shaping or forming something. By shaping or forming it, I take more than just the immediate constituents into my possession. This applies to the organic (breeding of cattle, etc.) as well as to the reshaping of raw materials and the "forces of nature." The point that needs to be emphasized is that marking something as my own is an action that extends my intention to ownership beyond the immediate thing itself, a principle that has been long accepted in legal theory and in social practice (and in fact is at the basis of our patent laws, etc.).

It is with the third category, however, that we come to the most interesting move. In a sense when I *disown* something (e.g., by selling it) I intend the thing in its entirety (I intend, so to speak, to be rid of it) and so presuppose the claim that it is/was most completely my own.

It is at this point that we can see clearly the missing half of our definitions of property. Note that it is generally held that there are two ways of *disowning* something:

(i)   I may yield it to the intention (will) of another, i.e., to another's claim to ownership (usually in exchange for something I deem valuable, though it may be an outright gift as long as the recipient accepts it as his or her own); or

(ii) I may abandon it (as *res nullius*, the property of no one? or as now the common property of all?).

The first option is clear enough and if we pursued that discussion the questions would center around the issue of what constitutes a fair exchange. But what about the second option? Where does the logic of disowning lead us? Consider the following case:

> Suppose S, being perceptive and industrious, notes that there is a good market for tiger skins (well tanned, handsome to the eye, and luxurious to the touch). Furthermore, there are wild tigers in S's vicinity and the tigers may rightfully be appropriated by anyone and thus become the private property of the one who appropriates them (there being plenty of tigers in the vicinity relative to the number of people, etc.). By virtue of S's physical strength, cunning, and dexterity (as well as industriousness), S is able to capture several of these tigers intending to breed them in captivity for their very fine skins. Suppose further that S is successful initially in breeding the tigers, but it soon develops that they do not live long enough in captivity to grow to a size to produce sufficiently luxurious skins. But S is undaunted and eventually, by ingenuity and much hard labor, is successful in breeding stock that is long-lived, very handsome and adequately large.
>
> Let's suppose further that as a result of this ingenious breeding process S produces a tiger, we can call it T_n, which has two very special and advantageous characteristics: (a) T_n regularly sheds its skin, leaving each time a very fine tiger skin ready to be tanned and sold; and (b) T_n appears to be immune to the aging process and even impervious to anything which might harm or even kill it. T_n appears to be indestructible, a source, it seems, of an infinite number of fine tiger skins.
>
> Can it be doubted that T_n is the private property of S, that S has the right to exclude all others from the use or benefit of T_n? If anything could ever satisfy the traditional property accounts like those of Kant, Locke, and Hegel, surely S's ownership of T_n could.
>
> Now let's imagine that one day T_n begins to show signs of a developing nasty temperament, and finally it becomes painfully clear to S that T_n is a serious danger to S (far outweighing the amazing advantages which T_n manifests), and as well a danger to those in S's immediate living unit, S's neighbors, and even S's whole community. But T_n is indestructible (or at least no one has yet found a way to do away with T_n). What is S to do? The danger is critical.
>
> Aha! S, using what precautions are possible, takes T_n one day to the village green and in the presence of the (not too happy) villagers makes the following announcement: "I, S, who have rightfully acquired this tiger, T_n, as my private property, do here and now publicly renounce, relinquish, and

abandon my property in T_n." We are assuming, of course, that S has attempted to transfer property in T_n to someone else, to yield S's property in T_n to the will of another and so into that person's possession, but understandably has found no takers.

Imagine then that the next day S's neighbor appears at S's door, cut and scratched and bearing the remains of a flock of sheep which had been destroyed during the night. "Look what your tiger has done," says the neighbor to S. "My tiger?" responds S. "I renounced and abandoned my property in that tiger yesterday. That's not *my* tiger." No doubt we would be more than a little sympathetic with the neighbor's reply: "The hell it's not *your* tiger!"

It is interesting to observe that Kant, Locke, and Hegel (to name only a few) all treat property *only* as if it were a good, i.e., as if the right to exclude all others was something always desirable (note our use of the term "goods"). Why is it that these pillars of modern Western social and political philosophy have apparently ignored what we might call the "garbage factor"? (Which is not to say that those involved with the practice of law and politics have likewise ignored this factor.) Is it because we no longer live in an age when people commonly throw their garbage out the window? Or because there are now so many of us? Or because of such things as radioactive nuclear wastes and breeder reactors? No matter. It is in any case clear that the initial definition of private property must now be revised along the following lines:

(1a)   x *is S's private property if and only if S has the right to exclude all others from the use or benefit of* x AND

(1b)   *each of these others has the right to be excluded from liability for the maleficence of* x.

The term "liability" ("responsibility" does equally well) is chosen for etymological reasons—the root of "liability" being *ligare,* to bind. It is not intended in any technical legal sense. This is what we may call the *double-edged exclusionary definition* of private property.

What will become obvious on reflection is that *if S's property is S's in precisely the same sense and for the same reason that S's action is S's, then the discussion of morality is also a discussion of property.*

Consider for a moment the question of the relation of intention to responsibility. In one sense I cannot be held responsible for an act that was not, in some significant sense, intentional. But I doubt that we want to take this in the strictest sense, i.e., that I have a right to recognize as my action—and to accept responsibility for—only those aspects of the deed of which I was conscious in my aim and which were contained in my original purpose. Surely, even though one may intend only to bring about a single, immediate state of affairs, there are consequences which are implicit within that state of affairs or connected with it empirically of which I ought to be aware and for which I am therefore morally responsible.

There is a clear parallel between how we deal with the question of someone's liability and how we deal with the beneficial additions to someone's property (by nature, chance, etc.) which, though subsequent to the time and intention of the acquisition of that property, are judged to be *part* of that property. It is directly analogous to the distinction between having an action imputed to me and being responsible for the consequences of an action. I may be responsible for a criminal act, though it does not follow that the thing done may be directly imputed to me. To apply this to our case of T_n, we might say that on the one hand we do not want to confuse S with T_n, though on the other hand we may want to hold S responsible for the consequences that follow.

Hegel observes: "To act is to expose oneself to bad luck. Thus bad luck has a right over me and is an embodiment of my own will (intention)."[8]

It is fair, we think, to paraphrase Hegel: "To acquire property is to expose oneself to bad luck."

The case of T_n, we argue, demonstrates that we are inclined to hold T_n's owner liable for the consequences, an inclination that finds expression in positive legislation in contemporary society. If we hold S liable for T_n, it is clear that what we are saying is that not only does S have rights in reference to T_n, but all others do as well. All the story of T_n does is to make explicit that the *double-edged exclusionary definition* represents what has always been, and indeed must be, implicit in the notion of private property.

The abandonment mode of disowning makes sense, then, *only if* property is *only* considered a good. Or rather we might say, it is morally justified only if what is abandoned *is* good. If it is acknowledged that property also entails liability for maleficence, then it follows (especially where the negative consequences of something are serious) that such a mode of disowning is really tantamount to ascribing to the thing in question the *de facto* status of common property of all—and that without the express (or implied) consent of those to whom the liability is transferred. Or perhaps we should say that the thing in question *ought* to be the common property of all, since in fact the negative consequences may fall more heavily on some than on others. Note that the definition of common property must also be revised to pick up the double-edged aspect.

(2a)   x *is the common property of* S_1, S_2, *etc., if and only if* S_1, S_2, *etc. together have the right to exclude all others from the use or benefit of* x, *and* S_1, S_2, *etc. each has the right not to be excluded from the use or benefit of* x

(2b)   *BUT not the right to be excluded from liability for the maleficence of* x.

IV

Given this interpretation of the logic of the notion of property, now reconsider a view which is current these days among some social theorists and popularized in Lodge's eclectic *The New American Ideology:* the view that the notion of (private) property is passé in our "post-industrial" era.

---

[8] Hegel, §119A.

Here Lodge suggests, as we have indicated above, that "(t)he value of property as a legitimizing idea and basis of authority has eroded . . . (and that it) is obvious that our large public corporations are not private property at all."

This "ideological" change, reflecting the operational changes in management practice in large "public" corporations, has been characterized as a *managerial revolution.* If we are to use a metaphor like "revolution" here, then it might be said that the managerial revolution is a revolution, to be sure, a revolution in the concept of property. That is, what seems to be implicit in the theory of the managerial revolution is not a move away from the notion of private property to some new basis of legitimation for the modern corporation, but rather a radical change in the concept of property itself. The implicit change (or revolution) is a *gerrymandering* of the concept of property out of parts of the concepts of private and common property. It would then appear to be something like the following:

(1a)   *S has the right to exclude all others from the use or benefit of* x *BUT*

(2b)   *these others do not have the right to be excluded from liability for the maleficence of* x.

This is, of course, a bit oversimplified, but recent cases like that of the Lockheed Corporation suggest that it is not far off the mark in characterizing our contemporary situation. We should entertain such (implicit) proposals for a gerrymandered definition of private property, we suggest, with considerable hesitation and even skepticism. Too easily giving up the notion of private property runs the danger of giving up the right to hold accountable for *x* those people who have the sole right to the use or benefit of *x*. What would be more rational (and not merely conceptually conservative, we are arguing) is to say that *when all others are to be held liable for S's* x, *then each of those others should also have the right not to be excluded from the use or benefit of* x—in other words, that *x* become common property. Or, one might say, logically some kind of social revolution is what is called for, not a conceptual revolution.

One of the many questions which now arise concerns the problem of symmetry (or fairness). Why should it be considered right to put a limit on liability (or to recognize a *de facto* limit, e.g., bankruptcy laws, etc.), but not to have some sort of similar limit on the use or benefits? (But would that not turn private property rights into common property rights, i.e., some procedure for fair taking/using?) The question becomes especially critical in situations where the negative consequences of something are actual while the benefits only potential. Thus, for example, S may declare the intention to assume liability for *x* commensurate with the potential benefits from *x* (or even commensurate with the total assets of S), but how does this help when the negative consequences are actual and the benefits only potential (or when the potential negative effects far outweigh the potential benefits)?

Lest one think that this is a purely hypothetical situation, consider the case of the 1957 Price-Anderson Act.

In 1954, when the government decided to encourage electric utilities to venture into nuclear power, the companies at first were enthusiastic; but after studying the consequences of a possible major nuclear accident, they and such equipment manufacturers as General Electric and Westinghouse backed off. They feared damage claims that could bankrupt them. Insurers refused then and refuse now to provide full coverage. And so the utilities told Congress they would build nuclear plants only if they first were to be immunized from full liability. Congress responded with the Price-Anderson Act of 1957. Because of this law—a law that legalized financial unaccountability—nuclear power technology exists and is growing today. . . . In 1965, when it recommended that the Price-Anderson Act be renewed, the Congressional Joint Committee on Atomic Energy "reported that one of the Act's objectives had been achieved—the deterrent to industrial participation in the atomic energy program had been removed by eliminating the threat of large liability claims." . . . In December 1975 . . . Congress voted to extend the law for ten more years.[9]

In the face of such policies we have attempted to demonstrate that the logic of property leads one from the notion of private property (the right to exclude) with a kind of inevitability to the notion of common property (the right not to be excluded)—unless one proposes gerrymandering the concept of private property. At least this is true with respect to certain kinds of things which have traditionally been seen to fall within the range of what can rightfully become (and remain) private property. A more elaborate specification of what kinds of things these might be is a topic that goes much beyond the scope of this paper. And, of course, there remains the task of filling out our incomplete notion of common property, i.e., formulating the principles for procedures for fair-taking and fair-using.

Property and Production
An Introduction to the Labor Theory of Property

DAVID P. ELLERMAN

INTRODUCTION

The purpose of this paper is to outline the modern development of the labor theory of property, and to briefly present a major application of the

[9] Morton Mintz and Jerry S. Cohen, *Power, Inc.* (New York: The Viking Press, 1976), pp. 513f. Other such liability exclusionary examples could be cited.

theory, the property theoretic critique of capitalist production. Most of the themes we will touch on can be illustrated using a certain pedogogical example: *the hired criminal example.*

An entrepreneur hires both labor and capital. For labor, he hires some workers for the performance of general services at a fixed wage and, for capital, he hires a van at a fixed rental. The van owner only rents out the van and is not personally or otherwise involved with the entrepreneur. The entrepreneur then employs his capital and labor to commit a crime, say, to rob a bank. After the crime, the bank robbers, i.e., the employer and his employees, are apprehended. But in court the employees tell the judge that they are just as innocent as the van owner. They say only the entrepreneur is responsible. They bring in economists and lawyers to testify, as experts, that "labor is a commodity" just like the services of the van, and that the workers and the van owner have symmetrical roles as sellers of certain commodities. It is the buyer who chooses the particular use of the commodities. The sellers of the services are to receive a fixed remuneration while the buyer assumes the risk of the enterprise. The suppliers of the hired inputs, the van owner and the workers, bear no responsibility for the results of the entrepreneur's enterprise. It's his business, after all.

The judge would, no doubt, be unmoved by this *hired labor defense.* He would point out that the hired worker's role is not really symmetrical with that of the van owner. The van owner could turn over the use of the van to the entrepreneur and not have any personal involvement in the van's use. If that were ascertained to be the case, the van owner would be innocent. However, a worker *cannot* turn over the use of his self to the entrepreneur and not have any personal involvement in the employment of his labor. Unless a worker is for some reason incapacitated and doesn't know what he is doing, a worker is inexorably involved and inescapably de facto responsible for the results of his intentional actions. Labor services are thus *not* a transferable commodity like the services of a van. Hence the judge would reject the hired labor defense.

If it were legally ascertained, say, by a jury trial, that the entrepreneur and his employees were in fact the people responsible for robbing the bank, then they *all* would be held legally responsible for the crime. The employees in work become the partners in crime. It isn't just the entrepreneur's business—after all.

In this hired criminal example, there need not be any criminal intent in the original contract. The criminal deed might have occurred within an on-going and otherwise normal employment relation. A common first reaction to this example is to assert that the employees are legally liable *because* an employment contract which involves the commission of a crime is null and void. But that puts the cart before the horse. The employees are legally liable for the crime, not because of the legal status of their contract, but because they committed the crime. Indeed, it must first be legally ascertained that the employer and the employees committed a crime in order to know that the commission of a crime was in fact involved in the employment relation. Their guilt is the reason for the nullification of the contract, not vice versa.

By rejecting the hired labor defense, the judge has, in fact, "dynamited" the legal foundations of capitalist production. In asserting that people are to be held legally responsible for the results of their intentional actions, the judge is applying the old labor theory of property ("People should get the fruits of their labor") in the courtroom. Unless the judge wanted to hold that the workers suddenly became machines like the van when the enterprise was not criminal, the judge would have to arrive at the same conclusion that *all* the people who worked together in the enterprise should have the legal responsibility for the results of their actions. Since, as the legal and economic experts might point out, the employer-entrepreneur has all the legal responsibility in a normal capitalist enterprise, the judge would have to conclude that this is unjust.

The judge's insight into the factual non-transferability of labor was really an insight into the old natural law doctrine of inalienable rights—in this case, the right to the results of one's actions ("fruits of one's labor"). A person cannot in fact transfer the use of his actions or "labor services" to another person the way that a van's services can be transferred—even when the enterprise is not criminal. The factual non-transferability of labor is the same if the activity is lawful or not. But the Law treats the two cases in diametrically opposite ways. When the enterprise is lawful, the employment contract is accepted as legally valid so the labor services are legally transferred and the workers, like the van owner, have no legal responsibility for the results of the enterprise. But unless the judge wanted to hold that lawfulness suddenly made labor services factually transferable like van services, the judge would have to conclude that the employment contract legally alienates that which is inalienable and thus that the contract is invalid on natural law grounds.

The hired criminal example is a parable that illustrates the labor theory of property and the critique of capitalist production based upon that theory. We will now develop these themes in more detail.

THE DISTRIBUTIVE SHARES METAPHOR

Conventional economic theory analyzes production in terms of the distributive shares paradigm—which pictures certain shares in the value of the product of production as being distributed to the suppliers of the various inputs. In particular, the capital owners, herein called "Capital," and the workers, herein called "Labor," are viewed as having basically symmetrical roles in that each gets a certain share of the pie. The traditional debate focuses on the determination of the share size.

As a description of property rights, the distributive shares picture is quite false. The simple fact is that one party, such as the employer in a capitalist firm, *owns all* the product, i.e., all the produced outputs. For example, Ford Motor Co. doesn't just own Capital's "share" of the Fords produced; it owns all of them. Capitalist economists are, of course, aware of this "legalistic" fact, but they feel called upon to metaphorically reinterpret the product as being "shared" or "distributed" in order to account for the income received by the input suppliers. How could one party, such as Capital, get all the product when there are several scarce inputs?

THE CONCEPT OF THE WHOLE PRODUCT

The simple facts (sans metaphor) will again suffice. Property can take either a positive or negative form as assets or liabilities, i.e., as property rights or property obligations. When economists speak of the "product," they refer only to the positive product—the assets produced in the production process (the outputs). But there is also a negative product. In order to produce the output assets, it is necessary to incur the liabilities for using up the inputs. And one can "own" or hold liabilities just as one can own assets. The fact which accounts for the other input suppliers' income without the shared pie metaphor is the fact that the one party who owns all the positive product also owns all the negative product, i.e., also holds all the liabilities for the used up inputs. For example, the Ford Motor Co. owns not only all the Fords produced but also holds all the liabilities for the inputs such as steel, rubber, glass, and labor used up in the production process. The other input suppliers, instead of being co-claimants of the product, are only creditors of that one party who owns all the positive and negative product.

We have seen that in order to accurately describe the property relations of production, it is necessary to expand the customary concept of "product" to include the negative product (input liabilities) in addition to the usual positive product (output assets). We will call this bundle of property rights and obligations, the *whole product.* In short, "whole product" = "positive product" + "negative product" = "output assets" + "input liabilities." In any productive enterprise, one legal party owns the whole product of production. Moreover, since the outputs were not created before and the inputs were not used up before, the whole product owner is the *initial* or *first* holder of that bundle of property rights and obligations. The legal phraseology for the initial acquisition of property, as opposed to the second-hand acquisition by transfer from a prior owner, is the *appropriation* of property. Hence we have the following basic structural characteristic of production property relations: *one party appropriates the whole product of a productive enterprise.*

WHO IS TO BE THE FIRM?

In a capitalist firm, the whole product is appropriated by the employer, typically the party herein called Capital consisting of the owners of the capital used in the production process. In a *socialist* firm, it is "Society" in its organized form, the government, which appropriates the whole product. In the type of firm which is called *self-managed, labor-managed, laborist,* or a *workers' cooperative,* it is the party herein called Labor consisting of all those who work in the enterprise who would appropriate the whole product. Hence the basic question which differentiates the systems of capitalist production, socialist production, or self-managed production is the question: "Who is to appropriate the whole product of production?" If we use the word "firm" as an abbreviation for "whole product appropriator," then the question could be paraphrased: "*Who is to be the firm?*" Capital, Society, or Labor?

Capitalist economists make no attempt to justify Capital's appropriation of the whole product. Instead, they evade the matter by using the distributive shares metaphor to misrepresent Capital and Labor as each getting a "share of the product." Since the size of the "pie shares" in the functional distribution of income is largely a function of prices, capitalist economists base their "story" on a theory of prices. However, the principal point about the neoclassical theory of prices is not that it is true or false, but that it is irrelevant to the debate over capitalist production. Capitalism is not a particular type of price system. Capitalism is a particular type of property system; the system which allows Capital, by means of the employment contract, to appropriate the whole product of a production process. The best of price theories would only determine the market value of the assets and liabilities in the whole product, but would not determine who is to acquire that bundle of property rights and obligations in the first place.

THE LABOR THEORY OF PROPERTY

The *labor theory of property* asserts that people have the natural right to the positive and negative fruits of their labor, i.e., that people have the natural right to own the positive fruits of their labor and the natural obligation to bear the negative fruits of their labor. In any given productive enterprise, the production of the outputs and the using up or consumption of the inputs are, respectively, the positive and negative fruits of the joint labor of the people working in the enterprise. Hence, the labor theory of property implies that the working community of the enterprise (i.e., Labor in the inclusive sense) has the natural right to the outputs and the natural liability for the inputs, i.e., that Labor should appropriate the whole product. Thus if labor is the just and legitimate basis for private property appropriation, then capitalist production—far from being allegedly "founded on private property"—stands in direct contradiction with the institution of private property. It is the system of production called *workers' self-management, labor-management, laborism,* or *workers' cooperation* which is implied by the basic property principle of appropriating the fruits of one's labor.

The theoretical attack on capitalist production has usually been in the name of a rather ill-defined group of theories collectively known as "the labor theory of value." But that broad heading includes two quite different "labor theories": (1) the marxist labor theory of value, and (2) the labor theory of property. We have already indicated the failure of *any* theory of value or prices, the neoclassical or the marxist theory, to come to grips with the basic structure of production property relations. It is only the property theoretic version of the "labor theory of value," the labor theory of property, which addresses the basic structural and non-value-theoretic question which separates self-managed production from capitalist production in its private or public enterprise forms, "Who is to be the firm?"

Within political economy, the labor theory of property was initially developed by the classical laborists such as Thomas Hodgskin and William Thompson in England and P.-J. Proudhon in France.[1] These early efforts have been largely obscured by Marx's mistaken attempt to develop the "labor theory" as a value theory—as if capitalism was a set of value relations instead of property relations. However, the full development of the labor theory of property was also impaired by two important deficiencies in the classical treatment: (1) the neglect of the negative part of the whole product, and (2) the failure to interpret the labor theory in terms of the juridical norm of legal imputation in accordance with de facto responsibility.

With regard to the neglect of liabilities, the labor theory has often been expressed in the rhetorical claim of "Labor's right to the whole product" where the expression "whole product" was taken as referring to only the positive product. But the claim hardly makes sense without the inclusion of the negative product. Suppose that, in a self-managed economy, firm A produces capital goods such as drill presses which are then used by firm B to produce consumer goods. How can the firm A workers appropriate the positive fruits of their labor unless the firm B workers appropriate the negative fruits of their labor (i.e., bear the liabilities for using up the machine services)? Unless the firm A workers are willing to give away their positive product for free (and live on air), the firm B workers must bear the negative fruits of their labor and satisfy those liabilities by purchasing or leasing the capital goods.

THE JURIDICAL PRINCIPLE OF IMPUTATION

The failure of the classical labor theorists to interpret the labor theory in terms of responsibility has been the single greatest impediment to the understanding and development of the theory. For example, the classical treatment of the labor theory notoriously failed to give a relevant and definitive differentiation of labor from the services of capital and land, e.g., the many attempts to show that "Only labor is productive" or that "Only labor creates value." Yet the differentiation is immediate on the responsibility interpretation since the non-human factors of production (capital and land) lack the capacity for responsibility. All the factors are

---

[1]Anton Menger, *The Right to the Whole Produce of Labour: The Origin and Development of the Theory of Labour's Claim to the Whole Product of Industry*, Macmillan and Co., London, 1899 (reprinted by Augustus Kelly).

productive in the sense of being causally efficacious, but *only labor is responsible*.

Anyone who can understand why guns and other instruments—no matter how efficacious—are not hauled into courts and charged with crimes can also understand that of all the factors of production, only labor is responsible. It is indeed a simple fact. Yet the capitalist and marxist debate on "the labor theory" has been so incredibly ingrown and dogmatic on both sides that the reader is invited to survey the entire past capitalist and marxist literature for any appreciation of the relevance of that simple fact.

We are concerned with *responsibility* in the ex post sense of the question "Who did it?"—not with "responsibilities" in the ex ante sense of one's duties or tasks in an organizational role. A person or group of people are said to be *de facto* or *factually responsible* for a certain result if it was the purposeful result of their intentional (joint) actions. The assignment of *de jure* or *legal responsibility* is called *imputation*. The fundamental *juridical principle of imputation* is that de jure or legal responsibility is to be imputed in accordance with de facto or factual responsibility. For example, the legal responsibility for a civil or criminal wrong should be assigned to the person or persons who intentionally committed the act, i.e., to the de facto responsible party (if any). Since, in the economic context, intentional human actions are called "labor," we have the following equivalence.

> *The Juridical Principle of Imputation:* People should have the legal responsibility for the positive and negative results of their intentional actions.
>
> *The Labor Theory of Property:* People should legally appropriate the positive and negative fruits of their labor.

This equivalence was perhaps not evident in the classical treatment of the labor theory of property because that treatment ignored the negative product, and yet it is the negative side of the imputation principle that is applied explicitly in civil and criminal trials.

In view of this equivalence, the labor theory of property emerges from the underground caverns of radical political economy into the center of the "Temple of Jurisprudence." The labor theory of property is not just some arcane doctrine ritualistically mentioned, usually in connection with Locke, in books on philosophy, law, or the history of thought; it is the standard principle of imputation applied, day in and day out, in the courts of law. Indeed, the idea of assigning legal responsibility in accordance with de facto responsibility is so basic and obvious that it usually isn't even formulated as a "principle." Instead, it is the exceptions to the rule that are labelled or flagged. That is, whenever on other grounds of public policy a party is held legally responsible for something that was not the result of their actions—as when a master is held legally liable for the tort of his servant—then the exception to the rule is explicitly labelled as "vicarious liability" or "strict liability" (see any lawbook on Agency).

MARGINAL PRODUCTIVITY THEORY

The equivalence between the labor theory of property and the juridical imputation principle pushes the roots of the labor theory back in history, far beyond Locke, to the time when Humanity emerged from the world-view of primitive animism. Animism attributed the capacity for responsibility not just to persons but also to non-human entities and forces. Accordingly, in order to escape the grasp of the imputation principle that imputes responsibility only to persons, capitalist economists have had to resurrect a metaphorical form of primitive animism. This "sophisticated animism" reaches its highpoint in the metaphorical interpretation of marginal productivity theory which views productivity in the sense of causal efficacy *as if* it were responsibility. Since the labor theory can be expressed in two equivalent ways, as the principle of property appropriation and as the juridical imputation principle, one might expect the corresponding two metaphorical versions of marginal productivity theory. The property version was developed by John Bates Clark[2] who viewed the inputs as generating property claims on shares of the product, and the imputation version was developed by Friedrich von Wieser[3] who viewed shares in the product as being imputed to the various inputs.

Wieser's contribution is remarkable because he is one of the few capitalist economists to have recognized (in print) the simple fact that only labor is responsible.

> The judge, . . . who, in his narrowly-defined task, is only concerned with the *legal imputation*, confines himself to the discovery of the legally responsible factor,—that person, in fact, who is threatened with the legal punishment. On him will rightly be laid the whole burden of the consequences, although he could never by himself alone—without instruments and all the other conditions—have committed the crime. The imputation takes for granted physical causality. . . .
> . . . If it is the moral imputation that is in question, then certainly no one but the labourer could be named. Land and capital have no merit that they bring forth fruit; they are dead tools in the hand of man; and the man is responsible for the use he makes of them.[4]

Since capitalist production was in obvious conflict with the juridical imputation principle, Wieser was presented with a dilemma. He chose to remain faithful to the professional mission of capitalist economists and thus he rejected the juridical imputation principle instead of capitalist production. The principle was "only" concerned with legal responsibility and judicial imputation. Capitalist apologetics clearly requires a different notion of imputation, an "economic imputation" in accordance with "economic responsibility."

[2]John Bates Clark, *The Distribution of Wealth*, Macmillan and Co., 1899.

[3]Friedrich von Wieser, *Natural Value*, tr. C. A. Malloch, G. E. Stechert and Co., 1930 (orig. published in 1889).

[4]*Ibid.*, pp. 76–79.

> In the division of the return from production, we have to deal similarly . . .
> with an imputation,—save that it is from the economic, not the judicial point
> of view.[5]

By defining "economic responsibility" as marginal productivity, Wieser
could at last draw his desired but rather tortured conclusion that competitive capitalism economically imputes the returns from production in accordance with economic responsibility.

Insofar as property rights are concerned, each input supplier's share
of the product is only a metaphor in the first place since the employer
appropriates the whole product. The Clark-Wieser theory that the size of
each input's metaphorical share of the product is justified by the input's
metaphorical responsibility ("To each what he creates") is the pinnacle of
capitalist apologetics. But it is the actual property relations of capitalist
production, i.e., the employer's appropriation of the whole product, that
need to be justified or condemned, and the relevant notion of responsibility is the non-metaphorical variety used every day as the basis for juridical
imputation.

THE PATHETIC FALLACY

There is also an older and more widespread animistic interpretation of
production which views the inputs as "agents of production cooperating
together to produce the product." This attribution of agency to natural
objects and forces is a common literary and artistic metaphor that Ruskin
called the *pathetic fallacy*. Examples include: "The wind was responsible
for the banging shutters" or "The waves pounded furiously on the shore."
Examples in the "literature" of economics are: "Together, the man and
shovel can dig my cellar" or "[L]and and labor *together* produce the corn
harvest."[6] In spite of the literary allure of the pathetic fallacy, it is still a
fallacy. It confounds the distinction, well-grounded in jurisprudence (but
virtually unheard of in economics), between the *responsible actions* of persons and the *behavior* of things. A shovel does not act together or cooperate together with a person to dig a cellar, because a shovel does not act at
all. A person uses a shovel to dig a cellar. Machines do not cooperate with
workers; machines are operated by workers. In general, things do not act
together with persons; things are acted upon and used by persons.

Instead of labor and the non-human inputs "cooperating together to
produce the product," the people who work in the production process use
up the non-human inputs in the process of producing the outputs. If we
describe "using up the inputs" as "producing the negative product," then
the factual non-animistic description of production is that Labor produces
the negative and the positive products, i.e., that Labor produces the whole
product.

[5]*Ibid.*, p. 76.
[6]Paul A. Samuelson, *Economics*, 10th ed., McGraw-Hill, New York, 1976, pp. 536–537.

THE EMPLOYEE AS A HUMAN TOOL

The equivalence between the labor theory of property and the juridical imputation principle allows us to use jurisprudential concepts and distinctions in the analysis of production—such as the distinction between the responsible actions of persons (labor) and the behavior of things (services of the non-human inputs). In particular, we can analyze the old charge that the employees are treated as things or objects in capitalist production. Things lack the capacity for responsibility so they can bear no legal responsibility for the results of their services. Instead, that responsibility is imputed back through the thing to the human user. That is exactly the legal position of the employees in a capitalist firm. The employees have none of the legal responsibility for the produced outputs (i.e., no legal ownership claim on the outputs) and none of the legal responsibility for the used up inputs (i.e., no legal claims against them for the used up inputs). Instead, that legal responsibility for the positive and negative results of the employees' actions is imputed back through them to the person or persons who "use" or "employ" them, the employer. Hence, the employees in a capitalist firm have, within the scope of their employment, precisely the legal role of tools or instruments.

This point could also be understood by considering a science fiction fantasy wherein employees were *actually* turned into human tools within the scope of their employment. Suppose that electrodes could somehow be inserted into each employee's brain so that a computer could drive them independently of their volition and involuntarily cause them to carry out the commanded tasks. During the off hours, the workers would be "unplugged" so they could lead their normal lives as consumers, citizens, and labor sellers. In such a system, labor would genuinely be devoid of responsible agency. Labor would truly be a commodity, like the services provided by a machine or animal, which can be bought and used by an employer without the original owner of the services incurring any responsibility for the results of the services.

The remarkable fact is that if all capitalist firms switched overnight to the employment of this dehumanized labor, the legal institutions of capitalism would hardly notice the difference. That is, the employees already have legal roles *as if* they were such part-time human tools so no changes in their legal roles would be required. Since the employees would then be genuinely devoid of responsibility for the results of their behavior, the legal structure that imputes all the legal responsibility for the used up inputs and the produced outputs to the employer would then be appropriate. As the employees would be "unplugged" during non-working hours, they could as usual combine in unions to collectively bargain about their wages and the conditions of their employment (but no union meetings on company time). Labor law would still guard the rights of labor sellers and curb the abuses of labor by the employers. Pundits could still celebrate each person's natural right to the original ownership of his labor services and his natural liberty to sell his own labor services by the voluntary employment contract to the highest bidder on the labor market.

In short, this new system would be essentially the same as normal capitalism, except that it would not violate the humanity of people during their work hours—since that humanity would have been suspended. By turning working people into part-time instruments, labor would be rendered morally safe for capitalist production. Since normal capitalism gives employees a legal role as if they already were such dehumanized instruments, it is easy to understand how capitalist production can be dehumanizing—how workers might feel alienated from their product as if it were not the fruits of their labor and how they might think of their work as so many hours taken out of their lives.

The employee in a (normal) capitalist firm and the slave both have the legal position of a human tool—but with two major differences. The slave was owned on a "full-time" basis, whereas the employee is only hired or rented. And the slave generally acquired the legal role of a chattel involuntarily. The voluntary contract to sell oneself—as opposed to renting oneself out—has now been legally invalidated.

> Since slavery was abolished, human earning power is forbidden by law to be capitalized. A man is not even free to sell himself: he must *rent* himself at a wage.[7] [Samuelson's emphasis]

It should hardly be surprising that people take on the legal role of an instrument when they *rent* themselves out by entering the employment contract.

The employee is legally treated as a human tool only so long as the activities are lawful. When the employer and employees break the law, then the legal authorities step in and hold the employees co-responsible together with the employer for the results of their activities. The "talking instrument" in work becomes the responsible person in crime. The slaves, of course, enjoyed the same miraculous metamorphosis whenever they committed crimes. As one abolitionist observed in 1853:

> The slave, who is but "*a chattel*" on all *other* occasions, with not one solitary attribute of personality accorded to him, becomes "*a person*" whenever he is to be *punished!*[8]

Legal philosophers and jurisprudents write volumes upon volumes which dissect human actions to establish degrees of de facto responsibility under conditions of impaired mental competence, mistaken information, duress, and so forth in order that the appropriate degree of legal responsibility may be assigned. Yet one would scan the entire legal and philosophical literature in vain to find the simple observation that the actions of the employees in a normal capitalist firm are fully deliberate, intention-

---

[7]*Ibid.*, p. 52.

[8]William Goodell, *The American Slave Code in Theory and Practice,* New American Library, New York, 1969, p. 309 (orig. published in 1853).

al, voluntary, and responsible—but that the employees are assigned zero legal responsibility for the positive and negative results of these actions. It is the staggering power of social indoctrination which structures people's perception of social reality so that certain aspects are seen very clearly while other aspects are quite invisible. Thus it is that lawyers and philosophers can spend a lifetime splitting hairs to properly apply the imputation principle to border-line cases and yet never even notice a direct one hundred per cent violation of the principle right under their noses.

CAPITALIST PRODUCTION AS A LEGALIZED FORM OF THEFT

The standard defense of capitalist production (i.e., wage labor) is that it cannot be inherently unjust because it, unlike chattel slavery, is based on a voluntary contract, the employer-employee or hired labor contract. Some critics (e.g., marxists) disagree with the factual proposition that the contract is voluntary—as if to agree with the underlying normative premise that wage labor would be permissible if it were really voluntary. But this customary debate about the voluntariness of the contract is quite sterile and irrelevant.

The point is that the employment contract is invalid either way. If wage labor "really" is involuntary and coercive, then it is, of course, wrong on those grounds. If wage labor is reasonably voluntary, as we assume it to be, then it is unjust as it directly violates the fundamental juridical principle of imputation. The labor services performed by the employees, directly or indirectly under the direction of the employer, are normal, voluntary, deliberate, and intentional human actions, i.e., they easily satisfy all the usual juridical criteria for responsible actions. Taking orders does not erase a person's de facto responsibility, as we saw in the hired criminal example. All the people who work in an enterprise, the employees and any working employers, have the joint *de facto* responsibility for the total results of their activities, i.e., for using up the inputs in the process of producing the outputs. But the employer takes all the *legal* responsibility for the used up inputs and the produced outputs (assuming that the activities were lawful). The employer legally appropriates the whole product *as if* the employees had *in fact* been mere instruments of production. Since one party, the employer, legally appropriates the property, the whole product, which another party, all who work in the enterprise, is de facto responsible for creating, wage labor is a legalized form of misappropriation or, in plain terms, theft.

Capitalist production is *not* a theft in the simple sense of a transfer of already owned property without the owner's consent. It is a theft in the sense of a wrongful appropriation of new property which is taken *ab initio* by a party other than the party de facto responsible for creating the property. When legal responsibility is imputed to a party other than the responsible party, that is a miscarriage of justice, a violation of the juridical imputation principle. The employment relation is an institutionalized form of that type of misimputation, where it is a bundle of both property rights and obligations that is misimputed.

Justice is at war with wage labor. The employer-employee relation inherently violates the basic norm of imputation. But how could this happen? Do the legal authorities deny the employees' de facto responsibility? Do the legal authorities claim that the employers (e.g., the corporate shareholders) are solely de facto responsible for the whole product? In short, what is the *modus operandi* of capitalist appropriation?

THE LAISSEZ FAIRE MECHANISM OF IMPUTATION

It would clearly be unfeasible for the legal authorities to render an explicit legal imputation, by having a judgment, ruling, or trial, in order to assign legal responsibility every time that some commodities were consumed or produced. Instead, the legal system must rely on the following:

> *Laissez Faire Mechanism of Imputation:* Unless some law has been broken, let the costs of an activity lie where they have fallen, and then let the party who bore the costs claim any appropriable positive results of the activity.

Thus if a party voluntarily appropriates the negative product, then that party has the legally defensible claim on the positive product. By depending on this jurisprudential invisible hand mechanism to govern lawful activities, the legal system can restrict explicit legal imputations to illegalities. The rationale for the laissez faire mechanism of imputation is that if any costs should fall into the wrong hands, then that presumably would involve an illegality (e.g., a crime, tort, or breach of contract) which, in turn, would prompt legal intervention by the "visible hand" of the law to explicitly impute the legal responsibility in accordance with de facto responsibility.

In a capitalist firm, the employer's appropriation of the whole product is a laissez faire appropriation. Within the confines of the laissez faire mechanism (i.e., when no law is broken), a party only needs to bear the costs of production (appropriate the negative product) in order to have the legally defensible claim on the positive product or outputs. Since no *explicit* legal imputation is involved in the employer's appropriation of the whole product, the legal authorities do not explicitly affirm or deny the de facto responsibility of the employees or the employer. The question of responsibility does not overtly arise at all—since it is an invisible hand mechanism. Moreover, the entire question of the appropriation of the whole product of production seems "invisible" to philosophers, lawyers, and economists.[9] Discussions of property appropriation generally ignore production and concentrate on the appropriation of unowned natural objects or land.

[9]See for example *The Economics of Property Rights,* ed. Eirik Furubotn and Svetozar Pejovich, Ballinger, Cambridge, MA, 1974.

Economists sometimes worry about the "original endowment" of input ownership, but they do not even formulate the question of appropriating the input-liabilities and output-assets created in production.

THE EMPLOYER-EMPLOYEE CONTRACT
AS AN INVALID CONTRACT

The key to the implicit denial of the employees' responsibility is the employer-employee contract. The owner of an instrument or machine, such as a car or van, can use the instrument personally and be responsible for the results *or* the owner can turn the instrument over to be used independently by another person who would then be responsible for the results. If a person could similarly alienate and transfer the "use" of his or her own person, then the employment contract would be a bona fide contract—like the contract to hire out a genuine instrument. *If* the employees could alienate and transfer their labor services to the employer so that the employer could somehow use these services without the employees being inextricably co-responsible, *then* the employer would be solely de facto responsible for the whole product and *then* the employer's laissez faire appropriation of the whole product would be jurisprudentially correct. But such a contractual performance on the part of the employees is not factually possible. All the employees can do is to voluntarily cooperate, as responsible human agents, with their working employer, but then the employees are inextricably de facto co-responsible for the results of the joint activity.

The inescapable joint responsibility of all the people who participate in an activity is a matter of fact. Judicial decrees, legislative enactments, and philosophical pronouncements will not change those facts. For lawful activities, the Law neither affirms nor denies those facts since the laissez faire mechanism reigns. When employees or, in legal jargon, servants commit civil or criminal wrongs at the direction of the employer, then the Law sets aside the invisible hand mechanism of imputation and renders an explicit legal imputation based on the facts insofar as they are ascertained.

> All who participate in a crime with a guilty intent are liable to punishment. A master and servant who so participate in a crime are liable criminally, not because they are master and servant, but because they jointly carried out a criminal venture and are both criminous.[10]

When the "venture" being "jointly carried out" is non-criminal, the employees do not suddenly become instruments (in fact). "All who participate in" the productive activity of a normal capitalist enterprise are similarly de facto responsible for the positive and negative results of the

---

[10]Francis Batt, *The Law of Master and Servant,* 5th ed. by G. Webber, Pitman, London, 1967, p. 612.

activity, i.e., for the whole product. The employer's legal appropriation of that whole product thus violates the basic norm of imputative justice. The Law does not "announce" the violation by solemnly decreeing that, as long as the employees' actions are lawful, the employees will be legally considered only as hired instruments being employed by the employer. Instead, the Law achieves the same results by accepting the employment contract as valid and by accepting the same inextricably co-responsible cooperation on the part of the employees as fulfilling the employment contract. No explicit decree, judgment, or imputation is necessary since the laissez faire mechanism has "taken over" again. The employer has borne all the costs of production, including the "labor costs," so the employer has the legally defensible claim on all the outputs. Thus the employer laissez faire appropriates the whole product of all the people working in the enterprise. That is the *modus operandi* of capitalist appropriation.

We have seen that in order to vouchsafe capitalist appropriation, the legal system must legalize a fraud in the sense of accepting a person as "fulfilling" a contract that implicitly puts the person in the legal role of a non-person or thing. A contract to sell oneself, as opposed to renting oneself out, would place a person in the legal role of a thing on a full-time basis. The contract to sell oneself is invalid on higher law or natural law grounds, and that invalidity is now recognized in positive law. The contract to hire or rent oneself out is similarly invalid on higher law grounds, but positive law still accepts it as "valid" and construes the employees' responsible cooperation as "fulfilling" the contract.

INALIENABLE RIGHTS

An *inalienable* right is a right that may not be alienated even with consent of the holder of the right. A right is inalienable if the voluntary contract to alienate the right is invalid. For example, any right held solely by virtue of being a person (as opposed to a thing) is inalienable on natural law grounds since one's status as a person is unchanged by any contract. A legal system can, of course, "validate" such a contract as a matter of positive law and thus treat an inalienable right as being legally alienable. For instance, in the period immediately preceding the Civil War, general legislation was passed in six slave states "to permit a free Negro to become a slave voluntarily."[11]

Most anyone can understand the concept of inalienability in the context of the hired criminal example. How absurd for the criminous employees to think that by signing a contract, they could "sell" their own actions and somehow transfer the responsibility for the results of their actions to someone else. But when the employees' actions are lawful, the absurdity becomes the legal reality as the employment contract is "vali-

[11]Lewis Cecil Gray, *History of Agriculture in the Southern United States in 1860,* Vol. I, Peter Smith, Gloucester, MA, 1958, p. 527.

dated" and all the legal responsibility for the results of the employees' actions is taken over by the employer. But since the de facto responsibility for the positive and negative results of one's intentional actions is non-transferable, whether the actions are lawful or not, the rights to the positive fruits of one's labor and the obligations to bear the negative fruits of one's labor are inalienable. Just as the positive law at one time "validated" the contract wherein a person could sell himself as a slave to a master, so today the positive law treats an inalienable right as being legally alienable by "validating" the contract to rent or hire oneself out as an employee or servant to an employer or master.

FINAL REMARKS

The standard defense of capitalist production is that it is based on a voluntary contract, the employment contract. But we have seen that the voluntary contract to hire oneself out, like the contract to sell oneself, is inherently invalid. The fraudulent mismatch, between the employees' legal role as hired instruments and their responsible performance, induces the malfunction in the laissez faire imputation mechanism. The contract sets up and allows the employer's misappropriation of the whole product. As usual, a fraud allows a theft to parade in the disguise of a voluntary contract.

Buddhist Economics

E. F. SCHUMACHER

"Right Livelihood" is one of the requirements of the Buddha's Noble Eightfold Path. It is clear, therefore, that there must be such a thing as Buddhist economics.

Buddhist countries have often stated that they wish to remain faithful to their heritage. So Burma: "The New Burma sees no conflict between religious values and economic progress. Spiritual health and material well-being are not enemies: they are natural allies."[1] Or: "We can blend successfully the religious and spiritual values of our heritage with

Chapter 4, "Buddhist Economics," from *Small Is Beautiful* by E. F. Schumacher. Copyright © 1973 by E. F. Schumacher. Reprinted by permission of Blond & Briggs, London, and Harper & Row, Publishers, Inc., New York.

[1]*The New Burma* (Economic and Social Board, Government of the Union of Burma, 1954)

the benefits of modern technology."[2] Or: "We Burmans have a sacred duty to conform both our dreams and our acts to our faith. This we shall ever do."[3]

All the same, such countries invariably assume that they can model their economic development plans in accordance with modern economics, and they call upon modern economists from so-called advanced countries to advise them, to formulate the policies to be pursued, and to construct the grand design for development, the Five-Year Plan or whatever it may be called. No one seems to think that a Buddhist way of life would call for Buddhist economics, just as the modern materialist way of life has brought forth modern economics.

Economists themselves, like most specialists, normally suffer from a kind of metaphysical blindness, assuming that theirs is a science of absolute and invariable truths, without any presuppositions. Some go as far as to claim that economic laws are as free from "metaphysics" or "values" as the law of gravitation. We need not, however, get involved in arguments of methodology. Instead, let us take some fundamentals and see what they look like when viewed by a modern economist and a Buddhist economist.

There is universal agreement that a fundamental source of wealth is human labour. Now, the modern economist has been brought up to consider "labour" or work as little more than a necessary evil. From the point of view of the employer, it is in any case simply an item of cost, to be reduced to a minimum if it cannot be eliminated altogether, say, by automation. From the point of view of the workman, it is a "disutility"; to work is to make a sacrifice of one's leisure and comfort, and wages are a kind of compensation for the sacrifice. Hence the ideal from the point of view of the employer is to have output without employees, and the ideal from the point of view of the employee is to have income without employment.

The consequences of these attitudes both in theory and in practice are, of course, extremely far-reaching. If the ideal with regard to work is to get rid of it, every method that "reduces the work load" is a good thing. The most potent method, short of automation, is the so-called "division of labour" and the classical example is the pin factory eulogised in Adam Smith's *Wealth of Nations*.[4] Here it is not a matter of ordinary specialisation, which mankind has practised from time immemorial, but of dividing up every complete process of production into minute parts, so that the final product can be produced at great speed without anyone having had to contribute more than a totally insignificant and, in most cases, unskilled movement of his limbs.

The Buddhist point of view takes the function of work to be at least threefold: to give a man a chance to utilise and develop his faculties; to enable him to overcome his ego-centredness by joining with other people in a common task; and to bring forth the goods and services needed for a

[2]*Ibid.*
[3]*Ibid.*
[4]*Wealth of Nations* by Adam Smith

becoming existence. Again, the consequences that flow from this view are endless. To organise work in such a manner that it becomes meaningless, boring, stultifying, or nerve-racking for the worker would be little short of criminal; it would indicate a greater concern with goods than with people, an evil lack of compassion and a soul-destroying degree of attachment to the most primitive side of this worldly existence. Equally, to strive for leisure as an alternative to work would be considered a complete misunderstanding of one of the basic truths of human existence, namely that work and leisure are complementary parts of the same living process and cannot be separated without destroying the joy of work and the bliss of leisure.

From the Buddhist point of view, there are therefore two types of mechanisation which must be clearly distinguished: one that enhances a man's skill and power and one that turns the work of man over to a mechanical slave, leaving man in a position of having to serve the slave. How to tell the one from the other? "The craftsman himself," says Ananda Coomaraswamy, a man equally competent to talk about the modern West as the ancient East, "can always, if allowed to, draw the delicate distinction between the machine and the tool. The carpet loom is a tool, a contrivance for holding warp threads at a stretch for the pile to be woven round them by the craftsmen's fingers; but the power loom is a machine, and its significance as a destroyer of culture lies in the fact that it does the essentially human part of the work."[5] It is clear, therefore, that Buddhist economics must be very different from the economics of modern materialism, since the Buddhist sees the essence of civilisation not in a multiplication of wants but in the purification of human character. Character, at the same time, is formed primarily by a man's work. And work, properly conducted in conditions of human dignity and freedom, blesses those who do it and equally their products. The Indian philosopher and economist J. C. Kumarappa sums the matter up as follows:

> If the nature of the work is properly appreciated and applied, it will stand in the same relation to the higher faculties as food is to the physical body. It nourishes and enlivens the higher man and urges him to produce the best he is capable of. It directs his free will along the proper course and disciplines the animal in him into progressive channels. It furnishes an excellent background for man to display his scale of values and develop his personality.[6]

If a man has no chance of obtaining work he is in a desperate position, not simply because he lacks an income but because he lacks this nourishing and enlivening factor of disciplined work which nothing can replace. A modern economist may engage in highly sophisticated calculations on whether full employment "pays" or whether it might be more "economic" to run an economy at less than full employment so as to

---

[5] *Art and Swadeshi* by Ananda K. Coomaraswamy (Ganesh & Co., Madras)

[6] *Economy of Permanence* by J. C. Kumarappa (Sarva-Seva Sangh Publication, Rajghat, Kashi, 4th edn., 1958)

ensure a greater mobility of labour, a better stability of wages, and so forth. His fundamental criterion of success is simply the total quantity of goods produced during a given period of time. "If the marginal urgency of goods is low," says Professor Galbraith in *The Affluent Society*, "then so is the urgency of employing the last man or the last million men in the labour force."[7] And again: "If . . . we can afford some unemployment in the interest of stability—a proposition, incidentally, of impeccably conservative antecedents—then we can afford to give those who are unemployed the goods that enable them to sustain their accustomed standard of living."

From a Buddhist point of view, this is standing the truth on its head by considering goods as more important than people and consumption as more important than creative activity. It means shifting the emphasis from the worker to the product of the work, that is, from the human to the subhuman, a surrender to the forces of evil. The very start of Buddhist economic planning would be a planning for full employment, and the primary purpose of this would in fact be employment for everyone who needs an "outside" job: it would not be the maximisation of employment nor the maximisation of production. Women, on the whole, do not need an "outside" job, and the large-scale employment of women in offices or factories would be considered a sign of serious economic failure. In particular, to let mothers of young children work in factories while the children run wild would be as uneconomic in the eyes of a Buddhist economist as the employment of a skilled worker as a soldier in the eyes of a modern economist.

While the materialist is mainly interested in goods, the Buddhist is mainly interested in liberation. But Buddhism is "The Middle Way" and therefore in no way antagonistic to physical well-being. It is not wealth that stands in the way of liberation but the attachment to wealth; not the enjoyment of pleasurable things but the craving for them. The keynote of Buddhist economics, therefore, is simplicity and non-violence. From an economist's point of view, the marvel of the Buddhist way of life is the utter rationality of its pattern—amazingly small means leading to extraordinarily satisfactory results.

For the modern economist this is very difficult to understand. He is used to measuring the "standard of living" by the amount of annual consumption, assuming all the time that a man who consumes more is "better off" than a man who consumes less. A Buddhist economist would consider this approach excessively irrational: since consumption is merely a means to human well-being, the aim should be to obtain the maximum of well-being with the minimum of consumption. Thus, if the purpose of clothing is a certain amount of temperature comfort and an attractive appearance, the task is to attain this purpose with the smallest possible effort, that is, with the smallest annual destruction of cloth and with the help of designs that involve the smallest possible input of toil. The less toil there is, the more time and strength is left for artistic creativity. It would be highly uneconomic, for instance, to go in for complicated tailoring, like the mod-

[7]*The Affluent Society* by John Kenneth Galbraith (Penguin Books Ltd., 1962)

ern West, when a much more beautiful effect can be achieved by the skilful draping of uncut material. It would be the height of folly to make material so that it should wear out quickly and the height of barbarity to make anything ugly, shabby or mean. What has just been said about clothing applies equally to all other human requirements. The ownership and the consumption of goods is a means to an end, and Buddhist economics is the systematic study of how to attain given ends with the minimum means.

Modern economics, on the other hand, considers consumption to be the sole end and purpose of all economic activity, taking the factors of production—land, labour, and capital—as the means. The former, in short, tries to maximise human satisfactions by the optimal pattern of consumption, while the latter tries to maximise consumption by the optimal pattern of productive effort. It is easy to see that the effort needed to sustain a way of life which seeks to attain the optimal pattern of consumption is likely to be much smaller than the effort needed to sustain a drive for maximum consumption. We need not be surprised, therefore, that the pressure and strain of living is very much less in, say, Burma than it is in the United States, in spite of the fact that the amount of labour-saving machinery used in the former country is only a minute fraction of the amount used in the latter.

Simplicity and non-violence are obviously closely related. The optimal pattern of consumption, producing a high degree of human satisfaction by means of a relatively low rate of consumption, allows people to live without great pressure and strain and to fulfill the primary injunction of Buddhist teaching: "Cease to do evil; try to do good." As physical resources are everywhere limited, people satisfying their needs by means of a modest use of resources are obviously less likely to be at each other's throats than people depending upon a high rate of use. Equally, people who live in highly self-sufficient local communities are less likely to get involved in large-scale violence than people whose existence depends on worldwide systems of trade.

From the point of view of Buddhist economics, therefore, production from local resources for local needs is the most rational way of economic life, while dependence on imports from afar and the consequent need to produce for export to unknown and distant peoples are highly uneconomic and justifiable only in exceptional cases and on a small scale. Just as the modern economist would admit that a high rate of consumption of transport services between a man's home and his place of work signifies a misfortune and not a high standard of life, so the Buddhist economist would hold that to satisfy human wants from faraway sources rather than from sources nearby signifies failure rather than success. The former tends to take statistics showing an increase in the number of ton/miles per head of the population carried by a country's transport system as proof of economic progress, while to the latter—the Buddhist economist—the same statistics would indicate a highly undesirable deterioration in the *pattern* of consumption.

Another striking difference between modern economics and Buddhist economics arises over the use of natural resources. Bertrand de Jouvenel, the eminent French political philosopher, has characterised

"Western man" in words which may be taken as a fair description of the modern economist:

> He tends to count nothing as an expenditure, other than human effort; he does not seem to mind how much mineral matter he wastes and, far worse, how much living matter he destroys. He does not seem to realise at all that human life is a dependent part of an ecosystem of many different forms of life. As the world is ruled from towns where men are cut off from any form of life other than human, the feeling of belonging to an ecosystem is not revived. This results in a harsh and improvident treatment of things upon which we ultimately depend, such as water and trees.[8]

The teaching of the Buddha, on the other hand, enjoins a reverent and non-violent attitude not only to all sentient beings but also, with great emphasis, to trees. Every follower of the Buddha ought to plant a tree every few years and look after it until it is safely established, and the Buddhist economist can demonstrate without difficulty that the universal observation of this rule would result in a high rate of genuine economic development independent of any foreign aid. Much of the economic decay of southeast Asia (as of many other parts of the world) is undoubtedly due to a heedless and shameful neglect of trees.

Modern economics does not distinguish between renewable and non-renewable materials, as its very method is to equalise and quantify everything by means of a money price. Thus, taking various alternative fuels, like coal, oil, wood, or water-power: the only difference between them recognised by modern economics is relative cost per equivalent unit. The cheapest is automatically the one to be preferred, as to do otherwise would be irrational and "uneconomic." From a Buddhist point of view, of course, this will not do; the essential difference between non-renewable fuels like coal and oil on the one hand and renewable fuels like wood and water-power on the other cannot be simply overlooked. Non-renewable goods must be used only if they are indispensable, and then only with the greatest care and the most meticulous concern for conservation. To use them heedlessly or extravagantly is an act of violence, and while complete non-violence may not be attainable on this earth, there is nonetheless an ineluctable duty on man to aim at the ideal of non-violence in all he does.

Just as a modern European economist would not consider it a great economic achievement if all European art treasures were sold to America at attractive prices, so the Buddhist economist would insist that a population basing its economic life on non-renewable fuels is living parasitically, on capital instead of income. Such a way of life could have no permanence and could therefore be justified only as a purely temporary expedient. As the world's resources of non-renewable fuels—coal, oil, and natural gas—are exceedingly unevenly distributed over the globe and undoubtedly limited in quantity, it is clear that their exploitation at an ever-increasing rate is an act of violence against nature which must almost inevitably lead to violence between men.

[8]*A Philosophy of Indian Economic Development* by Richard B. Gregg (Navajivan Publishing House, Ahmedabad, India, 1958)

This fact alone might give food for thought even to those people in Buddhist countries who care nothing for the religious and spiritual values of their heritage and ardently desire to embrace the materialism of modern economics at the fastest possible speed. Before they dismiss Buddhist economics as nothing better than a nostalgic dream, they might wish to consider whether the path of economic development outlined by modern economics is likely to lead them to places where they really want to be. Towards the end of his courageous book *The Challenge of Man's Future*, Professor Harrison Brown of the California Institute of Technology gives the following appraisal:

> Thus we see that, just as industrial society is fundamentally unstable and subject to reversion to agrarian existence, so within it the conditions which offer individual freedom are unstable in their ability to avoid the conditions which impose rigid organisation and totalitarian control. Indeed, when we examine all of the foreseeable difficulties which threaten the survival of industrial civilisation, it is difficult to see how the achievement of stability and the maintenance of individual liberty can be made compatible.[9]

Even if this were dismissed as a long-term view there is the immediate question of whether "modernisation," as currently practised without regard to religious and spiritual values, is actually producing agreeable results. As far as the masses are concerned, the results appear to be disastrous—a collapse of the rural economy, a rising tide of unemployment in town and country, and the growth of a city proletariat without nourishment for either body or soul.

It is in the light of both immediate experience and long-term prospects that the study of Buddhist economics could be recommended even to those who believe that economic growth is more important than any spiritual or religious values. For it is not a question of choosing between "modern growth" and "traditional stagnation." It is a question of finding the right path of development, the Middle Way between materialist heedlessness and traditionalist immobility, in short, of finding "Right Livelihood."

Suggestions for Further Reading

Two general sources on market systems and political systems are Albert O. Hirschman, *Exit, Voice and Loyalty: Responses to Decline in Firms, Organizations and States* (Cambridge, Mass.: Harvard University Press, 1970); and Charles E. Lindblom, *Politics and Markets: The World's Political-*

---

[9]*The Challenge of Man's Future* by Harrison Brown (The Viking Press, New York, 1954)

Economic Systems (New York: Basic Books, 1977). A good review of some recent concerns involved in the assessment of market-type distribution systems is to be found in Gerald Dworkin, Gordon Bermant, and Peter G. Brown, *Markets and Morals* (New York: Halsted, 1977).

An influential critique of recent efforts at regulating corporations is set out in Christopher D. Stone's *Where the Law Ends: The Social Control of Corporate Behavior* (New York: Harper & Row, 1975). A now-classic analysis of some of the problems involved in reducing the social costs of production is Ronald H. Coase, "The Problem of Social Cost," *Journal of Law and Economics* 3 (1960): 1–44. The nontechnical portions of Coase's article are reprinted in a book which has much else of interest on this topic: Bruce A. Ackerman, ed., *Economic Foundations of Property Law* (Boston: Little, Brown, 1975). Richard Posner's *Economic Analysis of Law,* 2d ed. (Boston: Little, Brown, 1977), chaps. 1–3, is also useful. Readers who wish to pursue the recent economic analysis of property rights should consult Eirik G. Furobotn and Svetozar Pejovich, eds., *The Economics of Property Rights* (Cambridge, Mass.: Ballinger, 1974). See especially "The Property Rights Paradigm" by Armen A. Alchian and Harold Demsetz. Harold Demsetz, "Toward a Theory of Property Rights," *American Economic Association Papers and Proceedings* (May, 1967), 253–257 is useful as well.

Lawrence C. Becker applies Honoré's analysis of ownership to the problem of who owns a large corporation in "Property Theory and the Corporation," in Michael Hoffman, ed., *Proceedings of the Second National Conference on Business Ethics* (Washington, D.C.: University Press of America, 1979). See also A. A. Berle and Gardiner Means, *The Modern Corporation and Private Property* (New York: Macmillan, 1932).

A collection of articles on workers' self-management is to be found in Gerry Hunnius, G. David Garson, and John Case, eds., *Workers' Control* (New York: Vintage, 1973). Edward Nell, ed., *Growth, Profits and Property: Essays in the Revival of Political Economy* (London: Cambridge University Press, 1980) includes some of Ellerman's recent work on the property theoretic analysis of orthodox economic theory as well as other pieces of interest.

In addition to the other essays in E. F. Schumacher's *Small Is Beautiful,* the reader may find of interest Ivan Illich, *Tools for Conviviality* (New York: Harper & Row, 1973).

GENERAL BIBLIOGRAPHY

We list here a few works of general interest to the student of property theory. An extensive bibliography (over 350 entries) by Gerald F. Gaus may be found in J. Roland Pennock and John W. Chapman, eds., *Property*, NOMOS XXII (New York: New York University Press, 1980).

ACKERMAN, BRUCE A. *Private Property and the Constitution*. New Haven: Yale University Press, 1977.

———, ed. *Economic Foundations of Property Law*. Boston: Little, Brown, 1975.

BARTLETT, J. V., ed. *Property: Its Duties and Rights*. 2d ed. London: Macmillan, 1915.

BEAGLEHOLE, ERNEST. *Property: A Study in Social Psychology*. London: George Allen & Unwin, 1931.

BECKER, LAWRENCE C. *Property Rights: Philosophic Foundations*. London and Boston: Routledge & Kegan Paul, 1977.

BENN, STANLEY I. "Property." In *The Encyclopedia of Philosophy*, edited by Paul Edwards. New York: Collier-Macmillan, 1967.

BERLE, A. A., and GARDINER MEANS. *The Modern Corporation and Private Property*. New York: Harcourt Brace & World, 1968.

BEUSCHER, JACOB H., and ROBERT R. WRIGHT, eds. *Cases and Materials on Land Use*. St. Paul: West, 1969.

CASNER, A. JAMES, and W. BARTON LEACH, eds. *Cases and Texts on Property.* 2d ed. Boston: Little, Brown, 1969.

DALTON, GEORGE, ed. *Tribal and Peasant Economics: Readings in Economic Anthropology.* Garden City, N.Y.: Natural History Press, 1967.

FURUBOTN, EIRIK G., and SVETOZAR PEJOVICH, eds. *The Economics of Property Rights.* Cambridge, Mass.: Ballinger, 1974.

HERSKOVITS, MELVILLE J. *Economic Anthropology.* New York: Alfred A. Knopf, 1952.

MACPHERSON, C. B. *The Political Theory of Possessive Individualism.* Oxford: Clarendon Press, 1962.

MANNE, HENRY G., ed. *The Economics of Legal Relationships: Readings in the Theory of Property Rights.* St. Paul: West, 1975.

SCHLATTER, RICHARD B. *Private Property: The History of an Idea.* New Brunswick, N.J.: Rutgers University Press, 1951.

SCOTT, WILLIAM B. *In Pursuit of Happiness: American Conceptions of Property from the Seventeenth to the Twentieth Century.* Bloomington: Indiana University Press, 1977.